THE SNODGRASS SITE OF THE POWERS PHASE
OF SOUTHEAST MISSOURI

Frontispiece. Members of the 1970 field crew at the Snodgrass site (left to right): James Price, Carol Price, James Krakker, Gary Mono, Richard Zurel, Pam Mears, Bruce Smith, Mike Jochim, Richard Malouf, Vida Goldstein, Terry D'Altroy, Barbara Luedtke, Nancy Hamblin Green, John Green, James B. Griffin.

ANTHROPOLOGICAL PAPERS

MUSEUM OF ANTHROPOLOGY, UNIVERSITY OF MICHIGAN

NO. 66

THE SNODGRASS SITE OF THE POWERS PHASE OF SOUTHEAST MISSOURI

BY JAMES E. PRICE AND JAMES B. GRIFFIN

ANN ARBOR, MICHIGAN

1979

©1979 Regents of The University of Michigan
The Museum of Anthropology
All rights reserved

Printed in the
United States of America
ISBN 0-932206-77-8

CONTENTS

LIST OF FIGURES

LIST OF TABLES

LIST OF PLATES

PREFACE

Archaeological research in Ripley and Butler Counties has been a consuming interest of James E. Price since 1960, and this interest has gradually expanded with his undergraduate training at the University of Missouri and his graduate work at the University of Michigan. James B. Griffin has had a long involvement in Eastern United States and Mississippi Valley archaeology. Price had field experience with Dr. Carl H. Chapman's field crew in 1962 and 1963. He did his first work at Powers Fort in late August of 1963 and other small tests in 1964 and 1965. Initial financial support was provided by the University of Missouri in 1966, and he received an Undergraduate Research Participant grant from the National Science Foundation. In his spare time he made a preliminary survey of the Little Black River and prepared a research paper for an undergraduate honors program. In late April 1966 Griffin heard Price present a paper on his work at the Central States Anthropological Society meeting in St. Louis and discussions there were followed by ones at the University of Missouri later that spring.

In the spring of 1966 local collectors began indiscriminate excavation on the Mississippian village at the Turner site, 23 Bu-21-A. Price investigated this and found that at least some structures on the site were burned. Further investigations of other village sites strongly indicated that they too had been burned. With $600 from the University of Missouri he began excavations on the Turner site during the summer of 1966 and this eventually expanded into the Powers Phase Project.

As the result of written communications, Griffin visited these excavations in 1967, was given a guided tour of the other then known village sites and of Powers Fort. Examination of the materials from the sites indicated the remarkable homogeneity of the material and along with the apparent short occupancy of the sites made them a unique opportunity to investigate the functioning of a Mississippian society within a tight time span. This strikingly anomalous situation provided a most unusual opportunity. We sat in a truck on the Turner site in late July, 1967, and roughed out a grant proposal to the National Science Foundation, for the Museum of Anthropology had provided a small amount of funds for the excavations in August 1966 and in the summer of 1967. Further support was provided in 1967 by the

University of Missouri in the form of field supplies and transportation. This was continued through the following years of excavation. Griffin and Chapman agreed amicably that the materials from the excavations would be divided between the University of Michigan and the University of Missouri.

In the fall of 1967, Price entered graduate school at the University of Michigan, and with the approval of the research request to the National Science Foundation an enlarged field program was begun by the Museum of Anthropology in the summer of 1968 with 18 individuals. After considerable discussion during the school term regarding the proper strategy, it was felt that sampling procedures should be applied to the adjacent Turner and Snodgrass sites. This was later changed to complete excavation of both sites and to test excavations at related villages and other types of settlements, as soon as it was recognized that complete excavation could be completed; since practically no similar Mississippian villages had been completely excavated, we decided to do the unusual. We regarded the project as a unique opportunity to obtain a reasonably accurate picture of two adjoining village sites.

During the early planning of the project and the allocation of distinctive contributions which we wished to have in a final report, our aim was at a higher level of accomplishment than we have been able to deliver. A major ethnobotanical analysis is still not completed, and an ethnohistorical study of the cultural patterns of late 17th and early 18th century Indian groups, along with an interpretation of the Powers phase behavioral pattern's relationship to them is still being studied. Our attempt to obtain palynological information met with limited success and a manuscript on the results from the Snodgrass site and environs has been prepared by Susan Fish. We were not able to obtain precise trace element analysis of the lithic material particularly of examples of tools and flakes believed to be of Mill Creek chert from southwestern Illinois. An analysis of the human skeletal material from the Turner, Snodgrass and Powers Fort sites has been made by Thomas K. Black and this will be revised for publication. Bruce Smith has published a major monograph and a number of papers with a strong data base from Powers phase faunal materials and his monograph on the Gypsy Joint site, a small Powers phase homestead, has been recently published (Smith 1978). It includes an ethnobotanical section by Wilma Koschik Wetterstrom.

We refrained from early publication for a number of reasons. The sites have had a minimum of clandestine excavation even though they are within easy driving distance of two major urban areas. Fortunately they are not productive from the standpoint of private collectors or dealers, and most of the tenants and property owners have been apprised of the damage and irrevocable harm that can be done by such activity. We also did not want to publish preliminary interpretations because the complexity of the Powers phase settlement and behavioral system became more apparent with each survey and excavation, not only year by year but almost month by month. In spite of various extensive and intensive surveys, for ten years new locations became known through surface vegetational changes, movement of surface soils or other unforeseen events.

ACKNOWLEDGMENTS

The Anthropology section of the National Science Foundation made three grants to the University of Michigan Museum of Anthropology in 1968, 1970 and 1973 for a total of $112,000. In addition, we benefitted from funds supplied to the Museum by that foundation's Undergraduate Research Participation Program from 1968 through 1972. We are indeed grateful for this support, for without it the project would not have been feasible. Throughout all excavations from 1968 to 1974, Griffin was principal investigator and Price the field and laboratory director. There was constant communication between the two during this period with responsibility and blame being shared. The several field and laboratory supervisors and the many students who participated all made significant contributions. We are particularly indebted to James Krakker, Bruce Smith, John Walthall, Suzanne Harris, Richard Malouf, Carol Price and Robert Luton for their vital assistance.

The preparation of this report has been almost entirely the work of James Price, while Griffin has acted in a general editorial capacity in the structure of the reports and as a critic of the manuscript. We are indebted to our colleagues in anthropology at the University of Michigan, the University of Missouri and other institutions and to the members of the field parties for innumerable helpful suggestions. The results presented herein are an amalgam of these ideas and procedures, limited by our ability to absorb and apply them to the Powers Phase Project.

We are also indebted to the following landowners in the area for permission to collect and excavate on their property and to the several tenants whose normal activities we regretfully disturbed from time to time. Special thanks must go to Mrs. A. H. Snodgrass and Dale Turner who permitted our operations to continue over the longest period of time.

LANDOWNERS

Mrs. Margaret Davis
Mr. Neil Flurry
Mr. David Kimbrough
Mr. Walter Koehler
Mr. Bob Lepold
Mr. Jim Lepold
Mrs. Richard Ovitt
Mrs. A. H. Snodgrass
Mrs. Jake Steinberg
Mr. Oneal Sullivan
Mr. Dale Turner
Mr. Malcolm Turner
Mr. Ronnie Wilborn
Mr. Carlton Woodard

PEOPLE WHO WORKED ON THE POWERS PHASE PROJECT

Gary Abernathy
Scott Albert
Linda Anderson
Russell Bailon
Virginia Balnius
Dorothy Bean
Anna Bennett
Thomas K. Black
Crawford Blakeman
Richard E. Blanton
Sheila Bobalik
Susan Burton
Elizabeth Butch
Brian Butler
Dan Caister
Gail Campbell
Janet Cofer
Michael Collins
John Cox
Terry D'Altroy
Nancy Davis
Kiffi Diamond
Diane Dickerson
Philip Dinehart
Alan Donn
Carol Donn
William Engelbrecht
Leslie Fedota
Gary Feinman
Paul Fish
Susan Kitchen Fish
Tommy Fisher
Steve Fleming
John Green
Dennis Grega
Meril Gregory
Vida Goldstein
Linda Hamblin
Nancy Hamblin
Suzanne Harris
Melody Haskin
Charles Hastings
Barbara Heminger
Steve Henson
Jeanette Hoffman
Timothy Hubert
Elizabeth Hunt
Ann Isaacs
Michael Jochim
Jill Johnson
Chris King
Walter Klippel
James Krakker
Steve Kranovit
Michael Kurtz
Dan Landis
Kathy Landis
Jack Lane
Harry Laughlin
Jack Leddick
Barbara Luedtke
Robert Luton
Mary Coliflower Malouf
Richard Malouf
Kathy Mastricola
James McClaury
Pamela Mears
William Messina
Rand Miller
Paul Minnis
Gary Mono
Margaret Mosenfelder
Karen Mudar
Sharon Odom
Kathy Parrent
Mary Petruchuis
Tom Porter
Karrie Potter
Richard Potter
Carol Price
Cynthia Price
Gary Price
Susan Price Leddick
Gerald Ramsey
Ilene Rosenberg
Victoria Rosenblum
Jane Sallade
John Scarry
Charles Scheffer
Barbara Sheldon
Sandy Smalley
Bruce Smith
Neil Sonenklar
Jay Sperber
Francis Stier
Leland Thompson
Richard Walling
John Walthall
Wilma Wetterstrom
Raymond Williams
Margaret Zadakof
Richard Zurel

I

MISSISSIPPIAN CULTURE AND THE POWERS PHASE

AN INTRODUCTION TO MISSISSIPPIAN CULTURE

Mississippian cultural traditions prevailed in eastern North America from ca. A.D. 700 through the historic period. Griffin (1967:11) breaks the fully developed culture of about A.D. 1500 into different large area complexes, namely Middle Mississippian, South Appalachian Mississippian, Plaquemine Mississippian, Caddoan Mississippian, Fort Ancient Mississippian, and Oneota Mississippian. Of these, Oneota is the most divergent from the Middle Mississippi societies. Some archaeologists regard the latter as the only "true" Mississippi.

Most known Mississippian phases seem to have focused around a permanent center, usually a fortified town with large mounds. Numerous villages, hamlets, farmsteads and hunting-gathering camps surround these centers, and their inhabitants were spread over a specific area near each town. Agriculture played an important role, for it allowed the maintenance of a permanent center. Cultivated plants became the primary food source, permitting a greater population density and perhaps a food surplus. This successful mode of subsistence probably released a segment of the population from the role of primary producers. It appears that the ceremonial centers united the population and provided ceremonial services for them. These centers also held specialists in administration, ceremonialism, and technology.

One can only conjecture concerning socio-political organization of these Mississippian groups. The degree of social stratification is unknown, but we can conclude from the archaeological record that there was status differentiation that probably correlated with an increase of ascribed status over achieved status. Some Mississippian leaders apparently had the power to coerce followers as members of lower classes, making public works possible. Individuals or families of high status lived in preferential locations and in bigger and better houses than the remainder of the population.

Religious behavior was concentrated in temples, and rituals were performed to control the supernatural. Most likely a ceremonial calendar existed in some form. Ceremonial paraphenalia was elaborate, as testified by graphic representations of dancers on objects of the Southeastern Ceremonial Complex.

Major Mississippian sites are marked by rectangular, flat-topped platform mounds that served as bases for temples, charnel houses, and other public buildings. Most often these platform mounds surround a plaza. Mound centers may be very large, ranging well above one hundred acres, as demonstrated by Cahokia (Madison County, Illinois) and Moundville (Tuscaloosa County, Alabama). Huge deposits of occupational debris testify to long occupation and a more-or-less stable population.

Mississippian dwellings were constructed of pole frames with cane mat walls and thatch roofs. Wattle and daub architecture occurs throughout the Mississippian areas but was not universally employed.

Mississippian mortuary practices were quite varied. The dead were interred in house floors, village "streets," cemeteries, and mounds. The most common position for the body is extended and supine. Cremation was occasionally practiced but is not very common. In several areas, such as the Nashville Basin in Tennessee, western Kentucky, and southwestern Illinois, the bodies of the dead were buried as bundles or as primary extended inhumations in stone box graves. Often grave offerings are elaborate for the more important members of the society. Jars, bowls, and bottles are the most common burial furniture.

Mississippian ceramics are varied in form and complexity and are manifested in jars, bottles, and bowls with incising, punctuating, engraving, and painting as surface treatment (see Phillips, Ford and Griffin 1951; Holmes 1903). Handles and various other appendages, as well as zoomorphic effigy forms, are common. Burned and pulverized river mussel shells appear to have been an almost universal tempering material during the Mississippi period.

Lithic industries were somewhat limited during the Mississippi period due to an apparent reliance on wooden artifacts. Stone tools occur in the form of projectile points (for arrows), perforators, scrapers, knives, and axes. Bone was often a substitute in the manufacture of most of these artifacts.

In summary, the Mississippian culture was a highly complex, well integrated cultural tradition which thrived throughout most of southeastern North America in late prehistoric times. Although it was widespread, it shares many common attributes such as shell-tempered pottery, platform mounds, plazas, and evidence of involvement in the Southeastern Ceremonial Complex. Large populations became concentrated in towns with a greater reliance on cultivated plants as a primary food source.

For more background information on Mississippian culture the reader should consult Cole et al. (1951); Chapman and Anderson (1955); Griffin (1967); Moselage (1962); Morse (1973); Phillips, Ford, and Griffin (1951); Sears (1956); Thomas (1894); Thruston (1890); Webb (1952); and Williams (1954).

THE PLACE OF THE POWERS PHASE IN MISSISSIPPIAN CULTURE

The Powers phase is a Middle Mississippian manifestation dating ca. A.D. 1275-1350 (see App. D) situated between the present-day towns of Naylor and Neelyville, Missouri, in the eastern portion of Ripley County and the western portion of Butler County. It extends from south of the Arkansas-Missouri line northward approximately 18 miles (Fig. 1). It lies on sand ridges south and east of where the Little Black River flows from the Ozark Highlands into the Mississippi Alluvial Valley.

The phase is named for Powers Fort, a large civic-ceremonial center near the present town of Naylor, Missouri and presently owned by Mr. Walter Koehler. Mention of it first appears in the archaeological literature in the *Twelfth Annual Report of the Bureau of American Ethnology* (1894) in which Cyrus Thomas describes archaeological investigations at the site. A somewhat inaccurate map made at that time is reproduced in Figure 2. The site is about 15 acres in size and at one time had a large ditch and fortification wall enclosing it. Within the fortified area are four mounds, a large flat-topped temple mound, and three subsidiary mounds badly damaged by cultivation and the early excavations. This mound center is the westernmost of its type in this northern area of the Lower Alluvial Valley (Williams 1966) and its configuration and other physical attributes, except accumulated midden, are similar to those of the St. Francis area of northeastern Arkansas and the Cairo Lowland of Southeast Missouri.

The Powers phase is like most other Middle Mississippian phases. Its material remains, i.e., ceramics, lithics, and architecture, do not depart drastically from those recovered from other sites of the Middle Mississippian complexes in the Central Mississippi River Valley. It is not indigenous to the Little Black River area but came there fully developed, bringing with it a cultural pattern which emerged earlier further east and south in the Mississippi River Delta.

Excavations of the Powers Phase Project have yielded information never before obtained in Mississippian studies. The research design proposed for the project called first for an archaeological survey to determine the settlement pattern of a complete Middle Mississippian society, from its civic-ceremonial center with a mound complex down to small ephemeral extractive sites. Such a survey helped to make clear the complex settlement pattern of

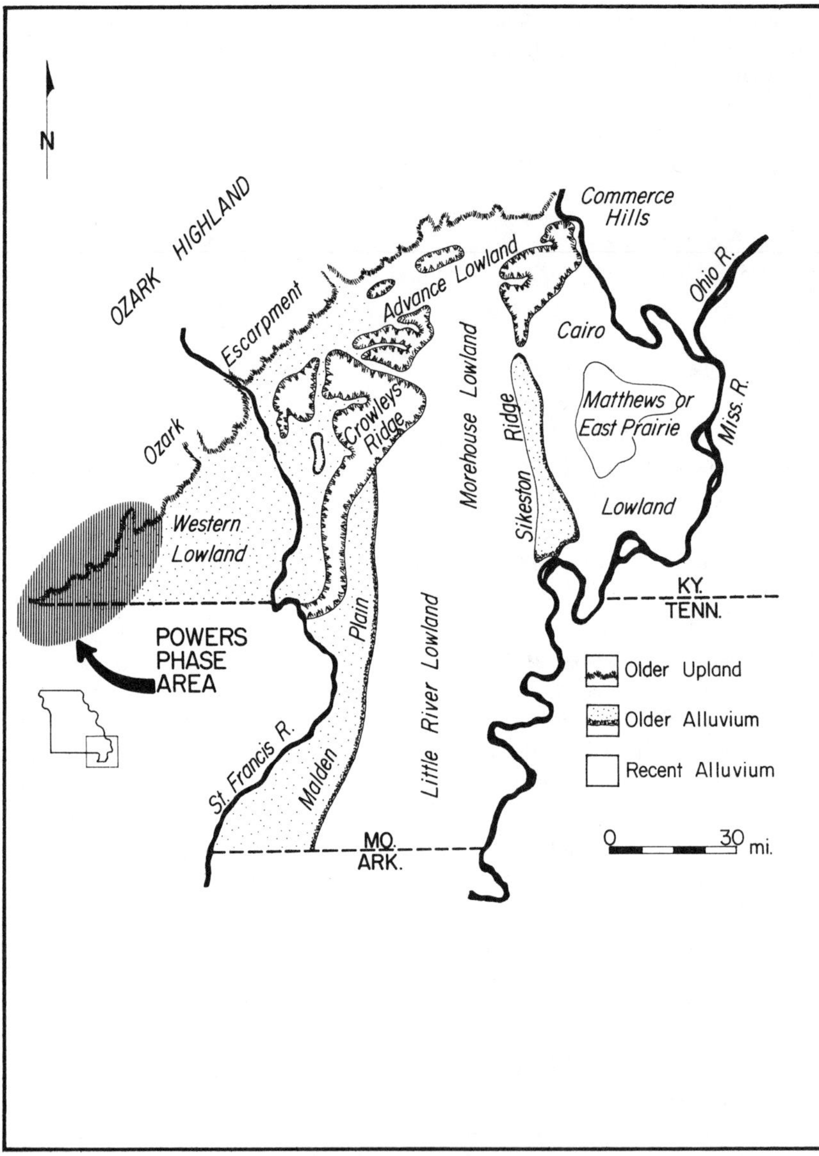

Figure 1. Location of the Powers Phase.

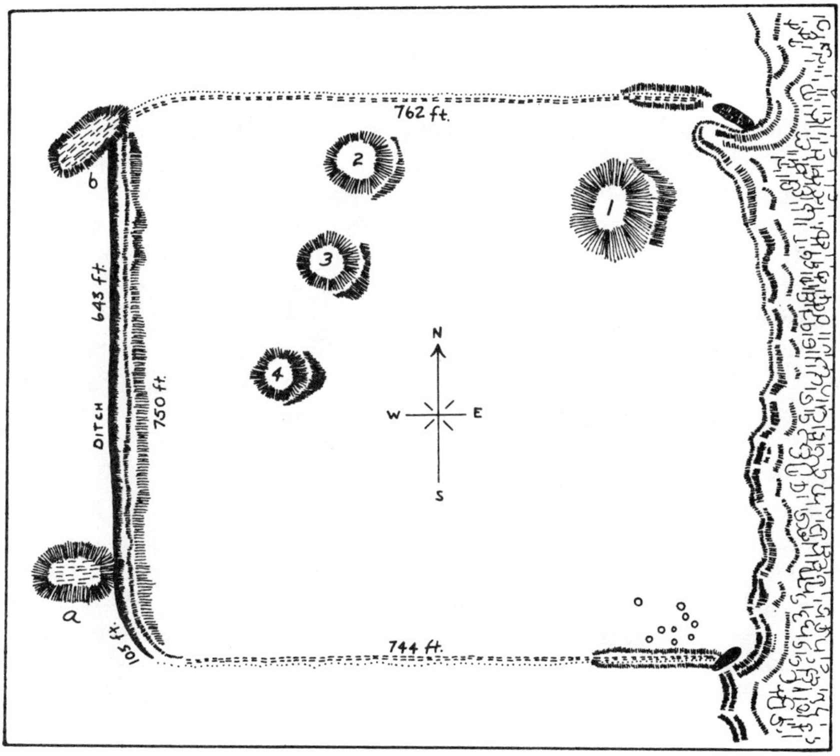

Figure 2. Powers Fort, Butler County, Missouri (map from C. Thomas, 1894).

a Mississippian phase, an achievement that had previously been open to conjecture. The next stage of the research was to excavate entire villages to recover complete community patterns. Traditional Mississippian research involved the excavation of only relatively small portions of sites, usually multi-component in nature, which yielded a few structure floor patterns and refuse pits. Traditional excavations have concentrated on mounds and small tests in large mound centers. Such excavations never demonstrated the contemporaneity of a large number of structures and features on the sites nor did they demonstrate the functional and spatial relationship of any feature to all other features within a single site. These were the objectives of the Powers Phase Project—to excavate an entire village and examine the community plan of one group of Mississippian people living in one settlement at one time. So short-lived were the Powers phase villages that this goal was feasible.

It can be assumed that the people of the Powers phase had a social system which has been extinct since the 14th century A.D. Yet that system remains inherent in the material remains they left behind. The spatial distribution of goods, structures, walls, and pits on a site can be assumed to result from people performing different social roles, but there is a great hiatus between this reflection of the social organization and the organization per se.

The Powers phase must have been culturally integrated at higher levels than the individual village level. It was politically unified across the whole phase area and functioned as a whole. A settlement pattern consisting of differential site size and content helps support the argument that in the Powers phase, socio-political authority was centralized and was integrated at higher levels than the individual settlements, resulting in a wide and elaborate economical, ceremonial, and ideological organization. This is supported by the occurrence of size-ranked and functionally differentiated sites. Powers Fort and its mound complex is the main town as it is larger, was occupied longer, and had more ceremonial activities. Subsidiary sites are located around it which contain little evidence of non-subsistence activities.

MISSISSIPPIAN SOCIAL ORGANIZATION

Most attempts to examine Mississippian socio-political organization have been made through ethnohistory and through lexico-reconstruction, from early accounts by explorers and naturalists (Mochon 1972:478). The ethnographic and ethnohistorical data concerning the southeastern United States are helpful concerning subsistence and technology since the coming of European peoples, but the use of these data for inferences concerning social behavior that reach into the archaeological past does not appear to be of great value. By the time such data were recorded in detail, these cultures had been greatly altered by the presence of the French, Spanish, and English. Undoubtedly there was so much social change that what was recorded may not have been in existence prior to contact with Europeans.

We must also keep in mind that what was recorded was interpreted through the eyes of an alien people with little or no scientific background by today's standards. In addition, the statements were usually written to support some particular viewpoint of benefit to the writer and his associates.

In traditional Middle Mississippian studies, a great deal of attention has been given to material culture such as ceramics, their types, and distribution of types. Very little attention utilizing archaeological data has been given to social organization. Differential status of individuals has been noted from archaeological morturary data by Peebles in his recent examination of the data from Moundville (1971), by Larson at Etowah (1971), and by Brown at Spiro (1971), all utilizing data from large civic-ceremonial centers. The Powers Phase Project represents the first major research project to excavate an entire Mississippian settlement and examine the distribution of its contents in an attempt to differentiate social segments that occupied it.

Many scholars dealing with the evolution and taxonomy of social organizations have established stages or categories to define them (Fried 1960, Sahlins 1958 and 1968, Service 1962, Leach 1954, White 1949, Steward 1955, and Beardsley et al. 1956). It is not our aim to correlate Powers phase socio-political organization to any of these cultural stages or taxa, since many of the criteria for these cannot be detected archaeologically. This volume provides evidence for a certain level of social complexity that existed among a prehistoric village population, and it is left to the reader to take the evidence and fit it to what he feels is the stage or taxon where it best fits.

The objectives of this report are two in number. The first objective is to examine the distribution of the contents of a Mississippian village, in an attempt to differentiate social segments through the presence and absence of attributes. The second objective is to provide evidence to determine the level of social complexity and patterned lifeways that existed among a prehistoric village population.

For several reasons, the Powers phase is an excellent case through which to investigate Mississippian culture. First, for all practical purposes it is the only major Mississippian manifestation in the Little Black River area, and its material culture can be easily distinguished from that of prior Woodland cultures (Barnes) that used sand-tempered wares and apparently had a much different subsistence base and settlement pattern. Second, the whole phase is of short duration, probably no more than fifty to a hundred years (see App. D). Third, all major village and town sites of the phase were consumed by fire, bringing the cultural activities to an abrupt and instantaneous halt and affording the archaeologist perfect time-space control. It is unknown, however, whether all sites burned the same day. Fourth, the area of the

Powers phase is under heavy cultivation, making almost all sites of the phase detectable through surface evidence and allowing adequate surface samples to be recovered, a situation lacking in many areas. Because of these factors the Powers phase provides an unusual and unprecedented situation for the study of Mississippian culture in the Mississippi alluvial valley and indeed, in the southeastern United States.

II

THE POWERS PHASE

ARCHAEOLOGICAL SURVEY OF THE POWERS PHASE AREA

Surface Reconnaissance

Price Survey, Winter 1966

An intensive surface survey was conducted along the Little Black River from 3 miles north of Ringo Ford southward to the Arkansas line, a total of approximately 18 miles. It was conducted section by section on foot. Areas where there was poor recovery or where the ground was covered by crops were noted and examined at a later date when surface conditions were more favorable. This survey was restricted to areas adjacent to Little Black River on both sides. A large portion of the braided channel area in eastern Ripley and western Butler Counties was also surveyed at this time. On this survey all sites from Paleo-Indian through Historic were noted and surface samples were recovered. The several Mississippian villages that were discovered contained identical material culture to that present at Powers Fort, which is located about a mile and a half from the Ozark Escarpment into the Western Lowlands.

During the survey, when local collectors began indiscriminate excavation at one village, it was noted that the village was burned. Further investigations on other sites demonstrated that they too had been destroyed by fire. Excavation was begun on the Turner site (23BU-21A) in the summer of 1966, and the Powers Phase Project was born.

Smith Survey, Spring 1969

Bruce Smith, a graduate assistant of the University of Michigan Museum of Anthropology, conducted a survey in the area to fill gaps in the Price survey and to expand reconnaissance southward into Arkansas and eastward on the sand ridges. He used the techniques employed on the Price survey, and ground conditions were very favorable for surface collecting, since most soybean and cotton fields were fallow during the winter after discing or plowing. Once a site was located, it was completely walked over and collected by following existing furrows or rows. A reasonable estimate is that in the area covered by the Price and Smith surveys, 90 percent of the sites were located. Any sites that escaped detection were probably small and extractive in nature.

During the Price and Smith surveys, a total of 157 archaeological sites were discovered. Of these, 80 contained Powers phase materials. The largest site is, of course, Powers Fort. Seven village sites of secondary size were discovered. Later an additional site was reclassified by Richard Malouf, then a research assistant of the University of Michigan Museum of Anthropology. This site was originally thought to be a hamlet. These villages range from 2.5 to 4 acres in size. Four small hamlets of tertiary magnitude were located, each smaller than 1.5 acres. The rest of the Powers phase sites, which were very small, yielded only a handful of pottery sherds These probably were temporary camps and individual farmsteads. A map of all sites located depicting their size order, is presented in Figure 3.

Intensive Controlled Surface Collecting

STAIN COLLECTION ON 23BU-21B, THE SNODGRASS SITE, SPRING 1968. This site was plowed and disced prior to surface collecting. A rain had fallen and washed surface objects clean; surface stains were noted over the entire site indicating the structures which had been built in shallow basins in the sterile subsoil and later burned. Each of these stains was carefully mapped with an alidade and plane table and a number assigned to it. Limits of stains were determined by viewing the site from a 60-foot tall tower and directing the workers by walkie-talkie radios. All surface materials collected from the stains were placed in numbered bags.

GRID CONTROLLED SURFACE COLLECTION ON 23BU-21B, SPRING 1969. The site was surveyed and gridded into squares 20 feet on a side, exclusive of the area that had been excavated previously in the 1969 field season. Workers attempted total recovery of all surface material. All sherds down to thumbnail size were collected, as well as all lithic and faunal remains.

Although the analysis of materials recovered is still incomplete, several conclusions can be drawn. (1) Site limits can be accurately determined by using these methods. (2) The locations of "courtyards" can be determined. (3) The general overall configuration or layout of structures can be determined. (4) Differential distribution of such artifacts as clay beads, drills, hoe flakes, and pottery can be determined.

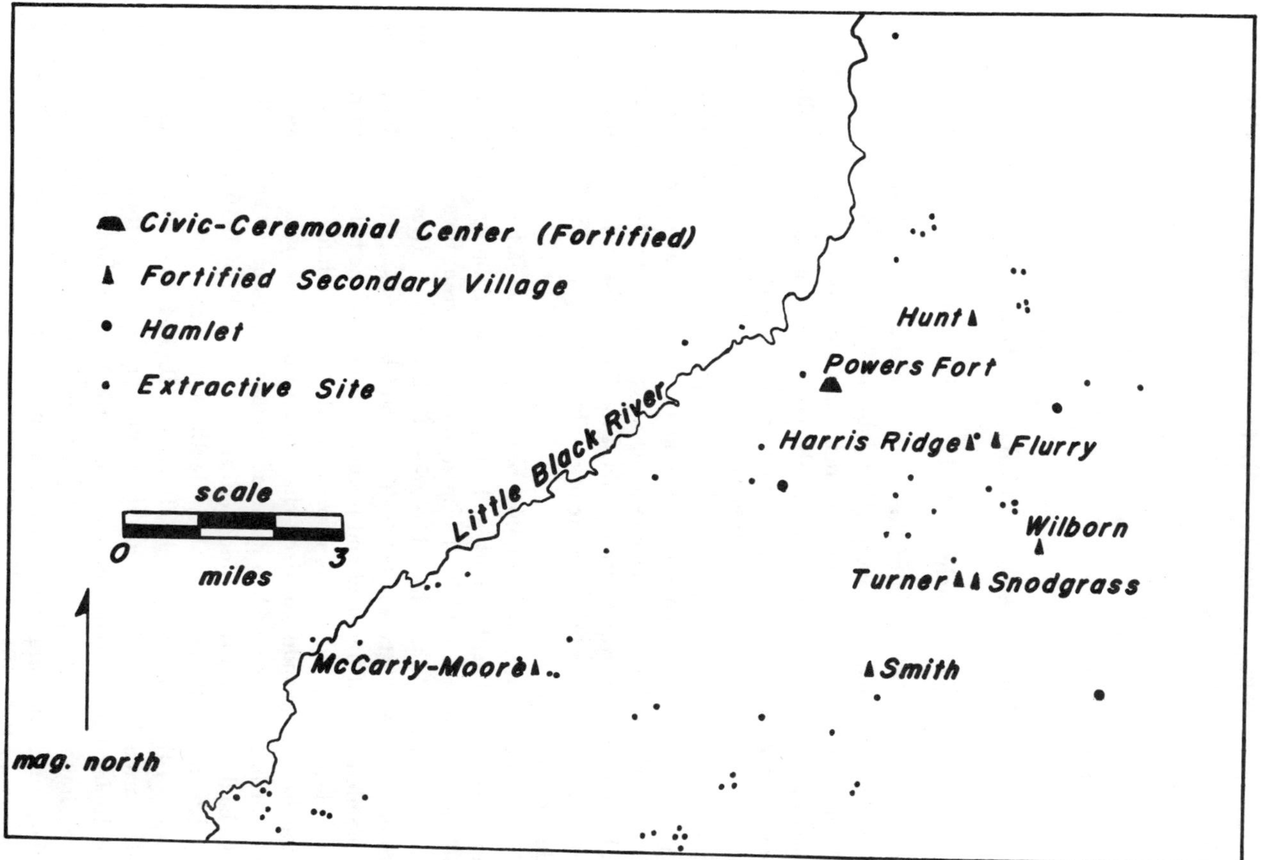

Figure 3. Powers phase settlement pattern.

RANDOM GRID CONTROLLED COLLECTION, POWERS FORT, (23BU-10), SPRING 1969. James MacLaury conducted a collection from Powers Fort using 20 squares, each 20 by 20 feet, randomly distributed across the site. Tentative observation of this material indicates that Powers phase dwelling areas are present, as well as areas occupied by Archaic and Woodland peoples prior to the building of Powers Fort.

ENVIRONMENTAL VARIABLES OF THE POWERS PHASE

Topography of the Little Black River Area

The Courtois Hills area of the Ozark Highland west of Little Black River is highly dissected, with very steep hills and narrow valleys. The Central Plateau area is not so greatly dissected, and valleys tend to be wider and the slopes more eroded. The streams in the Ozark Highland area are usually cold and clear. Small streams in the hollows may be intermittent and fed by wet weather springs. The major streams are rock and gravel bottomed and are fed by large springs. Big Springs, Greer Springs, Alley Spring, and Round Spring, some of the largest springs in the United States, are in this area. In the highland the drainage systems are primarily dendritic, and there is a large amount of runoff after a rain. Flooding of the valleys occurs at least once a year. These floods occur primarily in the spring and fall and are seldom of long duration.

The southeastern part of the Ozark Highland is part of a former plain that once sloped gently south and east, and present topography is the result of the erosion of this plain. The area closest to Current River is the roughest, because of deep dissection. The area of Little Black River is less hilly and forms a border between the highlands and lowlands. Little Black River is a combination of highland and lowland streams. In the hills it is fast running and clear, but it widens as it pours forth from the hills, filling many large sloughs and abandoned river channels. Little Black is a sluggish stream, except in flood stage when it spreads miles from its banks and overflows all the land except the sandy ridges (Hutton and Krusekopf 1916:11).

The main stream west of Little Black is Current River. Primary tributaries of this river are Fourche, Hurricane, Briar, Buffalo, Little Barren, and Big Barren Creeks. All except Hurricane start in the extreme western part of Ripley County and flow southeastward. North of Doniphan, deep gullies and draws are cut by Isaacs, Simpson, and Bills creeks. South of Doniphan the creeks are longer without an abrupt drop to the river (Hutton and Krusekopf 1916:10).

The topography and drainage of the lowland contrast greatly with that of the highland. The only elevations in the lowlands are low sand ridges.

Level flood plains in the area are interrupted by some higher land with a level to hummocky surface, but the general elevation is much less than that of the hills just across Little Black River. In some cases the difference between the elevation of the west and east banks of the river may be as much as 100 feet.

The bottoms of the streams are muddy, covered with logs and leaves, and the water is quite sluggish. Drainage systems are lateral, in contrast to the dendritic type of the hill country, and drainage is primarily crosswise to the main axis of the highland border. Whitewater River enters from the north and flows south to Morehouse Lowland; Castor River enters from the Ozark Highland northwest of Brownwood and flows southwest into the Morehouse Lowland. St. Francis River enters the lowland near Poplar Bluff, and the Current River enters it in Arkansas (Magill 1958:11). Floods would certainly have been a limiting factor to horticulture of the Powers phase and other Mississippian groups in adjacent areas, since they often occur during the summer months.

Sites of the Powers phase lie between those two vast regions (highlands and lowlands) on rolling sand ridges which were formed by braided channels of the Mississippi River over 7000 years ago according to an estimate by Fisk (1944). Recent research has demonstrated some of the ridges in the valley to be at least as old as 12,000 years (Saucier 1974).

Seven different geologic formations are present in the Little Black area. Six of them are Ordovician and one is Pleistocene. The six Ordovician formations are the Roubidoux, Smithville, Powell, Cotter, Jefferson City, and the Gasconade (Geologic Map of Missouri 1961).

The Roubidoux Formation is present in northern Ripley and northwestern Butler Counties. It is composed of sandstone, chert, and interbedded fine-grained dolomite. The Smithville, Powell, Cotter, and Jefferson City formations are present in the southern half of Ripley County west of Little Black River and are composed of fine-grained, silty, and cherty dolomite and oolitic chert. The Gasconade Formation, which lies in river valleys in the northern portion of both Ripley and Butler Counties, consists of coarsely crystalline cherty dolomite overlying a basal sandstone.

The Pleistocene formation forms the western part of the Western Lowland east of Little Black River. Here the deposits are alluvium, clay silt, and gravel. An overwhelming majority of the Powers phase sites are restricted to this formation.

The soils of the Little Black River area are of three types: Clarksville, Union, and Waverly-Calhoun. Clarksville soil covers the northwest half of Ripley County, except for an area of Union soil extending northwestward from the lowlands in the southeastern part of the county. The Clarksville soil of northwest Butler County is cut into two sections by a Union soil extension from the southeast.

The Clarksville soils (Krusekopf 1962:12) have very few level areas. Chert stones two to four inches in diameter are almost always present and make up 20 to 60 percent of the soil mass. The surface soil is gray to light brown in color and changes at a depth of approximately 6 inches to a gray-brown silty clay. Subsoil usually starts at about 12 inches and is a friable yellow-brown silty clay. Lower subsoils vary from a brittle gray silt loam to reddish brown clay loam or may consist of a mass of chert rock. The use of Clarksville soils for agricultural purposes is limited by topography, stone content, and fertility. Generally, it is very poor soil. Most of the land is not arable and is covered by forest in which pine is an important component. Soil quality would certainly have been a limiting factor for any westward expansion of the Powers phase or for farming in the adjacent highland area.

The Union soils (Krusekopf 1962:13) form a long belt which separates Clarksville and Waverly-Calhoun soils in Butler and Ripley Counties. Ridges and valleys have a deep soil mantle, but slopes may have been eroded, exposing outcrops. It is an area of sharp contrasts, of hilly land interspersed with forests. Stone-free soils have a silty texture and are light brown in color. The soil-forming material was a shallow loess, but in some places the source was limestone. Most of this soil is not suited for cultivation because of slope and severe erosion. Although creek bottom soil in this area is very fertile, it is subject to yearly flooding.

Waverly-Calhoun soils (Krusekopf 1962:16) start at the western edge of Crowley's Ridge and extend westward to the Ozark Highland. Soils are predominantly gray silt loams derived from loess washed from surrounding uplands. Waverly soils include the sand ridges around Neelyville and are most abundant in Butler County. Calhoun soils occur on low terraces and include most of the land between the St. Francis River and Crowley's Ridge. The soil is usually poorly drained, except on ridges. Many of the soils are thoroughly leached, are hard and brittle when dry, and are difficult to cultivate. Along the streams in the lowlands there are deposits of gumbo, which is organically rich and has the texture of clay, but would have been impossible to farm employing aboriginal techniques. The only favorable land for Powers phase farmers would have been on the ridges, and soil distribution was probably the prime factor in determining the settlement pattern.

Mineral resources of interest to aboriginal people, with the possible exception of clay, exist only in the hills of the Little Black River area. Hematite, galena, and limonite are totally absent in the lowland but are common in the Ozark region where they are mined commercially today (Ballinger and Persones 1948). Outcrops would have made these minerals readily available to the Powers phase people. Other important resources present in streambeds of the highland are chert and quartzite.

Climate of the Little Black River Area

There is a measurable difference in the overall climate between the Ozark Highland and the Western Lowlands. The averages presented in Table 1 indicate climatic variations of the region. It should not be assumed that these figures would hold true if extended into the past as much as 600 years, but, it does stand to reason that if there is a difference between the two areas today, similar proportions or ratios probably existed in the past. Differences are not great enough to affect maize cultivation. Rainfall was probably not a great limiting factor to Powers phase people, except when it came in too great or too small a quantity. From present rainfall conditions it is possible that part of the area covered by the phase could have had a drought while other areas had adequate rainfall.

High winds accompany summer thunderstorms and are hazards to standing crops. Although these are localized, they can level a corn field in a matter of minutes. No data are available on their frequency, but they occur almost exclusively during the growing season.

Little Black River is climatically as well as physically intermediate between the highlands and lowlands. The weather data demonstrate that the average temperature of the Ozarks is 56.8°F and of Boot Heel, 59.1°F. The average of 58.8°F for the Little Black River area falls between these two figures. The amount of precipitation is also intermediate but is closer to that of the lowlands. The highlands receive an average of 43.13 inches and the lowlands 46.21 inches. The Little Black River area receives 46.03 inches.

Killing frosts begin in late October but occur a few days sooner in the highlands than in the lowlands. This was probably not a critical factor to the Powers phase people, since most crops would have been harvested by October. Most nuts, with the exception of acorns, do not fall from trees until after a frost so this must have influenced the harvest of the nut crop.

In the highlands there is more snow and slightly more sleet and hail than in the lowlands (Sauer 1920:33). The highlands are also much more prone to drought, which does permanent damage to field crops during any part of the growth period.

The topographic variables are considerable, as can be deduced from the description of the area. Terrain ranges from rugged, deeply dissected Ozark hill country to the west to the broad delta of sand and mud to the east. Gradational forces, not to mention the poor soil, make farming impractical in the Ozark country. In the lowlands, the sand ridges are the only areas that could have supported aboriginal cultivation and this only above a certain elevation.

Drainage systems range from complex dendritic ones in the Ozarks to the lateral lowland streams and from fast flowing rock- and gravel-bottomed

TABLE I
TEMPERATURE AND PRECIPITATION DATA FOR THE POWERS PHASE AREA
(From The Decennial Census of U.S. Climate, 1965)

East Ozarks Division	*Temperature (°F)*
Average Temperature:	56.8
Average High:	78.2 in July
Average Low:	34.8 in January
Average Annual Precipitation:	43.13
Highest Recorded:	64.62
Lowest Recorded:	25.46
Highest Average:	5.01 in May
Lowest Average:	2.83 in December
Boot Heel Division	*Temperature (°F)*
Average Temperature:	59.1
Average High:	88.3 in July
Average Low:	34.8 in January
Average Annual Precipitation:	46.21
Highest Recorded:	76.94
Lowest Recorded:	25.46
Highest Average:	4.86 in March
Lowest Average:	3.12 in October

WEATHER DATA FROM POPLAR BLUFF, MO.
(McQuigg and Decker, 1963:21-23)

Temperature (°F)

Record High: 112 August — Record Low: -23 January

	Averages		Averages		
Jan.:	36.0	July:	76.4	Annual Average:	58.8
Feb.:	37.2	Aug.:	79.9		
Mar.:	40.4	Sept.:	78.0		
Apr.:	48.2	Oct.;	71.4		
May:	59.1	Nov.:	47.6		
June:	67.8	Dec.:	39.1		

Precipitation

Maximum in 24 hours: 6.17 inches

	Averages		Averages		
Jan.:	3.79	July:	3.33	Annual Average:	46.03
Feb.:	3.44	Aug.:	3.15		
Mar.:	4.54	Sept.:	3.40		
Apr.:	4.43	Oct.:	3.20		
May:	5.00	Nov.:	3.77		
June:	4.08	Dec.:	3.39		

to sluggish streams with mud bottoms. The Ozark streams are not only important for the resources they contain but also for the routes they provide into rugged country.

The soil quality ranges from the poorest to the most fertile in southeast Missouri. Clarksville soils are almost worthless for farming due to the high rock content and extremely thin topsoil, whereas the Waverly-Calhoun soils are excellent for farming because of their alluvial content. Since the latter soils are in the form of sandy loam in the Powers phase area, they were probably the easiest to exploit utilizing the aboriginal techniques of the Mississippian populations of the area.

Geological variables range from deposits rich in cherts, hematite, limonite, and galena in the Ozarks to the lowlands, which are completely devoid of all such materials. If such minerals occur in the lowland, they had to have been brought there through human effort.

Climatic variables are more difficult to deal with since temperature and precipitation averages tell us little about the direct influence of these variables on a sedentary village culture whose subsistence was based partly on hand cultivation. However, climatic variables become extremely important when total ranges are considered along with the frequency of occurrence of the extremes. The climate of the Little Black River area is fairly stable except for localized droughts and floods. Major droughts occur on the average about every 20 years, but small localized ones occur almost yearly. Hailstorms on the catastrophic level are usually localized, and data on their frequency are scarce. According to local residents, they tend to occur on the average of every 15 years.

The people of the Powers phase probably occupied an area with adequate rainfall, rich soil, and natural catastrophes frequent enough to cause major crop failures and damage occasionally. Such damages were probably very localized so that all fields of the phase were not harmed. Procuring data on the frequency of these climatic phenomena is almost impossible. As many of these phenomena are localized, the Powers phase culture may have had an exchange network to counteract their effects. When food resources failed in part of the system, foodstuffs may have been shifted from more productive areas within the system to sustain populations suffering from inadequate nutritional resources.

The most critical factors in this system are rainfall and soils, for these are the prime necessities for hoe cultivation without the aid of irrigation or fertilization. The topographic variable is likewise critical: there was limited space available for villages and horticulture because of swamps to the east, south, and between the ridges and because of the rugged hill country to the west.

EXTRACTIVE PROCESSES OF THE POWERS PHASE

Food

Vegetal products excavated from Powers phase sites include both wild and domesticated plants. Wild plants represented are acorns from several species of oaks, walnuts, butternuts, hickory nuts, persimmons, amaranth, and chenopods (S. E. Harris: personal communication). *Iva,* or marsh elder, is also present and Hugh Cutler, Missouri Botanical Gardens, has stated that the seeds are so large that they may have been domesticated (personal communication).

Wild plant foods were probably gathered in both the highlands and lowlands, since representatives of the above species grow in both areas today (Settergren and McDermott 1962). They were probably collected in baskets and transported back to the villages. Acorns, walnuts, and hickory nuts were shelled in the individual dwellings. That sand ridges adjacent to the sites functioned as fields for crops is evidenced by polished flakes of Mill Creek chert left by hoe sharpening on the sand ridges. However, from the quantity of flakes present in the structures, it appears that most resharpening of hoes was done in the dwellings.

The major portion of faunal food remains are from Eastern Whitetail deer, which were probably hunted in both the highlands and lowlands with only selected portions brought back to the villages (Bruce Smith: personal communication). Only bones of the limbs and head are found in great quantity. The humerus, calcaneum, astragalus, ulna, scapula, femur, cannon bone, and phalanges represent the limbs. An occasional atlas, axis, or cervical vertebra represents the head. Ribs and vertebrae are absent for all practical purposes. Often piles of one bone type, such as mandibles, antlers, or scapulae are found in structures (Bruce Smith: personal communication).

Other wildlife represented are opossum, beaver, squirrel, raccoon, eagle, waterfowl, fish, land terrapin, water turtle, and river mussel. Most of these creatures were probably present in both the highlands and lowlands, but in different frequencies. Fish, waterfowl, and water turtle could have come from the swamps and Little Black River. Mussels probably came from the river, as did beaver.

Stone for Tools and Weapons

The majority of chert utilized by the Powers phase people came from local stream beds, most likely that of Little Black before it empties into the lowlands. Cortex flakes indicate that cores were made of waterworn creek rocks of rather poor quality. The nearest chert source for people at Powers Fort was about 4 miles distant. Mill Creek chert from southern

Illinois and Dover chert from Tennessee are the only distant cherts that were procured. They occur in their natural state as large slabs and provided pieces sufficiently large for hoes and bifacially flaked knives that are found on Powers phase sites. The small amount recovered was probably obtained by exchange from neighboring groups rather than by expedition.

Quartzite is also present, but few tools appear to have been made of it. This too is of poor quality and was obtained from stream beds in the highlands.

Green granite was used for celts and hoes and must have been obtained from the glacial tills to the north in the area of the Missouri River, the most southern extent of glaciation. Some large green granite boulders are found in the Powers phase area, probably ice-rafted there in late Pleistocene times, and these cannot be overlooked as a possible granite source.

Sandstone for grinding slabs and tool abraders probably came from the highlands where such material occurs in quantity. Dolomite for axes likewise probably came from this area but was not exploited to a great degree.

Wood for tools could have been obtained from either the highland or lowland zones, and bone for tools was a byproduct of hunting.

Pigments

Pigments found on Powers phase sites are hematite, limonite, and galena. The first two are locally available in the highlands but the nearest galena source is in the Lead Belt of Missouri about 80 to 100 miles to the north. Pigments were used for painting and slipping pottery and for body paint.

Raw Material for Construction

Wood for structures, walls, and fortifications was probably obtained locally. Logs 9 to 12 inches in diameter were used for fortifications and ones averaging 6 inches in diameter were selected for intra-village walls and internal support posts for structures. Poles averaging 4 inches in diameter were used for wall wedges and stringers on structures. Walls and rafters of structures were made of poles averaging 3 inches in diameter. Smaller poles were used as lathing to which the thatch was applied. No limbs have been found in any architectural remains (limbs have their inner rings off center), so they must have been trimmed off and left in the forest or used as firewood (S. E. Harris: personal communication).

Cane for structure walls, baskets, and mats was probably procured from swamp margins where, until recently, large canebrakes grew. Remains of these have been found on both the Turner and Snodgrass sites. Grass for thatch was probably procured in the same areas that cane was.

A large quantity of material was needed to build the Snodgrass site. When all other villages and Powers Fort are considered, one can appreciate the amount of raw material that had to be extracted from the environment to construct all settlements of a small phase and provide firewood and general maintenance materials.

Clay

Clay for ceramics, cones, daub, etc. was obtained from the swamps. This is evidenced by the "buckshot" or iron concretions, which occur both in manufactured objects and the native clay. The clay is generally of poor quality and often large quantities of sand were used, in addition to shell, to temper it. Since wattle and daub architecture is not present in the Powers phase, not as much clay was needed for construction in this phase as appears in others further south and east during this same time period.

Water

Drinking water probably came from the swamps adjacent to the sites. Evidence for this is seen in the form of a red iron precipitate on the interior surfaces of water bottles. Such a precipitate would not be present had the people been storing river water.

THE MATERIAL CULTURE OF THE POWERS PHASE

Thousands of field specimens have been recovered by the surveys and excavations of the Powers Phase Project. At this time we can present a fairly complete inventory of the imperishable material culture employed by these peoples. The following is a presentation by category of the tools and facilities of the Powers phase:

Ceramics

The paste utilized in Powers phase ceramics is very heterogenous throughout all morphological types. It ranges from almost totally sand-tempered to wholly shell-tempered. The paste of the latter approximates that of Neelys Ferry Plain or Mississippi Plain. There is almost a total lack of surface decoration, and what little there is, is composed of incised lines, punctates, some cord-marking, and nodes. The nodes usually occur on the shoulders and rims of small and medium-sized jars. Some low-necked wide mouth water bottles have a red residue on their interior which looks like paint or slip but is in fact iron deposits from the iron-laden water of the area. At

Powers Forts there is more painted pottery than at any other site of the phase. These are painted red and occasionally red and white.

Vessel Forms

JARS. Jars range in size from miniatures to ones with a capacity of over 4 gallons (App. E). They usually have two strap handles which can be plain or binoded or rarely bifurcated. Some have small vertical holes through the top. Loop handles are rare and when present occur on small jars. A few lug handles are present on large jars. Large jars have "stir marks" in the bottom of the interior and sometimes charred food remains are present. They were probably used for cooking and for storage.

BOWLS. Greater variation occurs among this morphological type than among jars. They occur in two separate general types, low straight-sided ones that flare from a flat base and an effigy type. The first type ranges from 6 to 18 inches in diameter. The effigy bowls have nearly vertical sides and have rim-rider effigies usually in the form of a bird. A tab tail is usually present opposite the head on the rim.

BOTTLES. The most common bottle type is the short-necked wide mouth type with a globular body. The long-necked type, the traditional Mississippian water bottle, usually occurs only with burials, although fragments have been found in village refuse.

Secondary Usage of Ceramics

Many examples have been found in the structures where large jars or bottles, after they were broken, had been modified to make containers in the form of small shallow bowls.

Other Ceramic Objects

These include pottery trowels with plain or bifurcated handles, pottery beads, earspools, Kersey clay objects, and cones (Marshall 1965:123). The cones need special comment since they are unusual and occur in great quantity in this phase. They are solid ceramic objects that average 7 inches in height and usually have a hole in the side. They are found in the vicinity of fire hearths and probably functioned as supports for large cooking vessels. The hole was probably used in moving them while they were hot.

Chipped Stone Artifacts

The chipped lithic assemblages are composed of projectile points, knives, drills, and utilized flakes. Mill Creek chert hoes or spades are found as well as hoe flakes which are evidence of resharpening.

Ground Stone Artifacts

Greenstone hoes, axes, celts, handstones, and grinding slabs compose this assemblage.

Bone Tools and Artifacts

These are represented by deer ulnae awls, deer antler flakers, bird bone beads, and split bone awls. There is a great quantity of scapulae and mandibles which may have functioned as tools.

Matting and Cordage

Many woven mat impressions occur on the bottoms of some cones and on miscellaneous pieces of clay. Cord markings occur on a few sherds and on a Kersey clay object. One section of a split cane mat was found in a structure at the Snodgrass site. Elements of this mat are woven in a herringbone pattern.

THE POSITION OF THE SNODGRASS SITE IN THE REGIONAL SETTLEMENT PATTERN OF THE POWERS PHASE

The Snodgrass site is one of eight villages associated with Powers Fort, a large mound center, in Butler County, Missouri. These villages form a radial pattern to the east and south at a distance of from 2 to 5.5 miles from Powers Fort and are restricted to old braided stream areas or sand dunes (Figs. 3, 4). The Snodgrass site lies on the crest of a southward sloping sand ridge 3.2 miles southeast of Powers Fort and only 0.1 miles east of the Turner site which is another village in the settlement system. The Wilborn village lies to the northeast at a distance of 1.1 miles and the Smith site is located 1.8 miles to the southwest. Whether or not these sites were occupied contemporaneously is open to question at the present time.

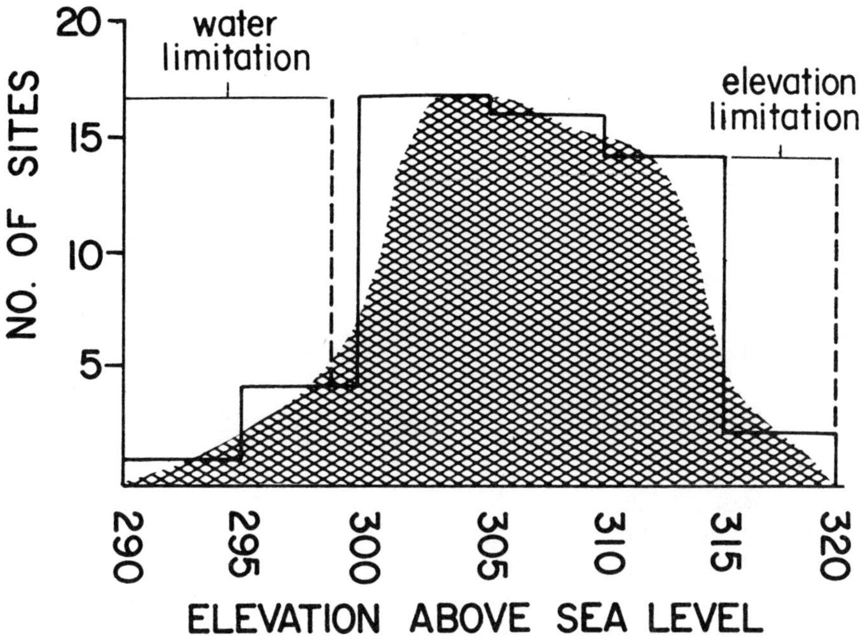

Figure 4. Site frequency at five-foot contour intervals.

III

EXCAVATION OF THE SNODGRASS SITE

SITE DESCRIPTION

The land on which the site lies has been under cultivation for approximately 70 years. It was cleared of large trees in the early 1900s and has been in row crops or pasture land to the present. At least one historic farmstead sat approximately in the middle of the site. Nails, brick fragments, and broken ironstone ceramics and glass are all that remain of this historic occupation, and since the evidence is scattered over a large area it is not possible from surface cultural debris to determine where the farm house originally sat. An historic cemetery, the Crab Cemetery, lies just north of the site.

Many years after the land was cleared, a farm lane bordered by a fence and trees ran from west to east across the north end of the site. The trees were cut and the fence removed in the 1940s. Since that time the field has been sown in row crops consisting of soybeans, cotton, and corn and cover crops of wheat, rye, and vetch. Watermelons have also been grown on the ridge. The site has been subjected to most modern farming practices, except for the chisel plow and subsoiler. The plow zone extends to a depth of 7 to 8 inches, and there are often tractor tracks and plow scars that extend deeper. Various fertilizers and chemicals have been used on crops growing on the site. Even though the site has been intensively farmed, it has not been badly damaged by these practices.

Some surface collecting has been done on the site over the years by amateurs and by the land tenant, Mr. Dale Turner, but other than projectile points, very little material has been removed. Mr. Ray Hastings of Doniphan, Missouri did a small amount of digging on the site, excavating a trench that ran from Burial 1 westward approximately 40 feet, terminating in Structure 5. In 1967 Mr. Dale Turner dug into two structures, 1 and 2, but the writer was on hand and finished the excavations so these data could be included in this report.

TOPOGRAPHY OF THE SITE AND ITS ENVIRONS

The site lies on a southwest to northeast axis along the crest of a sand ridge between 300 and 310 feet above sea level (Fig. 5). Contour lines, which reflect major modification of the sand ridge during construction of the site, roughly follow the outline of the village, indicating that the ridge was partially leveled during village construction. It is possible that soil removed from structure basins during construction was dumped along the sides of the sloping ridge. There is direct evidence of this on the east side of the site in the vicinity of the eastern courtyard; here it definitely appeared that underbrush had been piled, burned, and then covered with about 2.5 feet of soil. Another bit of evidence for this is that the clay subsoil is near the surface across most of the south end of the site, as if the topsoil had been removed prior to structure construction. Perhaps the best evidence for leveling of the ridge is the pattern of the contour lines on the site. Instead of being ellipitical like a normal sand ridge in the area, they roughly follow the outlines of the site. This is not debris or midden, since the site was occupied for too short a time for such an amount of debris to accumulate.

The soil in which the site lies and the soil on the surrounding ridges is a sandy loam at the surface. At a depth of approximately 2 feet, the soil is predominantly clay with iron concretions, locally called "buckshot," as inclusions. The topsoil is quite suitable for cultivation. It would have been easily tilled with hand tools in prehistoric times, although its fertility would have been quickly exhausted due to leaching of minerals in the sandy soil.

The Snodgrass site is almost completely surrounded by low, swampy areas unsuitable for cultivation because water stands on them for at least a portion of the year. Cottonwood, sycamore, willow, corkwood, and various other trees and shrubs grow in these areas. These swamps have been drained only within the last 30 years; older residents can remember catching fish and shooting ducks in them.

BASIS FOR EXCAVATION OF THE SNODGRASS SITE

Since the excavation of the Snodgrass site was seen as a unique opportunity, much consideration was given to the excavation and to a long-term research design. The primary objective of the Snodgrass excavation was to completely excavate a Mississippian village in order to leave no room for doubt concerning village planning and composition, distribution of goods, and the associations between elements. The site was chosen because it was adjacent to the Turner site where Price had excavated for two summers. This project would presumably provide data from two adjacent villages for

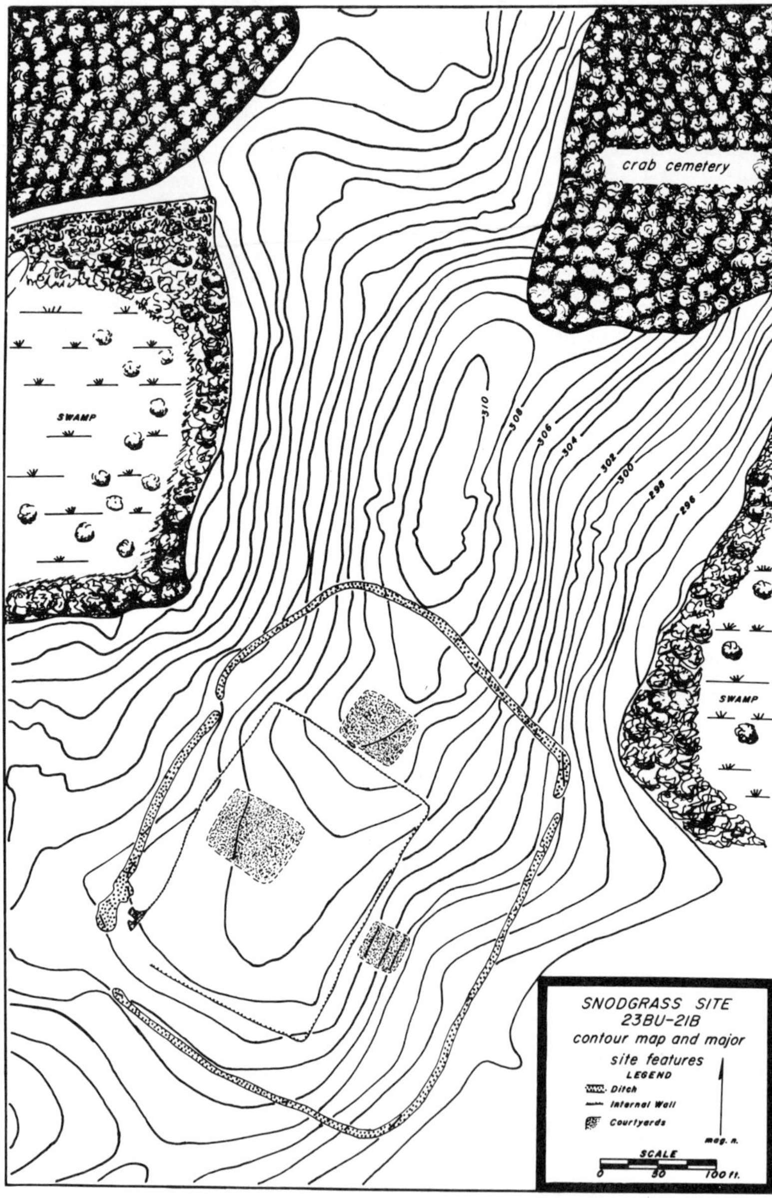

Figure 5. Contour map of the Snodgrass site.

comparisons of site size, structure size, community plan, and material goods. Also, friendly relations had been achieved between the excavators and the landowner and tenant, and permission to continue excavation was easily gained. Another reason for excavation of the site was that it had been relatively undisturbed by farming practices, roads, or pothunters. Thus, there was an excellent opportunity to delineate an entire Mississippian village and examine its contents. Urgings by well-intentioned colleagues to excavate as many villages as possible by a random sampling of squares was vigorously resisted. It was felt that the opportunity to completely excavate and record the features, artifacts and their relationships from one or more villages of a short-lived Middle Mississippi society far outweighed the knowledge to be acquired by a scientific numbers gamble. In no way could random sampling have told us what we know now about the Snodgrass and Turner sites.

PRELIMINARY RESEARCH ON THE SITE

The first excavations were made in August of 1967. Mr. Dale Turner, the farmer who leases the site for farming, dug holes into two structures on the site and uncovered some burned architecture and broken pottery vessels. These excavations were continued on a controlled basis by Price, for the University of Missouri Museum of Anthropology, and Structures 1 and 2 were totally excavated. Surface collections were also taken from the north end of the site.

Since the village was going to be entirely excavated, large excavation areas were chosen, with a minimum of 100 feet on a side. Sample units of this size would yield associations between structures, pits, streets, alleys, and other gross features of the site. As soon as one large area was stripped and excavated, another would be selected and excavation started there. Any unfinished excavation in these areas could be left from one season to the next for completion. This allowed recognition and excavation of all the areas used by the inhabitants, but also allowed us to be certain that there was no prehistoric evidence we had missed; it also provided a solid estimate of the amount of space within the wall that was occupied by structures or pits.

EXCAVATION TECHNIQUES EMPLOYED ON THE SNODGRASS SITE

Two types of excavation procedures were employed, one for preliminary detection of features and another for stripping large areas. The first method employed slit trenches which were cut deep enough through the plow zone to detect features. They measured 1.5 feet by 50 feet and were cut along a row of known structures, in order to obtain structure location, size, and orientation. When a structure or other feature was encountered, a cross slit trench was excavated in order to obtain dimensions of the structure or feature. Most of the site was tested in this fashion prior to stripping large areas.

The other method employed was stripping large areas of plow zone through the use of a tractor and rear-mounted earth bucket raised and lowered hydraulically (see Pl. 1). The scoop was lowered until it engaged the soil; the tractor was moved forward until the bucket was filled, then lifted, and the backfill dirt dumped in a designated area. The tractor work was followed by a row of workers with extremely sharp shovels removing what little remained of the plow zone and shoveling it ahead of them. The tractor was then backed up, the bucket lowered, and the shoveled soil hauled away and dumped. This proved to be very fast and efficient. The primary asset lay in the fact that the tractor never had to be driven over the area that had been trimmed clean with the shovels and the loose soil could be hauled away as fast as it accumulated in front of the shovelers. As soon as a feature was uncovered, it was outlined and recorded, thus making it ready for final excavation. When the designated area was uncovered, a staking crew, using a transit and two 100-foot steel surveying chains, set stakes at 10-foot intervals over the whole area. Next the features were recorded, utilizing the established stake grid for control. Next, stakes were driven at 5-foot intervals over large features such as structures. Structures were excavated with trowels, spoons, grapefruit knives, dental picks, and brushes. Two students were assigned to excavate each square. All large potsherds, diagnostic sherds, and architectural elements were left in place and recorded in two horizontal and one vertical dimension, in the form of a datum depth. Specimens were removed and bagged with exact provenience on the label. Samples of architectural charcoal were taken for laboratory identification and analysis.

Refuse pits were excavated with hand tools in diagonally opposing quadrants revealing two profiles at a right angle to each other. Most material was simply removed and bagged according to quadrant. If a pit was visibly stratified, it was dug in levels, keeping all material separate according to quadrant and stratum. Any obvious concentrations of material or associations were recorded. Soil samples were taken from the top, middle, and bottom of each pit.

Large features such as walls and ditches were excavated by first removing the topsoil from them and recording the horizontal dimension. Sections of ditches were cleared and cleaned out in order to locate postmolds and bastions.

Flotation was used on samples from pits and structure contents. For

Plate 1. Use of power equipment in plow zone stripping.

control, and near complete recovery of material, flotation was used on the contents of an entire structure, Structure 22, and on the contents of numerous pits. Other excavation and recovery techniques were similar to those used on most excavations and need not be discussed here, with the exception of a power sifter used to process the soil removed from structures. It consists of an aluminum frame with the sifting bed suspended by chains. It was driven by a 2 horsepower air-cooled engine with a chain drive. Such a sifter saved hundreds of man-hours of work per week, thus speeding up excavation time tremendously.

EXCAVATED AREAS ON THE SNODGRASS SITE, 1967-1972

As previously mentioned, the first excavations during the summer of 1967 were of a salvage nature. In the summer of 1968, when the first 100-foot square was opened, a road grader was first used to remove the plow zone. An area 100 x 12 feet was graded across the site. Hardly any features appeared in the shallow trench. Later it was discovered that the trench had cut across the northern courtyard, down a street, and stopped short of Structure 6.

The road grader proved to be much too bulky and hard to manage. Instead, a small tractor with a three-point hookup and a hydraulically operated blade was used to scrape off the plow zone, but it was too small to drag all the soil off such a large area. During the summer, a 100-foot square containing 11 structures was uncovered, but only 10 of the structures were completely excavated. A large portion of the fortification ditch on the east side of the site was excavated in addition to three bastions and a gate.

In the following summer (1969), a large area west of the first square was excavated. It contained 10 structures which later were either totally dug or extensively sampled. Structure 15, which lies south of the area, was also excavated as was Structure 26, the most southern and eastern structure in the site. Total flotation was begun on Structure 22 that season but was not completed until the following summer. A large section of the fortification ditch was excavated on the west side of the site, as well as a section of the white clay wall that surrounded the internal segment of the village. Most refuse pits were left for excavation during the following summer.

In the summer of 1970, the main objective of the research program was to delineate the entire village and all its large features by the use of small slit trenches and to uncover structures in various areas all over the site, in order to determine any variations in material goods throughout the site. The largest area opened was in the center of the village and on the southwest corner. Areas were also excavated in the northeast and northwest portions of the site. Seven structures were uncovered in the central area. The southwestern excavation revealed two structures and the large gateway in the southwest corner of the site consisting of a gap between the western and southern ditches. The western ditch was found to have a large expansion on the south end and a corresponding expansion was found at the south end of the white clay wall. Three structures were uncovered in the south central portion of the site and two structures were unearthed in the extreme northeastern portion of the site. Two additional structures were uncovered in the north central portion of the site. Portions of some structures were not excavated during that season but were left for completion the following summer.

The summer of 1971 brought full scale excavation. Large areas were stripped between previously excavated areas to provide a clear picture of the total village plan. Twenty-five structures were completely excavated, and excavations on unfinished structures from previous years were completed. With this accelerated excavation plan, less time was taken in structure excavation, but adequate controls were maintained. In 1972, four structures and several refuse pits were excavated. Fourteen structures remain unexcavated. They are Structures 6, 12, 32, 34, 35, 40, 57, 60, 68, 73, 74, 75, 79, and 81. Most of these have been badly disturbed by uprooted trees and by cultivation. Only about six of the remaining structures are worthy of excavation.

IV

NATURE OF THE ARCHAEOLOGICAL REMAINS AT THE SNODGRASS SITE

TYPES OF ARCHAEOLOGICAL FEATURES

Structures

Structures are the predominant architectural features found on the site. They can be easily detected due to their organic content, which makes them appear very dark in contrast to the light colored sand matrix in which they occur. All structures on the site are burned, and the ash and charcoal add to the dark coloration of structure fill. The structures are of a lowered floor type with structure foundation basins excavated into the ground from less than 8 inches to as much as 2 feet deep (Pl. 2). How the waste soil was disposed of by the builders is open to question. It may have been banked back against the walls of the finished structure or used as fill material to level the slopes of the ridge on which the site is situated. After the basin for the structures had been dug slightly larger than the intended finished structure, open-cornered wall trenches were often dug into the floor. Most structures bear little or no evidence for this, perhaps because of the sandy nature of the soil and the tendency for stains to "bleed" away.

Wall posts were set erect in the wall trenches or shoved slightly into the ground. A horizontal pole was lashed along the lower portions of the wall posts apparently at the height of the edge of the structure basin. This wedge presumably was to firmly secure the lower ends of the wall posts. Cross members were likewise lashed to the upper ends of the wall posts and members probably connected the walls with the large internal support posts. Mats constructed of a single layer of whole canes were then suspended on the interior side of the wall posts from the floor to the ceiling. There is no archaeological evidence that there was any additional covering on the structure walls other than the cane although there may have been a thin layer of thatching which would have burned away in the fire that destroyed the village. Bundles of swamp grass thatching covered the roofs of the structures and must have been lashed to rafters and lathing to be firmly secured in

Plate 2. Excavation of a structure.

place (Fig. 6). Doorways to structures were probably on the west side; there is very little archaeological evidence for doorways other than some small extensions of the structure basins on the west sides. On the east side of structures, the street is full of refuse pits preventing easy entrance from that direction. Other structures were directly adjacent to the north and south sides, making these unlikely locations for doorways.

No daub was used on the walls of the structures. The only evidence of daub is in the form of clay-encircled smoke holes in the roofs of structures. White swamp clay was plastered on the underside of the thatch and in the edges of the hole in the roof above the hearth area. Evidently this plaster prevented the sparks from igniting the roof. Remains of smoke holes are found in the southeast quarter of structures where they fell when the structures were destroyed by fire. The daub of these smoke holes is full of impressions of grass that had been added to the raw clay before it was plastered on the roofs. Often there are impressions of whole cane mats which must have covered the roofs under the thatch at least in the area of the smoke holes, if not over the entire roof.

There is very little evidence concerning the nature of the material used to lash together the structural elements of houses on the site, but in Structure 4 there was a piece of bark still wrapped around two elements of the structure.

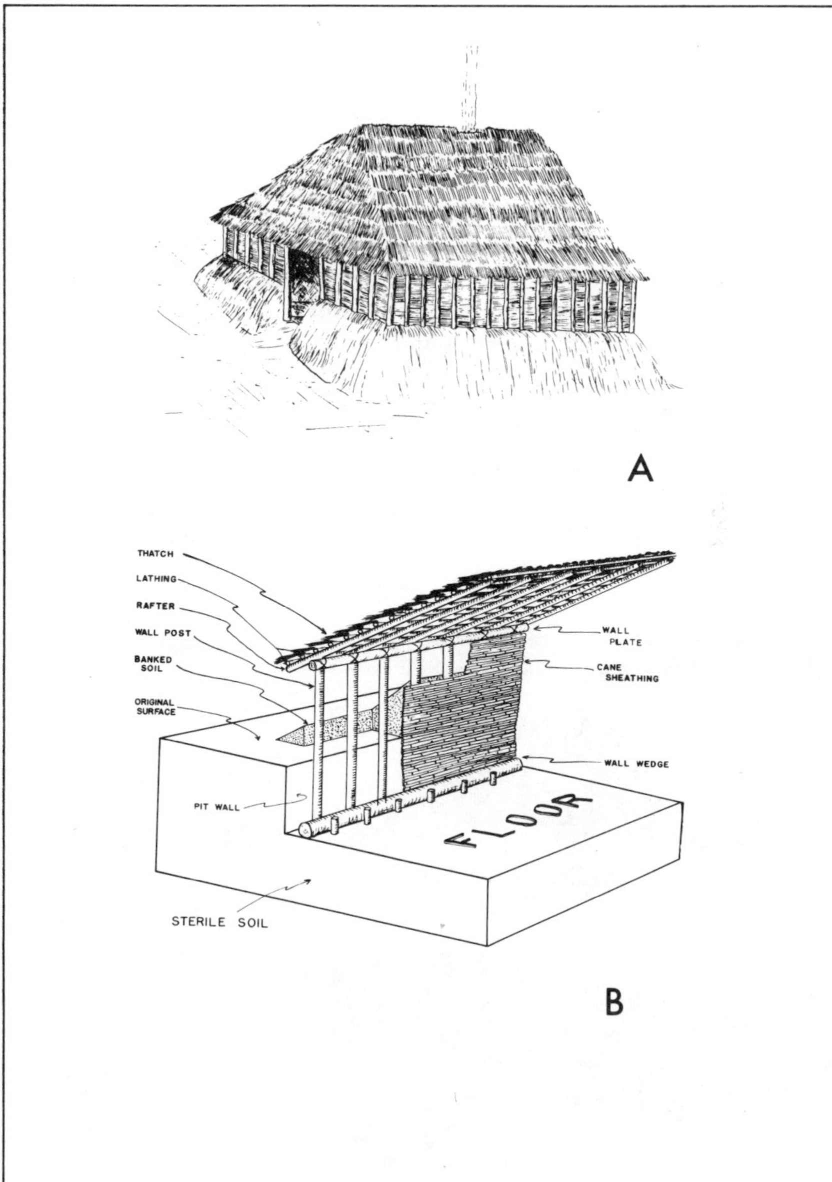

Figure 6. Snodgrass structures: A. Probable reconstruction, B. Architectural elements.

Internal support posts are much larger than wall posts. These are usually nine in number placed in three rows of three posts each. They often are over 6 inches in diameter and sometimes as much as 15 inches across. Some of them extended to a depth of 18 inches into the floor of the structures although most extended no more than 6 inches. A typical structure, Structure 3, is illustrated in Figure 7.

Refuse Pits

Round pits were excavated in the streets adjacent to the east wall of structures. They are basin shaped with outward flaring walls and are seldom deeper than 1 foot. They range in diameter from less than 2 feet to over 7 feet (Pl. 3). Figure 8 illustrates a typical pit. Contents of pits generally consist of pottery sherds, animal bones, chert and quartzite flakes, and broken hammerstones and anvilstones. There is seldom evidence of stratification in the pits. Two bore evidence of having been only partially filled at the time the village was burned. Burned poles, cane, and thatch from collapsed structures form distinct strata in these pits. There is no evidence that the pits were ever

Plate 3. Excavation of a pit.

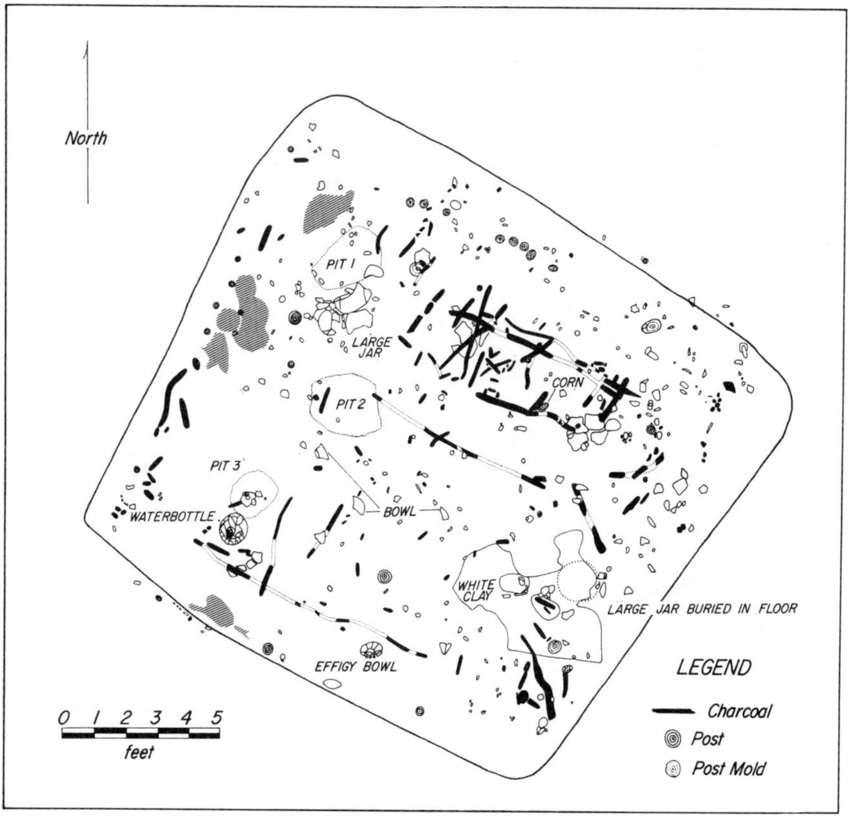

Figure 7. Snodgrass site, structure 3, 23 Bu-21B.

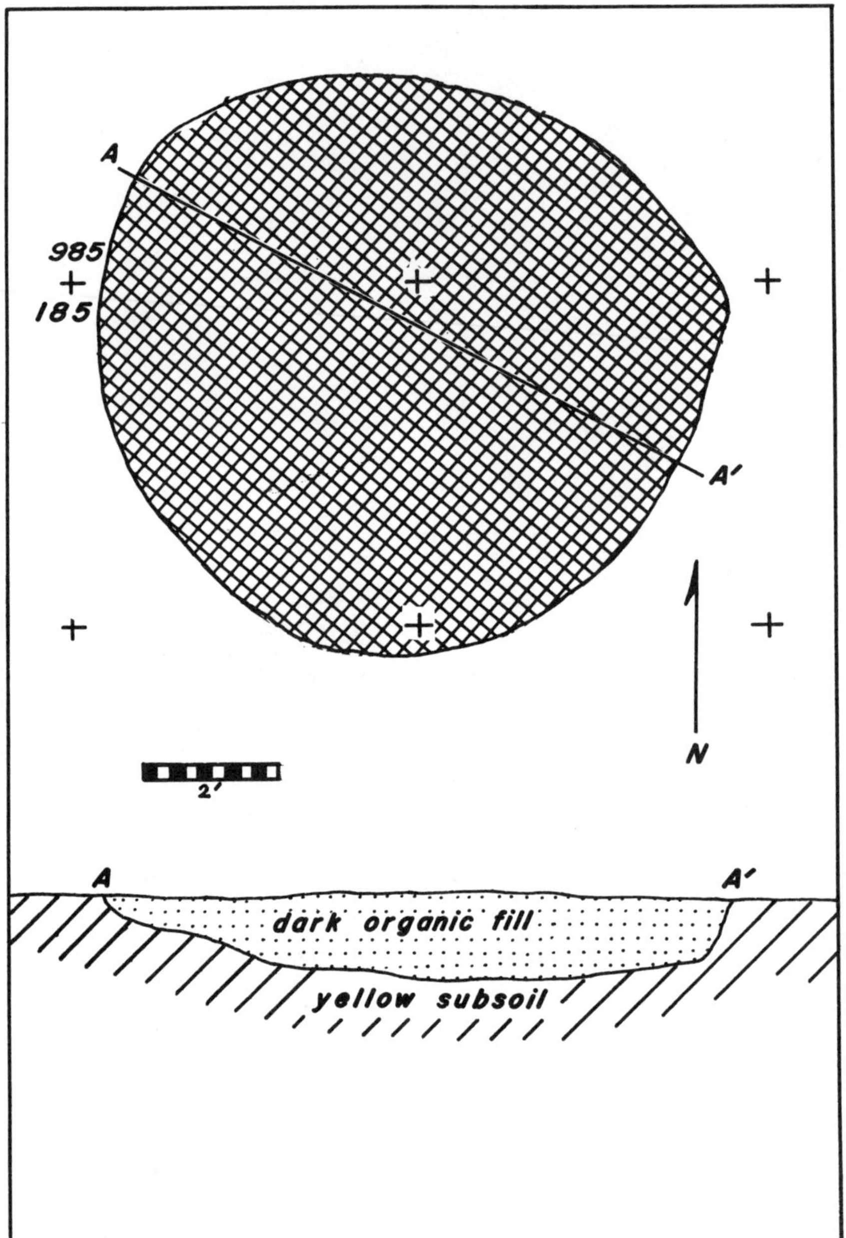

Figure 8. Pit 7, a typical pit.

lined or that they were ever used for storage, with the exception of one pit that contained white swamp clay which may have been stored there for future use. Many more refuse pits occur in the internal segment than in the external segments of the village. The significance of this will be discussed later.

Walls

There is direct evidence for only one wall within the site. It surrounds 38 structures and the major courtyard of the village. Since only a few postmolds have been found where the wall once stood, posts must have been spaced rather far apart. The evidence for existence of the wall is white swamp clay that must have been plastered on it. The wall was probably no more than a flimsy screen made of posts with interwoven cane or branches that were covered with a white swamp clay plaster. After the village burned the wall eroded, and clay spread on the ground, washing into adjacent pits and structures. Burrowing animals took the clay down into the subsoil of the site which makes the location of the wall easily detectable. A gap in the wall at the southwest corner corresponds to the major gateway between the fortification ditches. Access to the internal segment must have been gained through this opening. A bastion must have stood at the south end of the western white wall. Here a large circular stain of white clay and bits of charcoal present evidence for a superstructure of poles plastered with white clay which was probably a tower or guard house for protection of the gate. Most of the white wall had been destroyed by recent farming at the north end of the internal compound where it crossed the crest of the ridge. Here all that was left was white clay in rodent burrows in the subsoil. Clay from the white wall was concentrated most heavily in the basins of Structures 23, 24, and 25 and southward from there along the west side of the internal segment. Here the clay from the white wall had dissolved and washed into the structure basins. From the evidence, it appears that the wall here was probably not large, probably no more than 6 feet high based on the volume of clay in the structures. The significance of this wall will be discussed later in this work.

Ditches and Bastions

The site is surrounded by a large ditch which is roughly rectangular in ground plan. It varies from 4 to 8 feet wide and averages over 2 feet in depth (Pl. 4). The ditch is filled with a dark organic soil, which distinguishes it from the surrounding matrix of yellow sand and clay (Fig. 9). In cross section it is basin shaped with walls that slant upwards to the surface. The south end of the western ditch increases considerably in width and forms a large bulbous

Plate 4. Excavation of a fortification ditch.

area. At this point there is a large gap between the west and south ditch, which formed a gate to provide access to the village. A natural ridge on the approach to the village was used as a route leading into the gateway.

How the gateway was protected is unknown. There was probably a series of palisades set in the ground that gave only a narrow and perhaps a winding passage into the village. A bastion may have been in the large bulbous area to help protect the entrance. This section of the ditch was not excavated to its bottom, but a cross section was cut north of the bulbous portion; here the ditch was deeper and wider than elsewhere around the circumference of the site. A considerable amount of refuse in the form of animal bones and sherds was found in the bottom of the ditch. Such refuse was very scarce in other portions of the ditch.

Soil from the ditch was probably piled up on the village side of the ditch, but there is no archaeological evidence for this. Any earthwork would have been plowed away long ago.

Three bastions were excavated along the east ditch. A semicircle of logs had been set erect on the bottom and walls of the ditch with the open side facing inward toward the village. This half circle was then filled with yellow subsoil clay and packed down to form a foundation for the bastions. They

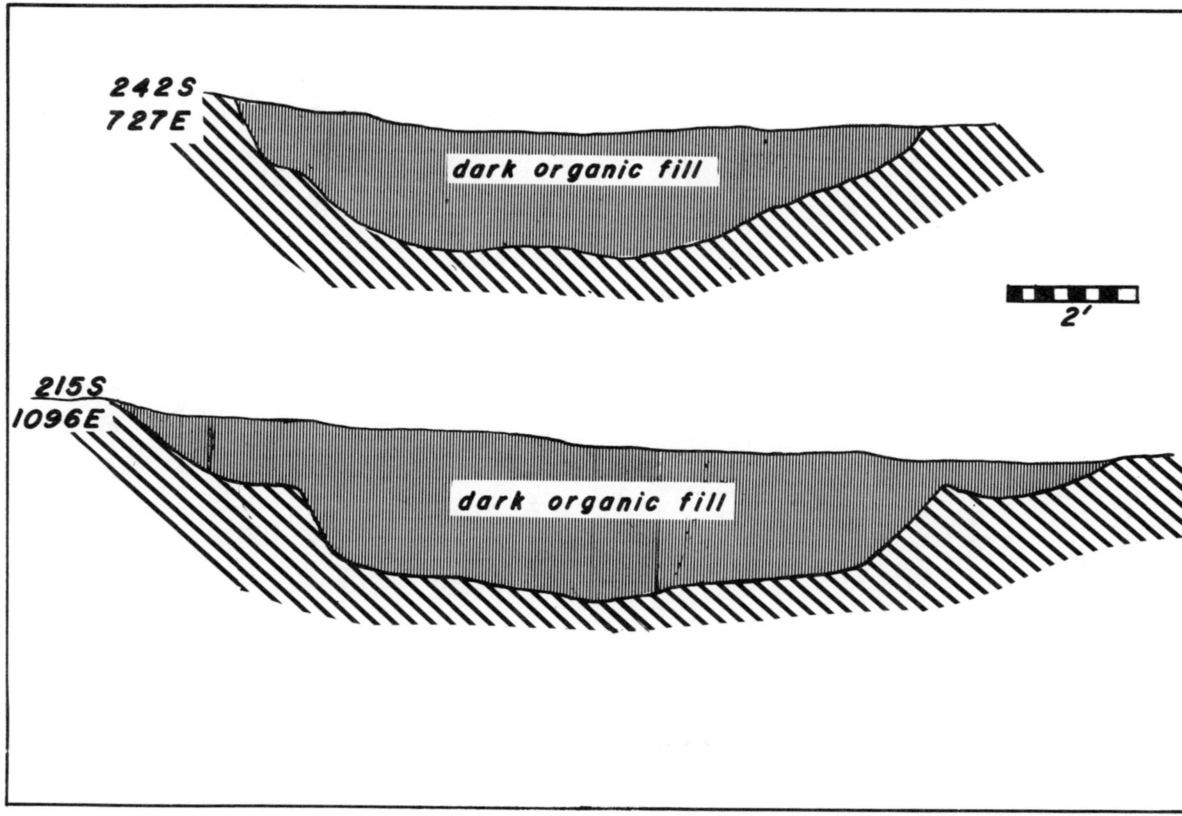

Figure 9. Fortification ditch cross sections.

were spaced approximately 75 feet apart along the ditch. This distance was probably determined by the range at which arrows could be launched with a high degree of accuracy.

Courtyards

Three open areas or courtyards occur within the village (see Fig. 11). The largest, an almost perfect square, 75 feet on a side, is on the western edge of the internal compound separated from the white wall by a single row of structures. It is essentially undisturbed by intrusive features except on the western side where refuse pits and a hearth (Pit 32) adjacent to the western row of structures were dug into it. An amorphous fill area, located in the south central area of the courtyard, probably represents an area leveled with fill during the construction of the village.

The exact function of the courtyard is unknown. It may have served as a gathering area for meetings or for rituals. The remains of a cremated body were found scattered at the northwest corner of the courtyard in Pits 28 and 30, at the southeast corner of structure 19. Most of the remains were cranial fragments with very little postcranial material represented.

The northern courtyard is likewise 75 feet in a northwest-southeast axis by approximately 60 feet on a southwest-northeast axis. It is bordered on the north, east, and west by structures and on the south by the white clay wall of the internal compound. This courtyard too was devoid of cultural material and pit disturbance.

The eastern courtyard centrally interrupts two northeast-southwest rows of structures on the eastern side of the site. It is approximately 55 feet long in a northeast-southwest axis and 50 feet wide in a northwest-southeast axis. The western edge of this courtyard is comprised of a large land fill area approximately 2.5 feet in depth with unknown boundaries, since it was not totally uncovered. It is bordered on the west by the white wall and on the north, south, and east by structures. On the east side there is a wider than average gap in the row of structures which leads toward the eastern fortification ditch. This courtyard is also devoid of cultural material and intrusive pits.

The exact function of these courtyards is open to question, but it is likely that they served the same function in each segment. They may have been vacant areas left within the village as planned spaces for expansion. As the population increased such areas could have been used for structures.

Burials

Burials are few in number. Only six adult burials were found in the entire village. Adults were placed in shallow pits in an extended, supine position.

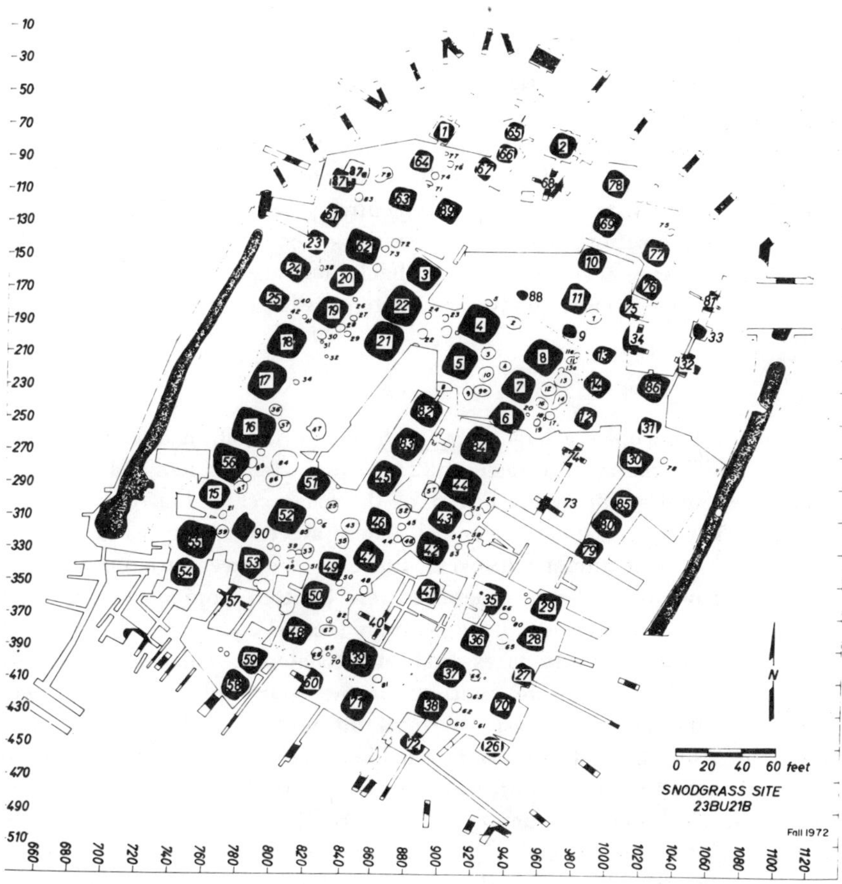

Figure 10. Snodgrass site, 23 BU–21B, Fall 1972.

All except one had the head pointing to the southeast in the same direction as the east-west axis of structure rows. The remaining head was pointed northeast along the same axis as the north-south rows of structures. Adults buried outside structures had one or two pottery vessels placed around the head, shoulders, or on the chest. Only small jars and shallow bowls are represented; long-necked water bottles are absent. Infant burials occur only under structure floors and, like the adults, are in an extended-supine position. Grave furniture for infants consists of miniature vessels and large body sherds.

STRUCTURE DIMENSIONS AND SIZE DISTRIBUTIONS

The Snodgrass site contains 90 structures, presumably used primarily as dwellings for basic family units (Fig. 10). Thirty-eight of these structures lie within a compound bounded by a white clay plastered wall. Within the site, structures range in size from 20 square feet (Structure 88) to 472.5 square feet (Structure 84) in the east central part of the village. Based on structure size, location, and the placement of courtyards, the site can be divided into three segments that probably reflect social divisions. These will be described individually and criteria will be provided for their delineation.

Segment 1

Segment 1 occupies a large area inside the fortification ditches and encompasses 38 structures averaging 322.63 square feet in size and lying primarily west and south of the center of the village (Fig. 11). This segment was definitely systematically planned. There are ten structures in each of three rows in a northeast-southwest direction and seven structures in the remaining row where three structures were omitted from the second row from the west to allow room for a centrally located courtyard. This segment also has rows of four structures, each aligned along a northwest-southeast axis except where they are omitted for the courtyard. A structure was omitted in the third east-west row from the north and the second north-south row from the east but was inserted between rows, two structures from the south end, to make a northeast-southwest row that still contained ten structures. The inserted structure is Structure 40. The spot where it should have been, at the north end of the segment, was filled with a large refuse pit containing bone, pottery, lithics, and a quantity of corn stalks and cobs.

Another deviation in the plan is a small structure (Structure 90) which was built in the south end of the first "street" from the west and is centrally located from the corners of Structures 15, 52, 53, and 55.

Two structures (17 and 18) in the western row of this segment were set back westward half a structure width to make more room for the courtyard. Since the structures in the western row were built immediately adjacent to the white wall, their doors must have opened onto the courtyard.

An unexplained phenomenon occurs in the two eastern rows of the segment. These rows swing eastward just off the southeast corner of the courtyard. Structures 42 and 46 are shifted eastward from the row and Structures 41 and 47 shift even farther to the east. Structures to the south of these continue in normal rows with the same axis as the structures on the northern side of the shifted area. Structures in the last two northwest-southeast rows on the south end of the segment tend to be smaller than other structures in the segment and may indeed form a separate subsegment separated from the rest of the segment by a wider east-west "avenue" in which Structures 40 and 90 were constructed. Structures in the last two rows tend to be smaller than 260 square feet of structure basin area.

The only detectable opening into the segment is in the southwest corner of the white clay wall. Access was probably gained by going through a system of embankments protected by a bastion which stood on the south end of the western white wall.

Structure basins in Segment 1 tend to be larger than 240 square feet, except Structures 41, 42, 43, 48, 54, and 90 which all lie toward the south end of the segment either in the shifted area or in the last southeast-northwest

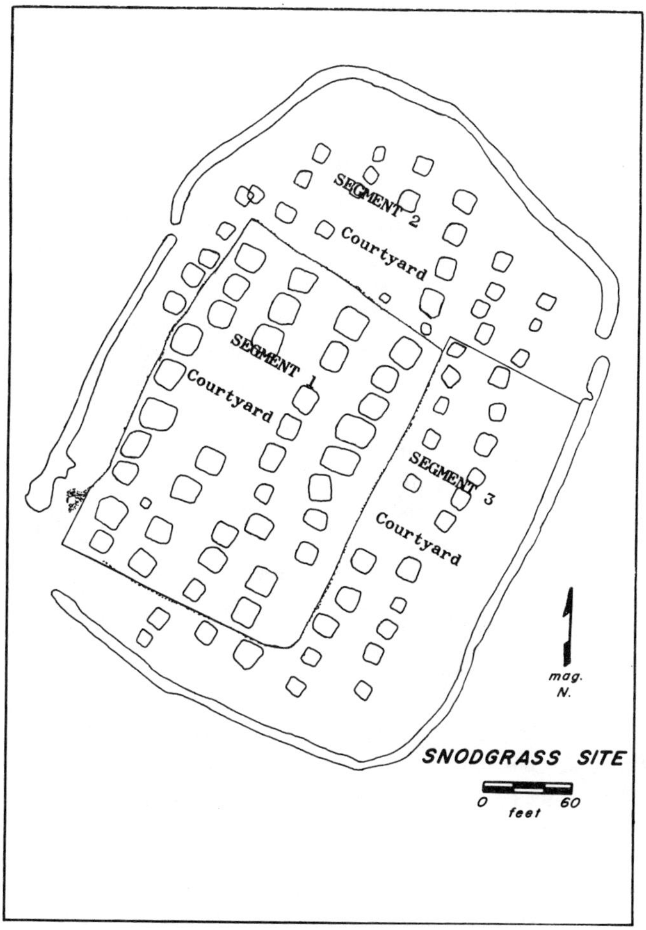

Figure 11. Location of village segments.

row (with the exception of Structure 90, which is unique because of its small size).

Segment 2

This segment lies on the north end of the site and surrounds a courtyard centrally located on the south side. This segment is not planned as regularly as Segment 1. It is bounded on the north, west, and east by the fortification ditch and on the south by the white wall and an offset row of structures in Segment 3. It contains 28 structures averaging 166.79 square feet in size. Only four structures (11, 34, 68, and 2) are larger than 240 square feet. This segment contains seven rows of structures in a northwest-southeast axis and essentially four more or less complete rows along a northeast-southwest axis. The rows align with the rows of Segment 1.

The western row consists of six structures along the northwestern side of the white wall (Structures 23, 24, 25, 61, 87a, and 87b). Some of these structures are specialized and will be discussed later. Structures 87a and 87b are the only superimposed structures on the site. The second row from the west contains three normally-spaced structures and the third row contains four irregularly spaced structures. Structure 67 is shifted northward, creating a large northeast-southwest gap in the row. Row 4 contains two structures on the north side of the courtyard and row 5 contains four regularly-spaced structures. Row 6 contains four structures, one of which (Structure 75) is out of order in the east-west rows and appears to have been inserted into the "alley" between Structures 34 and 76. It is possible it is an earlier structure, but this is unlikely. The last row, or the easternmost, contains three structures in a normal row.

A large space separates this segment from the fortification ditch everywhere except on the west side. A portion of this space was probably occupied by an earthern embankment surrounded by wooden palisades.

Segment 3

This segment lies along the eastern side of the site and along the south side of the southern portion of the white wall. A courtyard is centrally located along the eastern side. Segment 3 is bounded on the north by Segment 2 and on the east and south by the fortification ditch.

Admittedly, the criteria used for separating Segments 2 and 3 are rather arbitrary. The affiliation of Structures 9, 13, 86, and 88 is open to question. Two of these structures (13 and 86) were assigned to Segment 3 because they are offset to the west at least half a structure width from structures in rows to the north in Segment 2. Also there are no corresponding structures on the west side of Segment 2 to complete a row across the site. The four structures appear to be a series filling a small wedge of space at the northeast corner of the white wall, because they become progressively smaller from east to west. It is possible they did not belong to either Segments 2 or 3 and should be a separate segment. Two structures do, however, align better with structures in Segment 2 then with those in Segment 3.

The average size of structure basins in Segment 3 is 192.79 square feet. All structures, with the exception of Structures 71, 86, 29, and 38, are smaller than 240 square feet.

This segment is basically only two rows wide, extending in a northeast-southwest direction interrupted only by the centrally located courtyard. A single northwest-southeast row consisting of Structures 59, 60, 71, and 72 extends along the south side of the white wall. A single structure (58), lies to the south of Structure 59. The courtyard is smaller than those in Segments 1 and 2.

When structure size in square feet and structure location are plotted, it becomes apparent that a significant dichotomy existed within the village (see Figs. 12, 13). Structures larger than 240 square feet in basin size occur primarily inside the white wall, Segment 1. The average size for structures in Segment 1 is 322.63 square feet. Those in Segment 2 are 166.79 square feet, and structures of Segment 3 average 192.79 square feet. Structure measurements and locations are presented in Appendix A. On the average, structures inside the white wall tend to be almost twice as large as those outside, and the possible significance of this variation will be discussed later.

SITE AND STRUCTURE ORIENTATION

Villages and structures of the Powers phase are oriented in a similar fashion. The long axes of villages tend to be oriented in either a northeast-southwest or northwest-southeast direction. The corners of sites and structures are roughly oriented to the cardinal directions. To determine the north-south orientation of rows of structures on the Powers phase sites, lines were drawn on site maps through the centers of structures along a row. A magnetic north line was drawn across the site map and structure row orientations were calculated from it. Surface stain maps were used for the Flurry and Wilborn sites (Figs. 14, 15), since they have not been as extensively excavated as the Turner and Snodgrass sites (Figs. 16, 10). These four sites demonstrate a remarkable similarity of orientation, indicating that a common criterion was employed in their planning. This orientation is likewise demonstrated by Mounds 2, 3, and 4 at Powers Fort (Fig. 2). It should be noted here that Cyrus Thomas' 1894 map is wrong in several points. A map made by the Powers Phase Project in 1969 indicates that the

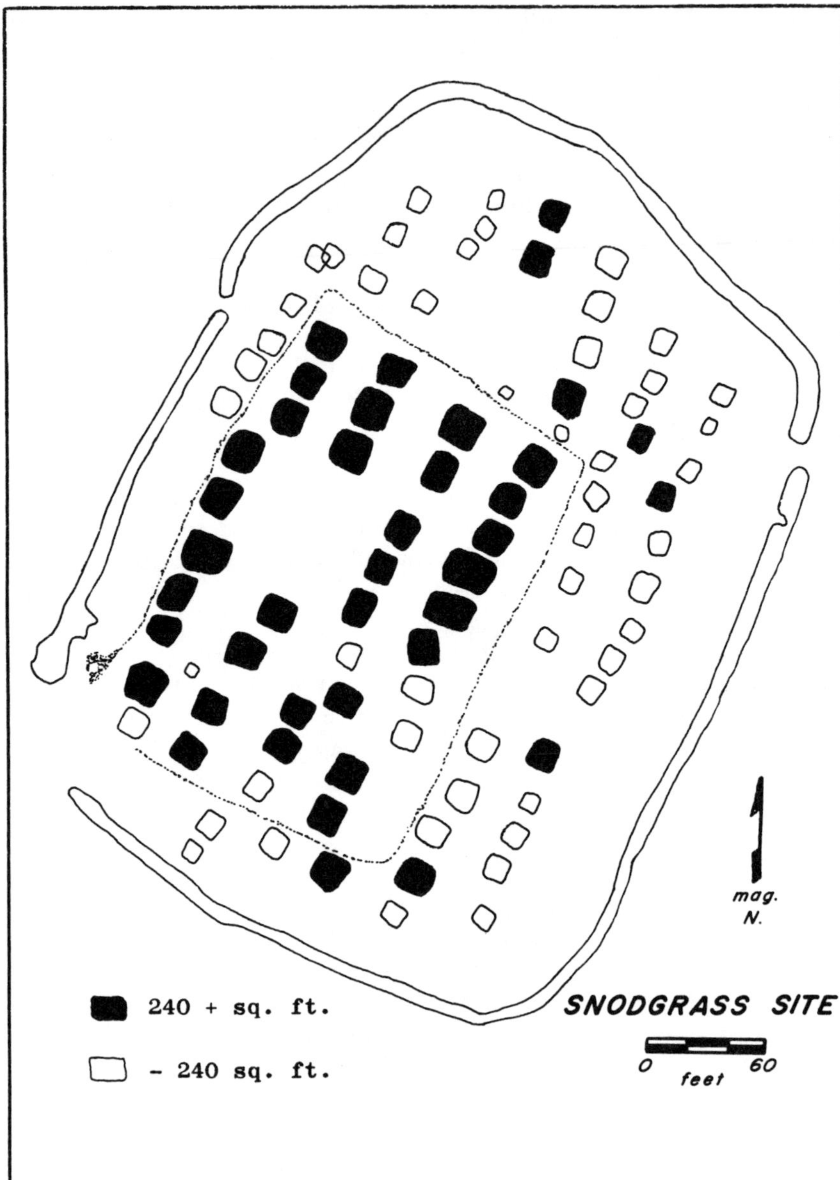

Figure 12. Distribution of structure size.

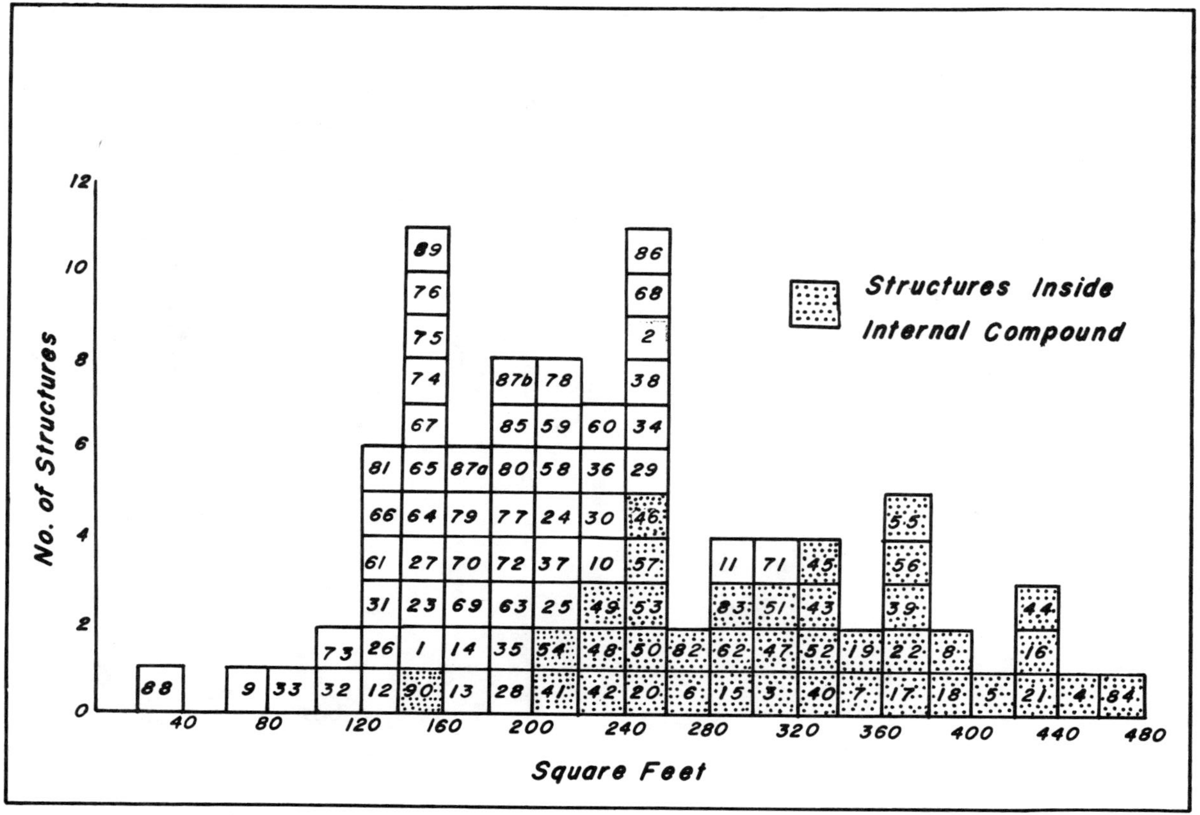

Figure 13. Structure size distribution of the Snodgrass site.

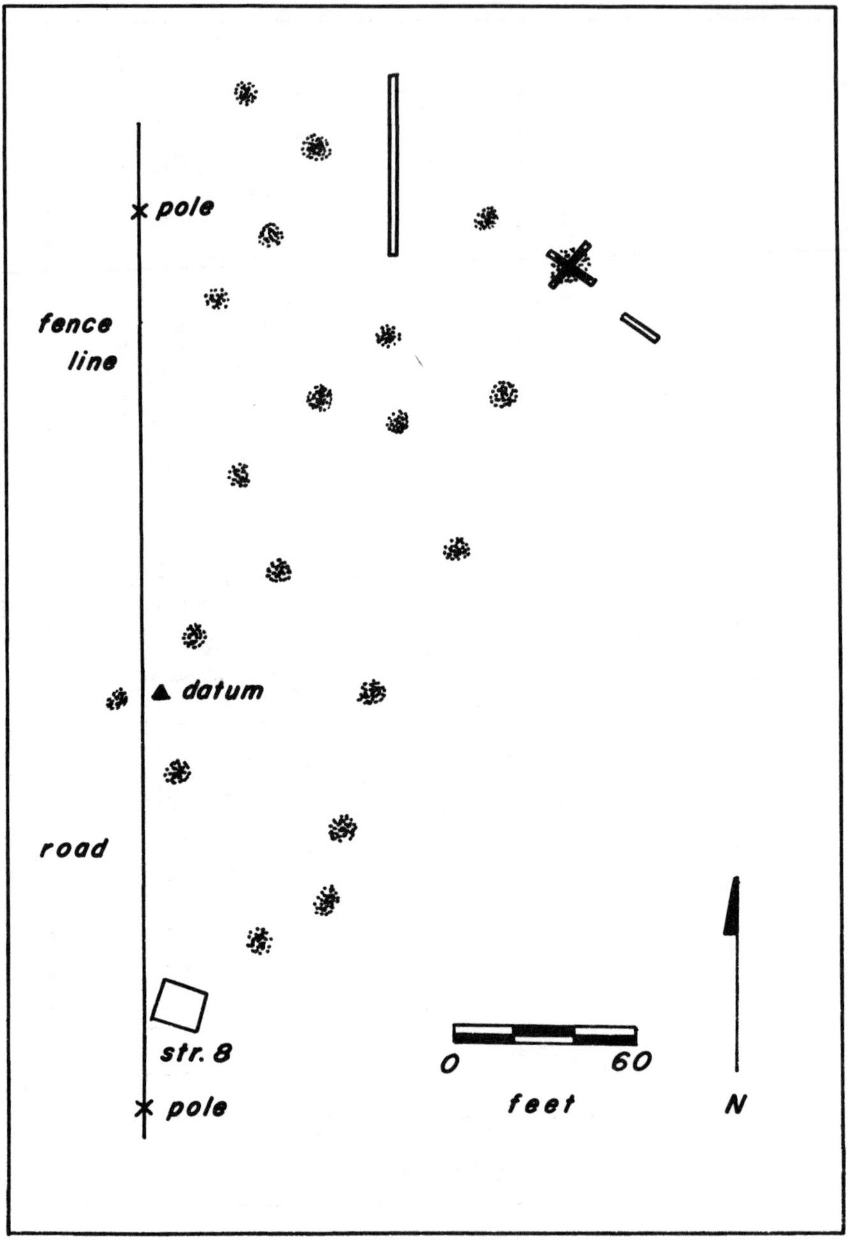

Figure 14. Flurry site, 23BU69. House stains and 1970 excavation.

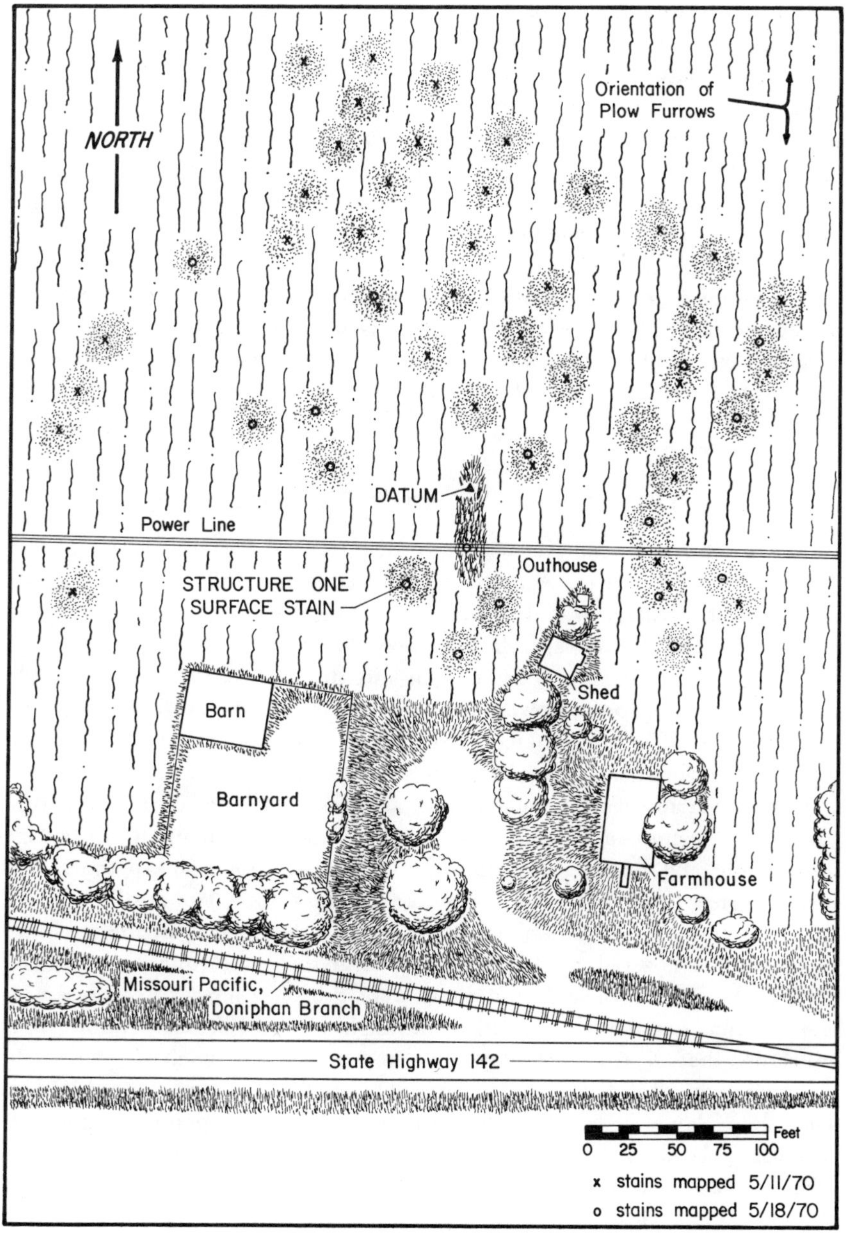

Figure 15. Wilborn site 23BU77. Map of surface stains.

angle between Mounds 2 and 3 is 25° east of north. Mound 4 has been essentially destroyed by plowing. Table 2 presents data on site orientation from five Powers phase sites and demonstrates the remarkable similarity of alignment. The angle of structure rows in the Snodgrass site ranges between 27° and 30° east of magnetic north. On the Turner site the angle is from 26.5° to 28.5° (Fig. 16), and on the Wilborn Site from 25° to 28.5° east of magnetic north (Fig. 15). Only a portion of the Flurry site was available for mapping, and the structure rows in that area are between 24° and 33° east of magnetic north (Fig. 14).

It is more than likely that the criterion for site alignment was based on an astronomical phenomenon since there is no topographic feature on the horizon that could have been used. A detailed study is needed to determine the point of reference used by the Powers phase people in planning their settlements.

DESTRUCTION OF THE SNODGRASS SITE BY FIRE

All structures on the site with the exception of Structures 23 and 87a in the western row were consumed by a raging fire. All evidence suggests that the entire village was destroyed by a single fire on a single day. Since pole, cane, and thatch are all extremely flammable materials when dry, the village was probably consumed in minutes. In such a village, a single structure catching on fire would be an immediate threat to every structure. Particles of burning thatch carried by even a slight breeze could spread the fire throughout the village in a very short time.

Charred architectural remains that fell on the floors of the structure basins demonstrate a common destruction pattern throughout the village both inside and outside the internal compound. Fire attacked the southeast corners of the structures and weakened them first. The north and west walls fell toward this weakening point and lay smoldering in the structure basins, to be covered by blowing sand until they were uncovered by the excavators. The north and west walls were the ones most often preserved, and this pattern remains consistent throughout the village; therefore, it is concluded that all structures were consumed at the same time.

Other evidence demonstrates complete destruction on the same day. The white clay wall which surrounded the internal compound, Segment 1, was baked hard on both the inside and outside before it collapsed into Structure 24 near the northwest corner of the internal compound. This demonstrates that Structure 24 was burning outside the wall while Structures 19 and 20 were being consumed on the inside.

Throughout the village, structures that were adjacent to the white wall contain white clay deposited in them as the remains of the wall eroded after

TABLE II
POWERS PHASE SITE ORIENTATION

Site	Orientation of Structure Rows NE/SW*	Location	Orientation of Structure Rows NW/SE*	Location
SNODGRASS	27.0° E of N	West row inside white wall	22.5° S of E	Southernmost row in village
	29.0° E of N	2nd row from west	30.0° S of E	Northernmost row in village
	30.0° E of N	3rd row from west		
	27.0° E of N	East row inside white wall		
	27.0° E of N	Eastern row in village		
	30.0° E of N	Western row in village		
TURNER	26.5° E of N	Eastern row	21.0° S of E	Northern row
	27.5° E of N	2nd row from east	31.0° S of E	Southern row
	28.5° E of N	Western row		
WILBORN	27.0° E of N	Western row	29.0° S of E	Northern row
	25.0° E of N	2nd row from west	Southern rows covered by farm house	
	27.0° E of N	3rd row from west		
	27.0° E of N	5th row from west		
	28.5° E of N	Eastern row		
FLURRY	Between 24.0° & 30.0° E of N	Eastern row	27.5° S of E	Northern row
	Approx. 33.0° E of N		Not enough stains mapped to reveal any other alignments	
POWERS FORT	Approx. 25.0° E of N —Centers of Mounds 2 & 3, Mound 1 destroyed by farming			

*All measurements of degrees taken from magnetic north.

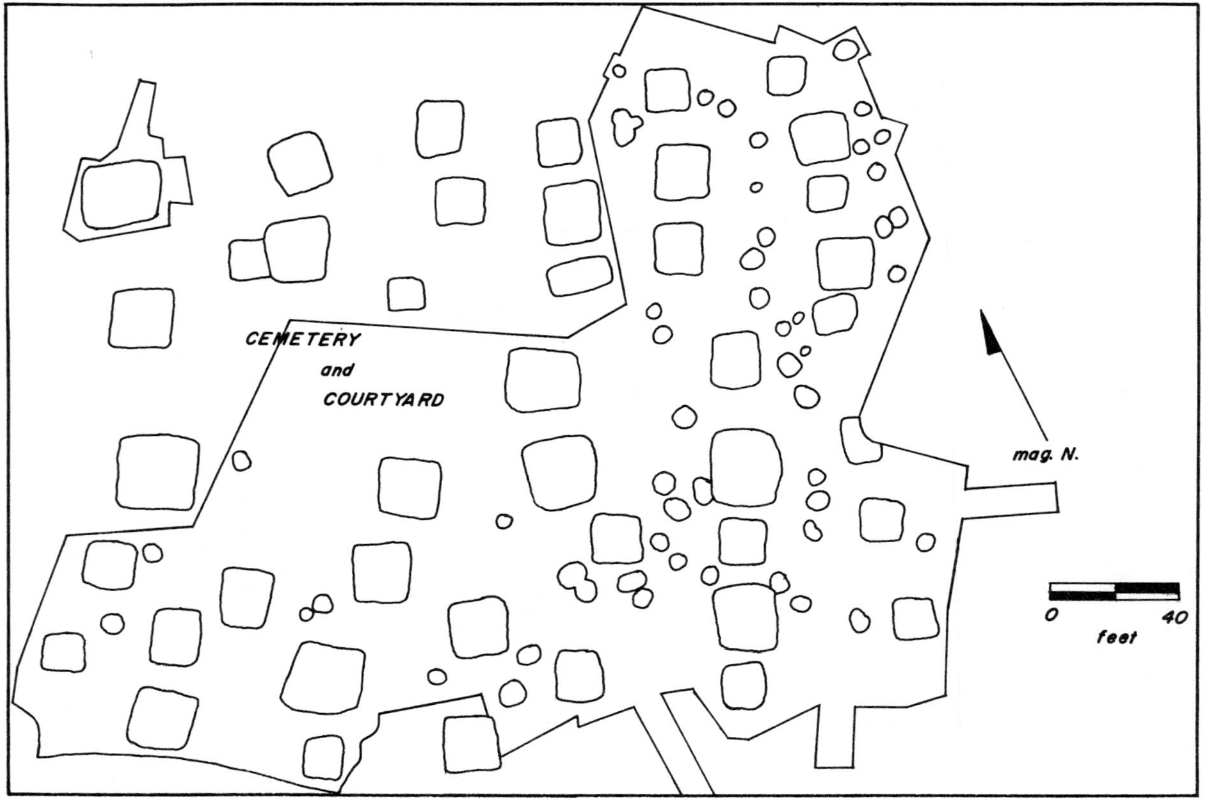

Figure 16. Turner site.

the fire. Therefore, it would seem that structures both inside and outside the wall burned at the same time.

All structures, with the exception of two, appear to have been in use until the fire destroyed them. The other two, Structures 23 and 87a, had been abandoned and used as refuse dumps.

Since the village was probably quickly destroyed, inhabitants would have had very little time to save goods and foodstuffs once it started, yet the structures had almost all easily portable goods removed prior to the fire. Other than refuse and lost artifacts, most small articles such as axes, hoes, and vessels were either removed prior to the fire or were salvaged after it. Articles left behind include large jars, bowls, water bottles, ceramic cones, grinding slabs, and hammerstones, and predictably, artifacts that had been buried in the floor remain. Thus, it would appear that the inhabitants expected the fire and may actually have set it intentionally, since they had removed small vessels that would have been broken in the collapsing structures. Broken examples of such vessels are common in the refuse pits, and the paucity of whole speciments found in the burned structures indicates that most were removed prior to the fire.

Structures in the village were destroyed at the same time, but there are unanswered questions concerning the contemporaneity of their construction. The whole village was short-lived, probably occupied for no more than two years. Lack of refuse, structure repair, or overlapping refuse pits all testify to this. Anyone familiar with Middle Mississippi sites in this area is aware that normally there are large quantities of pottery sherds on the surface. This is not the case on the Snodgrass site where surface collection yielded no more than a dozen large sherds. The Snodgrass occupancy must have been short indeed.

V

DISTRIBUTION OF PROJECTILE POINTS ON THE SNODGRASS SITE

PROJECTILE POINT TYPES

Projectile points are one of the most common lithic artifacts on the Snodgrass site. Since projectile points are generally made by men, they are used in this study in an attempt to delineate stylistic areas of male-oriented artifacts within the village, in contrast to variations in pottery styles, a result of female manufacture. There is no direct evidence that males made the projectile points and that females made pottery, but it is assumed that each did so on the Snodgrass site since these are almost universal sex role functions at this level of cultural development among North American Indians and many other groups as well.

The Snodgrass points were first examined to determine the range of attributes present in the population and establish attribute clusters which would possibly segregate them into different stylistic types. Observed attributes are length, width, serration, notching, stem shape, length, width, and method of manufacture.

Ten metric attributes were chosen for computer analysis. These are total length, shoulder width, base width, blade width, stem width, minimum stem diameter to base, width at midsection, stem length, thickness at stem and shoulder juncture, and thickness at midsection. Computer analysis consisted of plotting histograms of the ten quantified variables, and plotting two at a time those variables which seemed most likely to demonstrate evidence of the existence of different populations. One hundred and seventy-one projectile points from several Powers phase sites were used. Projectile points with five missing measurements were omitted. In every case the histogram of each of the ten variables demonstrated normal bell-shaped curves, some being rather narrow while others were spread out. Eight plots of two variables each were made. Each plot had a main group of points which could roughly be represented by a straight line with a few widely scattered points. The scattered points did not represent the same projectile points in every plot, but were rather a projectile point which had only one or two exaggerated measurements. The main body of points on each plot demonstrated one of two things, depending upon the particular plot. Either the two variables varied together, as one increased the other increased at the same rate, as would be expected (in a larger point both measurements would be correspondingly larger), or one measurement remained within certain limits as the other varied (Computer Print Out Sheets, Michigan Terminal System, 102870; Files of the Powers Phase Project).

The data indicate that a single population of projectile points is represented. Normal distributions indicate randomness within certain limitations, while the straight functions indicate a continuum over which one characteristic was sought in the manufacture of Powers phase points.

This study demonstrates that the Powers phase points are very homogeneous throughout the phase with certain variations resulting from the skill of the makers. There appears to be little variation from site to site based on metric data. The hopes of differentiating stylistic types within the Snodgrass site looked very slim using these techniques. Yet when all points of known provenience were placed on a large site map on the areas where they were found, certain stylistic variables were noted. It was decided to set up a visual typology ignoring metric data. Three basic shapes were noted, triangular, stemmed, and cornernotched. Points were first segregated into these categories. A few points did not fit the established taxa. Two willowleaf points (Fig. 17:2) fit into a separate category but are in such minority that they need only superficial attention. The eight triangular points (Fig. 17:1) appear to be consistently alike and may indeed be merely blank forms prior to notching or stemming. The stemmed and cornernotched points are separated on form of shaft attachment at the base. Stemmed points are those on which the sides of the basal tang extend parallel to or converge away from the shoulder of the blade. Cornernotched points are those on which the sides of the tang expand away from the shoulder.

Stemmed points were then divided into types based on width and shape of stem. These categories were narrow-stemmed (Fig. 17:3), medium-stemmed (Fig. 17:4), broad-stemmed (Fig. 17:5), contracting-stemmed (Fig. 17:6), and stemmed points with incurvate blade (Fig. 17:7). These appear to be fairly discreet categories with little overlap between narrow, medium, and broad stems. The size of the stem was analyzed in relation to the total size of the point. Narrow-stemmed points (Type 3) tend to be almost as wide as they are long. Medium-stemmed and broad-stemmed points (Types 4 and 5) are consistently alike except for differences in stem width. Contracting-stemmed points (Type 6) are the most discreet of the stemmed types. Stems appear to be slightly thicker than on other stemmed forms. Stemmed points with incurvate blade (Type 7) tend to be smaller than

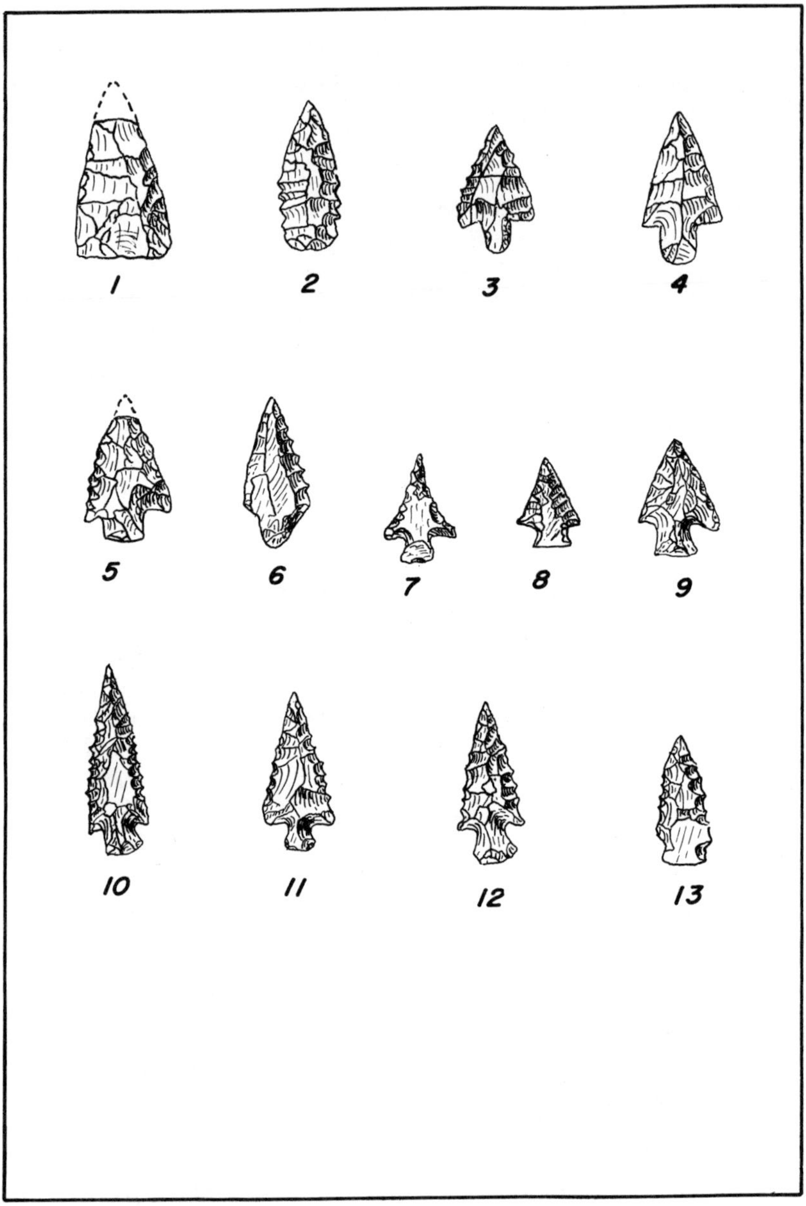

Figure 17. Projectile point types—Type 1: triangular; 2: willowleaf; 3: narrow-stemmed; 4: medium-stemmed; 5: broad-stemmed; 6: contracting-stemmed; 7: stemmed with incurvate blade; 8: small cornernotched; 9: deeply cornernotched; 10: large points with small corner notches; 11: cornernotched with narrow stems; 12: cornernotched with wide stems; 13: shallow cornernotched.

other stemmed forms. They are easily recognized since they are the only points in the population whose blade outline is incurvate in form. Deeply cornernotched points (Type 9) are generally well made and are larger than most types within the population (Fig. 17:9). Large points with small corner notches (Fig. 17:10) have corner notches that are small in relation to the total size of the point (Type 10). On cornernotched points with narrow stems (Type 11) the notches take up most of the basal area, leaving a small expanding stem for hafting purposes (Fig. 17:11). Cornernotched points with wide stems (Type 12) have corner notches deeper than the shallow cornernotched points but have a wide stem which separates them from cornernotched points with narrow stems (Fig. 17:12). Very shallow cornernotched points (Type 13) have very slight notching on the corners of the base (Fig. 17:13). Some are of very poor workmanship and may actually be rejects.

There are 208 points in the Snodgrass site collection that can be assigned to types. Six of these are triangular; 2 are willowleaf; 53 are stemmed types; and 95 are cornernotched types.

The distribution of the total projectile point population is certainly nonrandom on the site. Most projectile points occur in Segment 1 inside the white clay wall (Fig. 18). Within the segment most projectile points occur around the courtyard (Fig. 18). Of the points of known provenience that are both whole and capable of being typed and broken and unassignable to types, 174 points occur within Segment 1. The largest concentration of points is in the two rows of structures east of the courtyard. Structure 84 contained the most, 15 points. Just to the south of Structure 84, Structure 44 yielded 11 points. Immediately adjacent to the eastern edge of the courtyard Structure 82 contained 7 points, Structure 82, 8 points, and Structure 45, 12 points. Collectively these five structures contained 53 points, or 30.5% of all points in Segment 1. Another concentration of points occurs on the west side of the courtyard in Structures 16 and 17. Structure 16 yielded 7 points and Structure 17 contained 7 points. On the north side of the courtyard Structure 21 contained 7 points. Structure 8 in the northeast corner of the segment contained 12 points. Structure 47 off the southeast corner of the courtyard yielded 6 points. Structure 55 in the southwest corner of the segment contained 5 specimens. Structures 51 and 52 off the south side of the courtyard contained 5 and 11 points respectively. Structure 62 had 5 specimens, 18 had 6, 56 had 10, and Structure 7 had 5. All other structures contained 3 or less projectile points. With the exception of Structure 55, structures in the last two northwest-southeast rows of the south end of Segment 1 contained very few projectile points. In fact, only 12 points came from these rows. If the quantity of projectile points reflects the amount of hunting activity by households, evidence from the Snodgrass site, Segment 1, would indicate that males engaged in hunting-associated tasks in structures around the courtyard.

Eighteen projectile points came from Segment 2, the northern segment. Six of these came from structures east of the courtyard and the remaining 12 came from structures west of the courtyard. Ten of these 12 points came from structures adjacent to the white wall, along its northwest side and corner. These came from Structures 87a, 87b, 61, 23, 24, and 25. Projectile point types from these structures are shared with structures in the northwest quarter of the internal compound, Segment 1.

Twenty-four projectile points came from the eastern segment, Segment 3. Fourteen of these came from south of the courtyard and the remaining 10 came from areas north of the courtyard.

The scarcity of projectile points in Segments 2 and 3 would indicate that either very little hunting activity was conducted by people living outside the white wall or that this area was occupied for such a short time that very few projectile points were lost or discarded. The low number of projectile points from these areas makes it impossible to analyze the distribution of types in these areas with any level of confidence. Types are shared by the areas both inside and outside the white wall, but the samples from Segments 2 and 3 are so small that no clustering of types seems evident with the exception of a cluster of 3 points of Type 6 in Segment 2, just off the northwest corner of Segment 1.

Clustering of projectile point types is quite obvious within Segment 1. Certain types cluster in adjacent structures in an obviously nonrandom distribution while other types are randomly distributed throughout the segment.

DISTRIBUTION OF PROJECTILE POINT TYPES

Distribution of Type 1

Triangular points, Type 1, cluster in the southwest quarter of Segment 1 (Fig. 19). One specimen came fron Structure 55, 1 from Structure 53, and 2 from Structure 51. Two specimens occured outside the cluster, 1 in Structure 21 and 1 in Segment 3 in Structure 30.

Distribution of Type 2

The two specimens of Type 2, willowleaf, came from Segments 1 and 3 (Fig. 20). The specimen from Segment 1 came from Structure 44, and the other came from Structure 38 in Segment 3. With so few specimens of this type their distribution is meaningless.

Distribution of Type 3

Ten narrow-stemmed points, Type 3, occur rather randomly within Segment 1 (Fig. 21). However, none were found in the last two rows at the south end of the segment. Specimens were found in Structures 8, 22, 82, 44, 16, 51, and 47 in Segment 1.

Distribution of Type 4

Medium-stemmed points, Type 4, cluster well east and southeast of the courtyard in Segment 1 (Fig. 22). Single specimens occur in Structures 51 and 46. Two came from Structure 45 and 3 from Structure 84. Elsewhere in the village single specimens came from Structure 21 in Segment 1, and from Structure 87a and 10 in Segment 2.

Distribution of Type 5

Broad-stemmed points, Type 5, occur both on the east and west sides of the courtyard in Segment 1 (Fig. 23). Single specimens were found in Structures 45, 84, 17, 19, 90, and 4 in Segment 1. Structures 27 and 30 and Pit 78 yielded single specimens in Segment 3. Two specimens were found in Structure 25 in Segment and 3 came from Structure 8 in Segment 1.

Distribution of Type 6

Contracting-stemmed points, Type 6, cluster nicely in the northwest quarter of Segment 1 (Fig. 24). One specimen came from Structure 17, 2 from 18, 2 from 21, 1 from 22, and 1 from 62. A single specimen came from Structure 7 in the northeast corner of Segment 1. Two points came from Structure 52 on the south side of the courtyard in Segment 1, and 1 came from Structure 56 on the southwest corner of the courtyard. Other specimens were found in structures just off the northwest corner of Segment 1 in Segment 2. Single specimens came from Structures 23, 87a, 87b, and from Pit 77.

Distribution of Type 7

Stemmed points with incurvate blades, Type 7, occur only in structures immediately adjacent to the courtyard in Segment 1 (Fig. 25). Single specimens came from Structures 82, 45, and 16.

Distribution of Type 8

Small cornernotched points, Type 8, occur mostly in the eastern portion of Segment 1 in Structure 56 in the western portion and in Structure 37 in Segment 3 (Fig. 26). Single specimens came from Structures 7, 8, 84, 47, and 56 in Segment 1 and from Structure 37 in Segment 3.

Distribution of Type 9

Deeply cornernotched points, Type 9, occur around the courtyard in Segment 1 (Fig. 27). Single specimens came from Structures 15, 16, 17, 21, 45, 44, and 84 and 2 came from Structure 52.

Distribution of Type 10

Ten of the 18 large points with small corner notches, Type 10, cluster east of the courtyard in Segment 1 (Fig. 28). Three specimens came from Structure 47, 2 from 84 and 44, and 1 each from Structures 83, 45, and 46. Elsewhere in the segment, single specimens came from Structures 55, 17, 19, and 8. Single specimens came from Structure 10 in Segment 2 and from Structures 85, 36, and 71 in Segment 3.

Distribution of Type 11

Cornernotched points with narrow stems, Type 11, occur mainly on the east side of Segment 1 (Fig. 29). Single specimens came from Structures 7, 8, 83, and 42. Two specimens each came from Structures 44 and 82 and 3 came from Structure 84. On the west side of the segment, single specimens came from Structures 15 and 16, and 2 came from Structure 56. Off the northwest corner of Segment 1, in Segment 2, this type clusters in Structures 61, 23, and 24. Two specimens occur in Segment 3—one each in Structures 31 and 85.

Distribution of Type 12

Cornernotched points with wide stems, Type 12, occur almost everywhere in Segment 1 and nowhere else in the village (Fig. 30). Single specimens were found in Structures 48, 44, 84, 8, 4, 3, 18, 16, and 5, and on the surface between Structures 4 and 5. Two specimens each came from Structures 39, 20, 56, 52, and 83. Three specimens each came from Structures 55, 45, and 17. Four specimens were found in Structure 62.

Distribution of Type 13

The distribution of shallow cornernotched points, Type 13, is limited to the eastern half of Segment 1, especially in the second row from the east side (Fig. 31). Single specimens came from Structures 50, 49, 45, 82, 44, 21, and 5. One specimen each came from Structures 77 in Segment 2 and Structure 30 in Segment 3.

Distribution of Type 14

Projectile points with the base broken off, Type 14, are rather randomly distributed in Segment 1 (Fig. 32). Single specimens were found in Structures 48, 53, 47, 41, 42, 15, 45, 16, 21, 22, 5, 52, 82, and on the surface west of Structure 49. A single specimen also came from Pit 86. Two specimens each came from Structures 18 and 8. One specimen each came from Structures 30 and 86 in Segment 3.

Distribution of Type 15

Projectile point tips, Type 15, cluster in structures on the east side of the courtyard in Segment 1 (Fig. 33). One specimen each came from Structures 41, 43, and 82, and 1 was found on the surface between Structures 43 and 44. Two specimens each came from Structures 7 and 84 and 3 specimens came from Structure 44. Other single specimens came from Structures 56, 18, 51, and 52 and from Pit 33. Single specimens were found in Structure 77 in Segment 2 and in Structure 31 in Segment 3.

Distribution of Type 16

Unfinished projectile points, Type 16, cluster on the south and east sides of the courtyard of Segment 1 (Fig. 34). In this area single specimens were found in Structures 56 and 45, while 2 specimens each were found in Structures 52 and 83. Elsewhere in Segment 1, a single specimen was found in Structure 8. Structure 87a yielded the only specimen of this type from Segment 2. Specimens were found in Segment 2 in only two structures, Structures 28 and 70. Three came from Structure 70 and 1 from Structure 28.

Distribution of Type 17

Type 17, blank forms, primarily occur within Segment 1 (Fig. 35). They tend to be in structures adjacent to the courtyard and in structures on the east side of the segment. Single specimens came from Structures 16, 51, 53,

82, 8, 41, and the surface near Structure 46. Two specimens came from both Structures 56 and 84. Three came from both Structures 56 and 84. Three came from both Structures 44 and 62. In Segment 2, single specimens came from Structures 76, 81, and 33. In Segment 3, single specimens came from Structures 37, 70, and 28.

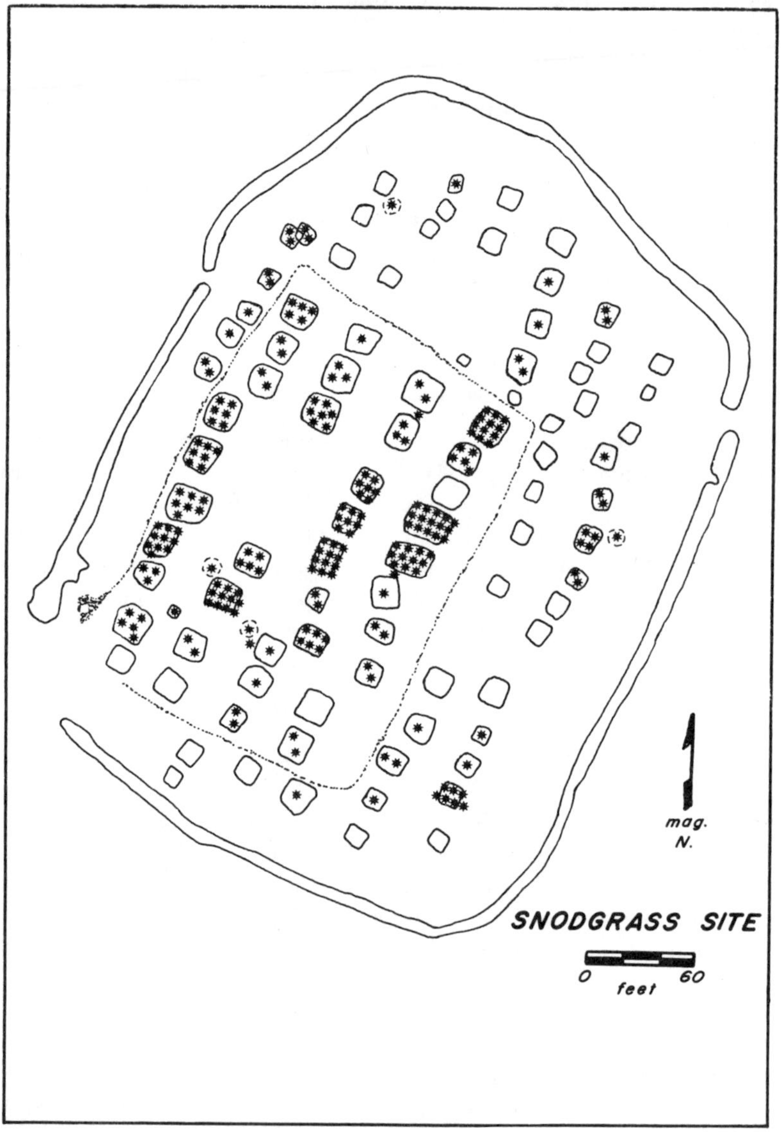

Figure 18. Distribution of projectile points at the Snodgrass site.

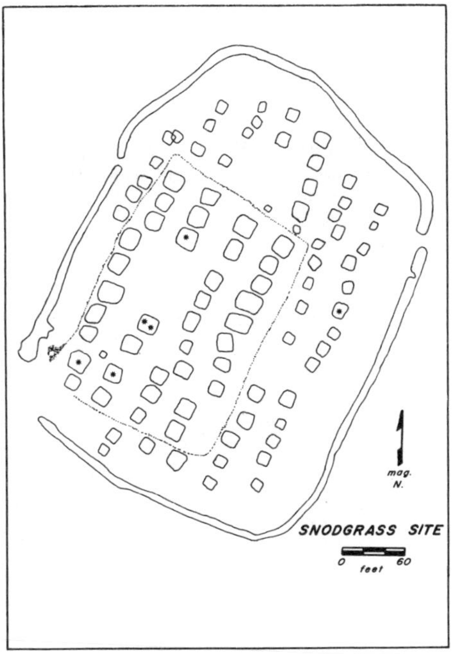

Figure 19. Distribution of projectile points: Type 1, triangular.

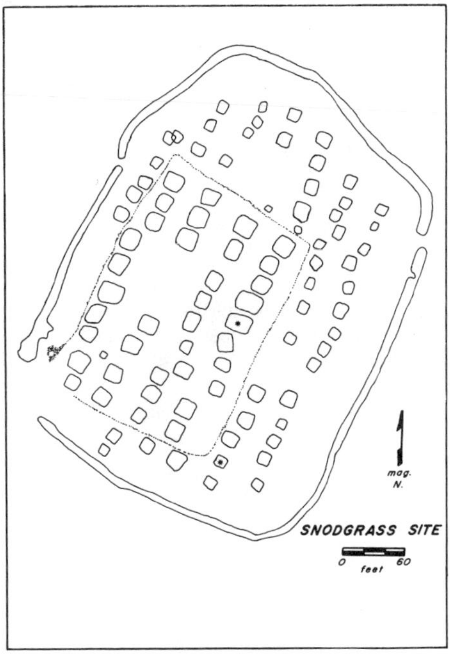

Figure 20. Distribution of projectile points: Type 2, willowleaf.

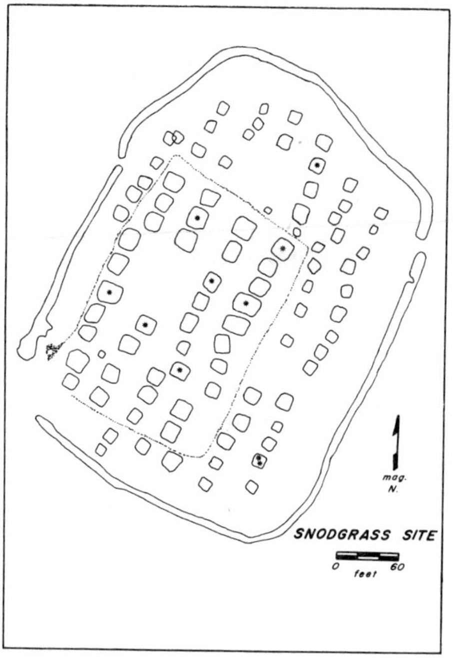

Figure 21. Distribution of projectile points: Type 3, narrow-stemmed.

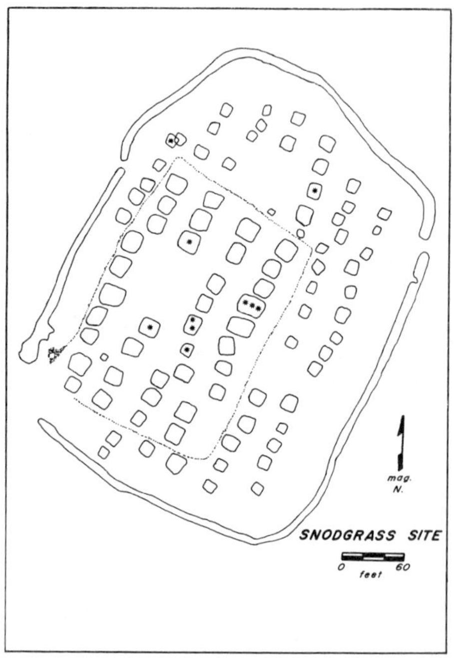

Figure 22. Distribution of projectile points: Type 4, medium-stemmed.

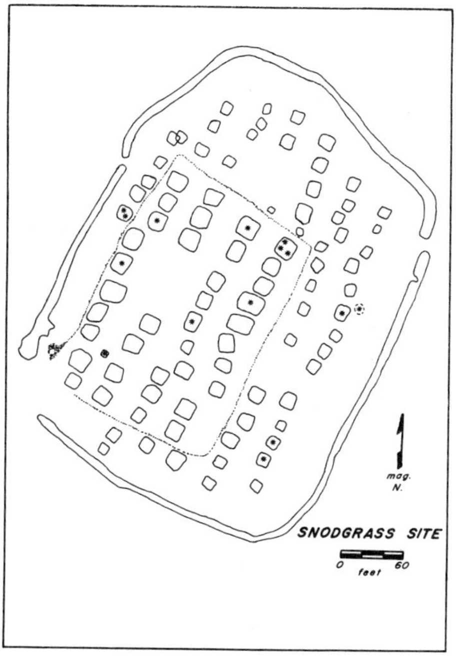

Figure 23. Distribution of projectile points: Type 5, broad-stemmed.

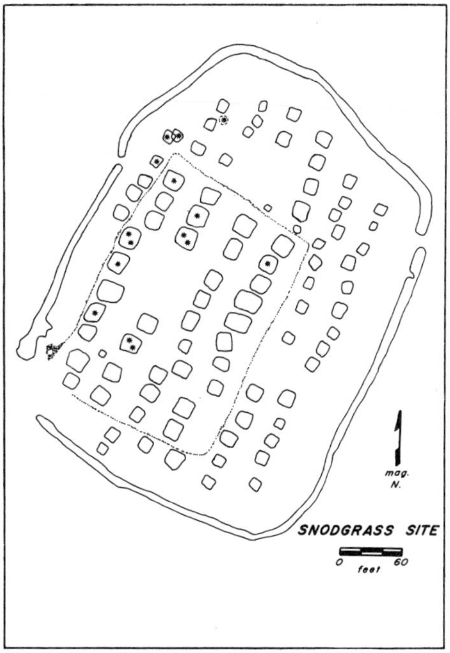

Figure 24. Distribution of projectile points: Type 6, contracting-stemmed.

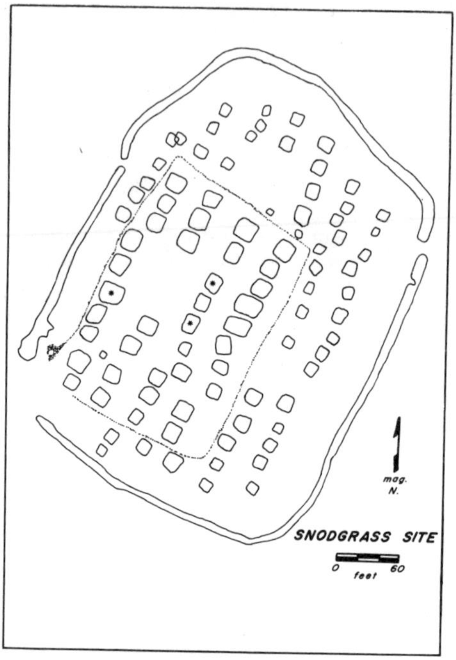

Figure 25. Distribution of projectile points: Type 7, stemmed with incurvate blade.

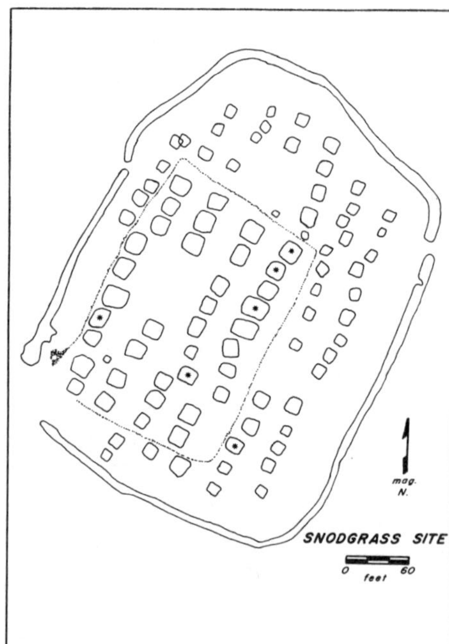

Figure 26. Distribution of projectile points: Type 8, small cornernotched.

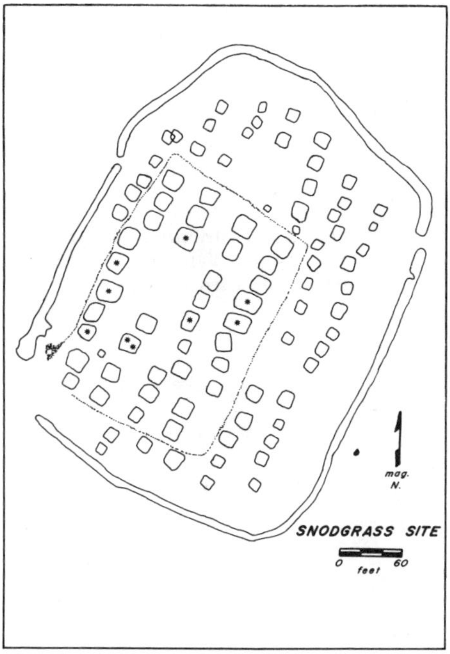

Figure 27. Distribution of projectile points: Type 9, deeply cornernotched.

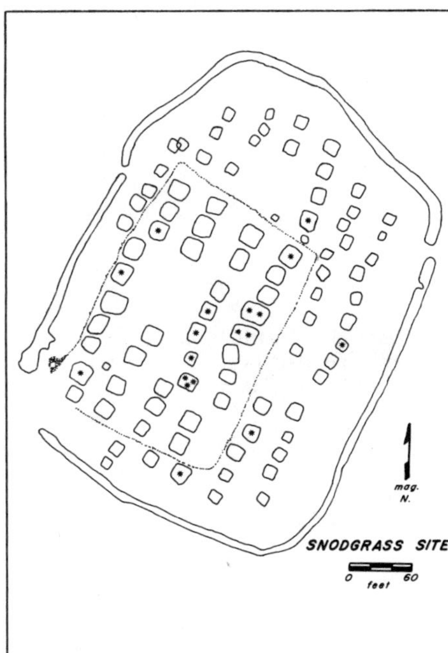

Figure 28. Distribution of projectile points: Type 10, large points with small cornernotches.

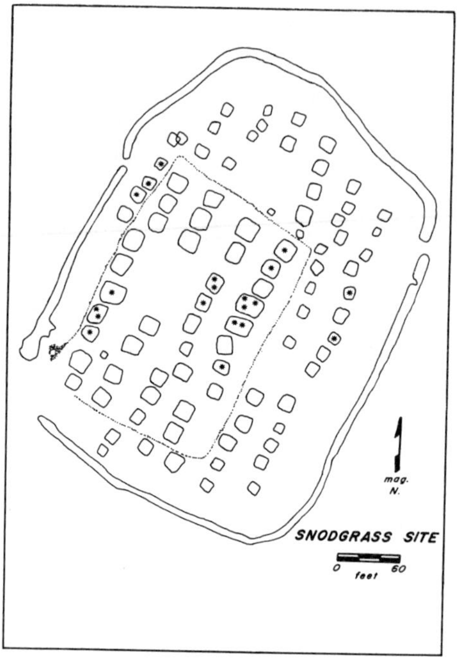

Figure 29. Distribution of projectile points: Type 11, corner-notched with narrow stems.

Figure 30. Distribution of projectile points: Type 12, corner-notched with wide stems.

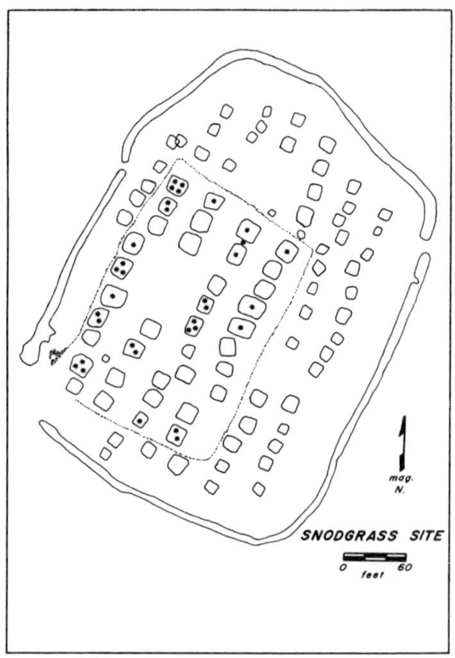

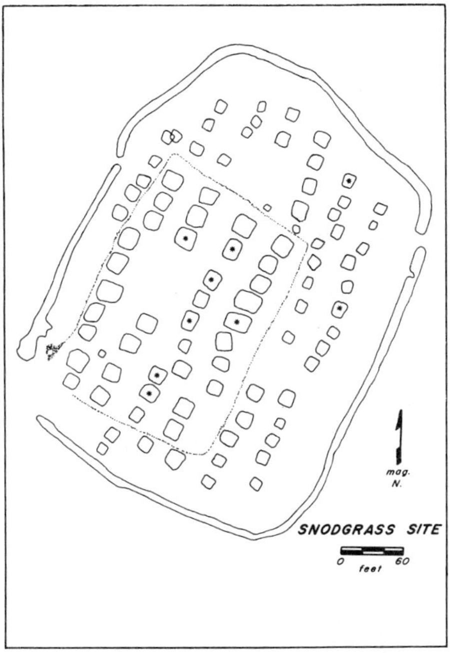

Figure 31. Distribution of projectile points: Type 13, shallow cornernotched.

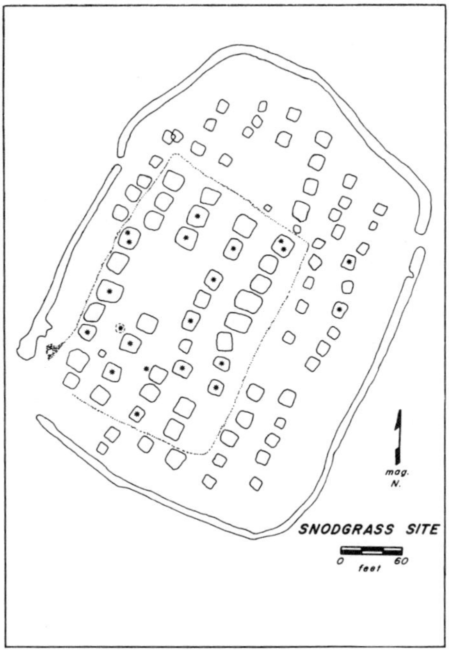

Figure 32. Distribution of projectile points: Type 14, points with broken bases.

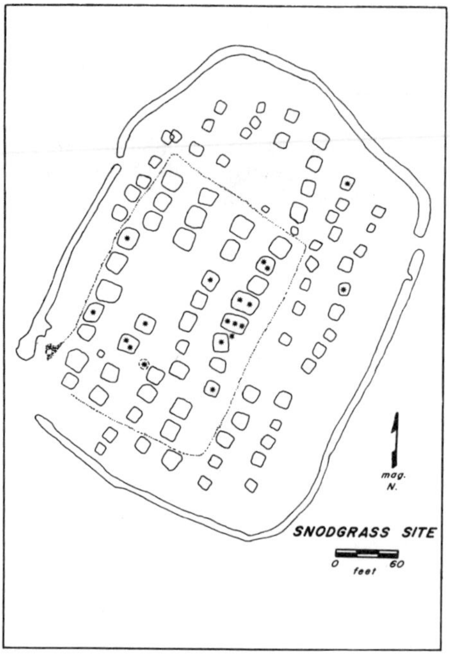

Figure 33. Distribution of projectile points: Type 15, projectile point tips.

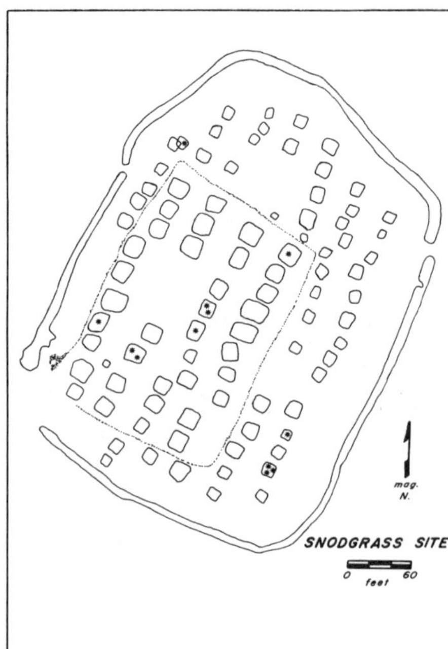

Figure 34. Distribution of projectile points: Type 16, unfinished points.

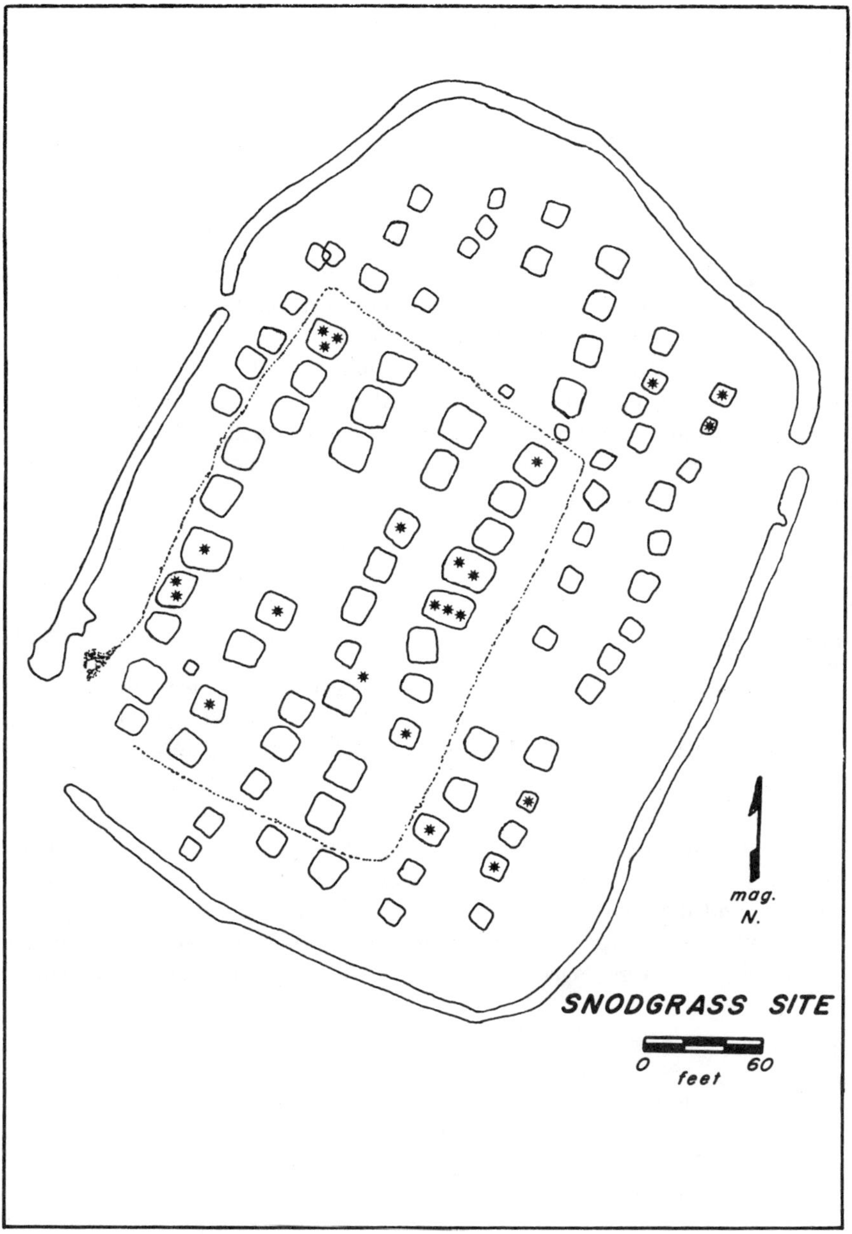

Figure 35. Distribution of projectile points: Type 17, blank forms.

Conclusions Concerning the Distribution of Projectile Points and Possible Explanations

Conclusion 1

Most projectile points occur within the white-walled area, Segment 1.

POSSIBLE EXPLANATION. More man-hours of hunting-oriented activity took place within the white-walled area, Segment 1. Hunting-oriented activity is defined as any activity which involves the preparation, maintenance, or storage of articles for hunting purposes. Considering the very small quantity of blank forms and unfinished specimens, projectile points must have been manufactured away from the site, perhaps on extractive sites where most hunting activity was conducted. Points found on the site must be specimens lost in daily activity or discarded after they were broken. Since deer bone from the site indicates that deer were butchered at the kill site or hunting camp, arrows were probably removed there, and if the point was broken, it may have been replaced there and the broken one discarded. This would account for the number of whole specimens on the Snodgrass site.

Conclusion 2

Within Segment 1, projectile points tend to cluster in structures adjacent to the courtyard and in Structures 44 and 84 on the east side of the segment.

POSSIBLE EXPLANATION. More man-hours of hunting-oriented activity took place in structures around the courtyard and in Structures 44 and 84. This explanation is based on the premise that more projectile points were lost or discarded in areas where more projectile points occurred in the functioning hunting activity of the Snodgrass population. Occupants of structures around the courtyard and in structures on the east side of the segment may have been engaged in more hunting activities than other households of the village or were engaged in such activities over a longer period of time.

Conclusion 3

Structures in the two southernmost northwest-southeast rows in Segment 1 have very few projectile points compared to other structures in the segment.

POSSIBLE EXPLANATION. Less hunting-oriented activity was conducted in these structures compared with other structures in the segment.

ALTERNATE EXPLANATION. The last two rows of structures were not occupied for as many man-hours as others in the segment, therefore, fewer projectile points were lost or discarded. This could have resulted from these two rows being an addition to Segment 1 after the others had been built and occupied for a period of time.

Conclusion 4

Most projectile points occur on the east side of the courtyard in Structures 82, 83, 45, 44, and 84 and in the northeast corner of the segment in Structure 8.

POSSIBLE EXPLANATION. More hunting-oriented activity was conducted by members of these households. The greatest diversity of projectile point types also occur in these structures. These structures may have been the loci where returning hunters brought their game for redistribution if there was such a mechanism within the Snodgrass society.

Conclusion 5

In Segment 2 most projectile points occur in the structures along the northwest edge of Segment 1 and in the first row east of the courtyard.

POSSIBLE EXPLANATION. Structures adjacent to the northwest corner of Segment 1 had almost as many man-hours of hunting-oriented activity conducted in them as structures inside the white wall in Segment 1. They may have been inhabited by specialists from inside the white wall since one structure, Structure 25, was a pottery maker's house and another, Structure 24, contained several large jars; another, Structure 23, contained nothing but refuse indicating it had been abandoned. Ceramic attributes in the form of notched rims tie these structures to the occupants inside the white wall.

Conclusion 6

There is a lower density of projectile points in Segment 2 than in other segments of the village.

POSSIBLE EXPLANATION. Fewer man-hours of hunting-oriented activity were conducted in this segment than in other segments of the village. This might be true if Segment 2 was occupied for a shorter period of time than the other segments. The fact that points are rather randomly distributed might be explained by a situation under which there were no individual structures where hunting-oriented activities were focused.

Conclusion 7

There is considerable clustering of projectile point types within the village.

POSSIBLE EXPLANATION. Single individuals or a number of related individuals of households made different styles of projectile points which were lost or discarded in or around the structures they occupied or in structures in which they conducted hunting-oriented activities. Various households were involved in such activities east of the courtyard; therefore, there is a mixture of types there.

ALTERNATE EXPLANATION. Projectile point types were functional types for various types of hunting or warfare. A single household made more than one type. This would account for a mixture of types in households east of the courtyard. This is unlikely, however, since the workmanship varies from type to type. Certain types appear to have been made by a single individual or a limited number of individuals duplicating the same style and same skill of flaking.

Conclusion 8

Most blank forms, Type 17, occur in the northern half of Segment 1, east of the courtyard in Segment 2, and south of the courtyard in Segment 3.

POSSIBLE EXPLANATION. Blank projectile point forms represent evidence for projectile point manufacture. They represent a stage in the preparation of a point. Blank forms were probably discarded or lost in the areas where they were being prepared or stored. A distribution plot of such blanks should represent areas where such activities occured.

Conclusion 9

Unfinished specimens, Type 16, occur in structures on the south and east sides of the courtyard in Segment 1 and in Structure 70 in Segment 3.

POSSIBLE EXPLANATION. Like blank projectile point forms, unfinished specimens are evidence of projectile point manufacture. The unfinished specimens appear to have been discarded when the maker encountered some flaking difficulty in thinning the specimen or broke it. If points were discarded in the areas where they were being made, then most manufacturing activity took place south and east of the courtyard in Segment 1 and in Structure 70 in Segment 3.

Conclusion 10

Projectile point tips, Type 15, cluster in the center of the easternmost row in Segment 1.

POSSIBLE EXPLANATION. Projectile point tips obviously represent broken specimens. Tips could result from mistakes in manufacture, but all the tips in the population appear to have come from finished specimens. Tips could be the result of projectile points being broken when they were shot into an animal. None of the tips fit on projectile point bases found on the site, so bases must have been discarded elsewhere, possibly in the field or on hunting camps. Tips found on the Snodgrass site may have been extracted from animal carcass segments brought in from hunts. This might indicate that occupants of households east of the courtyard in Segment 1 did more hunting than other occupants of the village or that meat from the hunt was brought to these households for division and distribution throughout the village.

Conclusion 11

Projectile points with bases broken off, Type 14, occur randomly inside Segment 1. Only two specimens occur outside Segment 1, both in Segment 3.

POSSIBLE EXPLANATION. Broken projectile points represent points broken in use, probably in hunting. The distribution plot indicates that most households had occupants who probably hunted. Evidence points to the fact that occupants of Segment 1 were involved in many more man-hours of hunting than those in other segments.

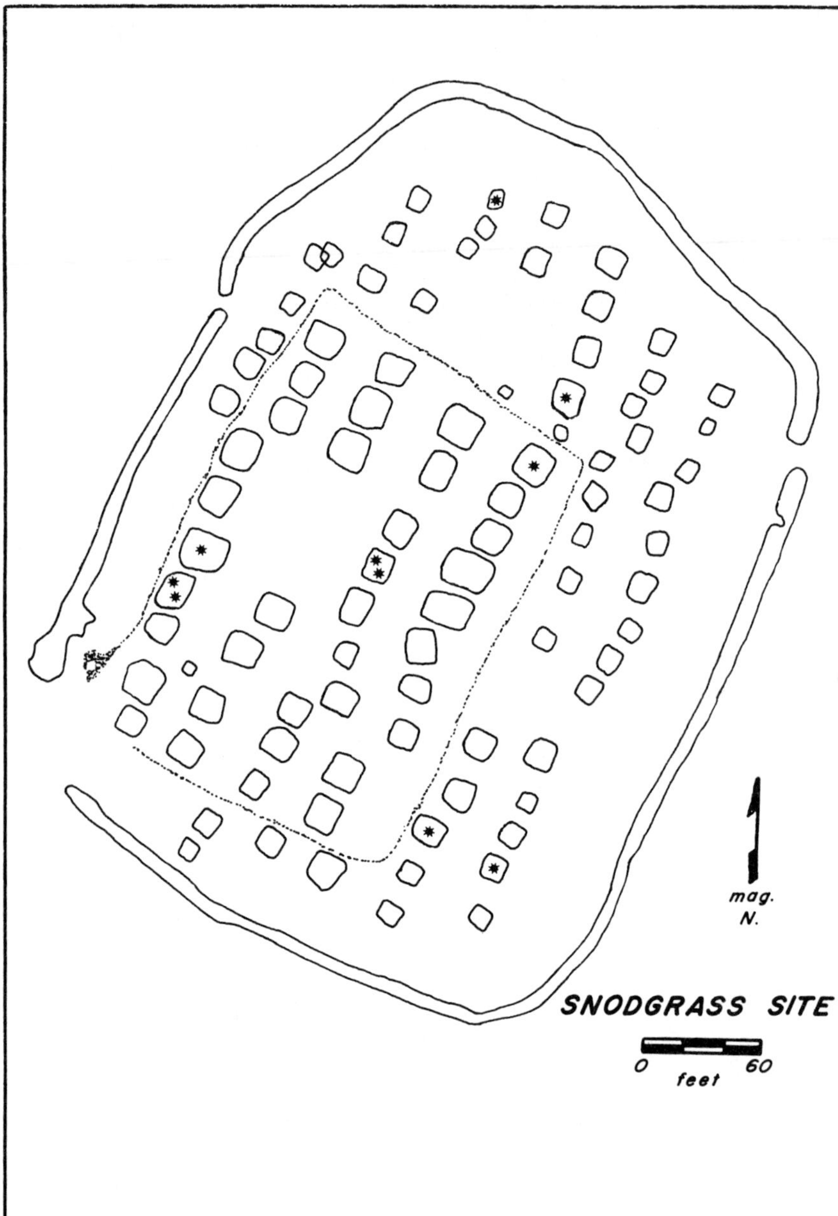

Figure 36. Distribution of projectile points: unclassifiable.

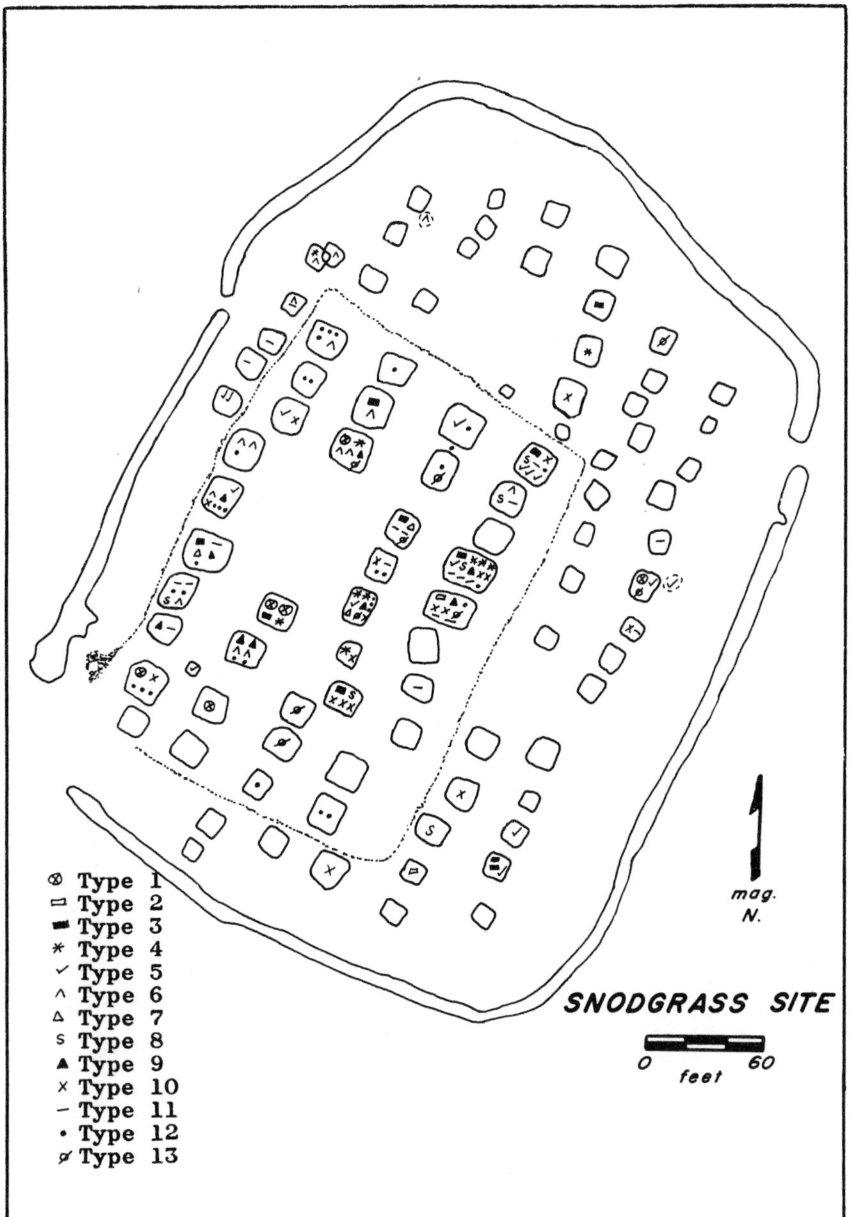

Figure 37. Distribution of projectile points: Types 1-13.

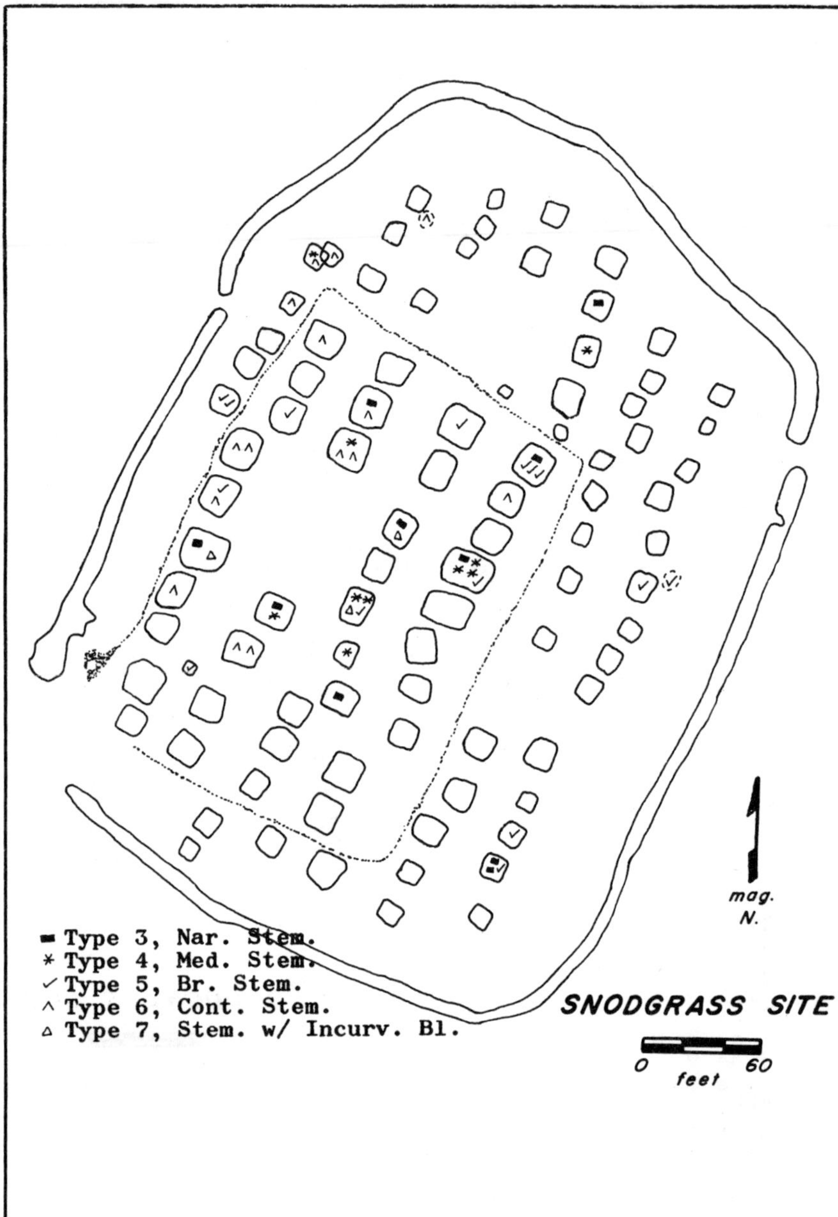

Figure 38. Distribution of projectile points: Types 3, 4, 5, 6, and 7.

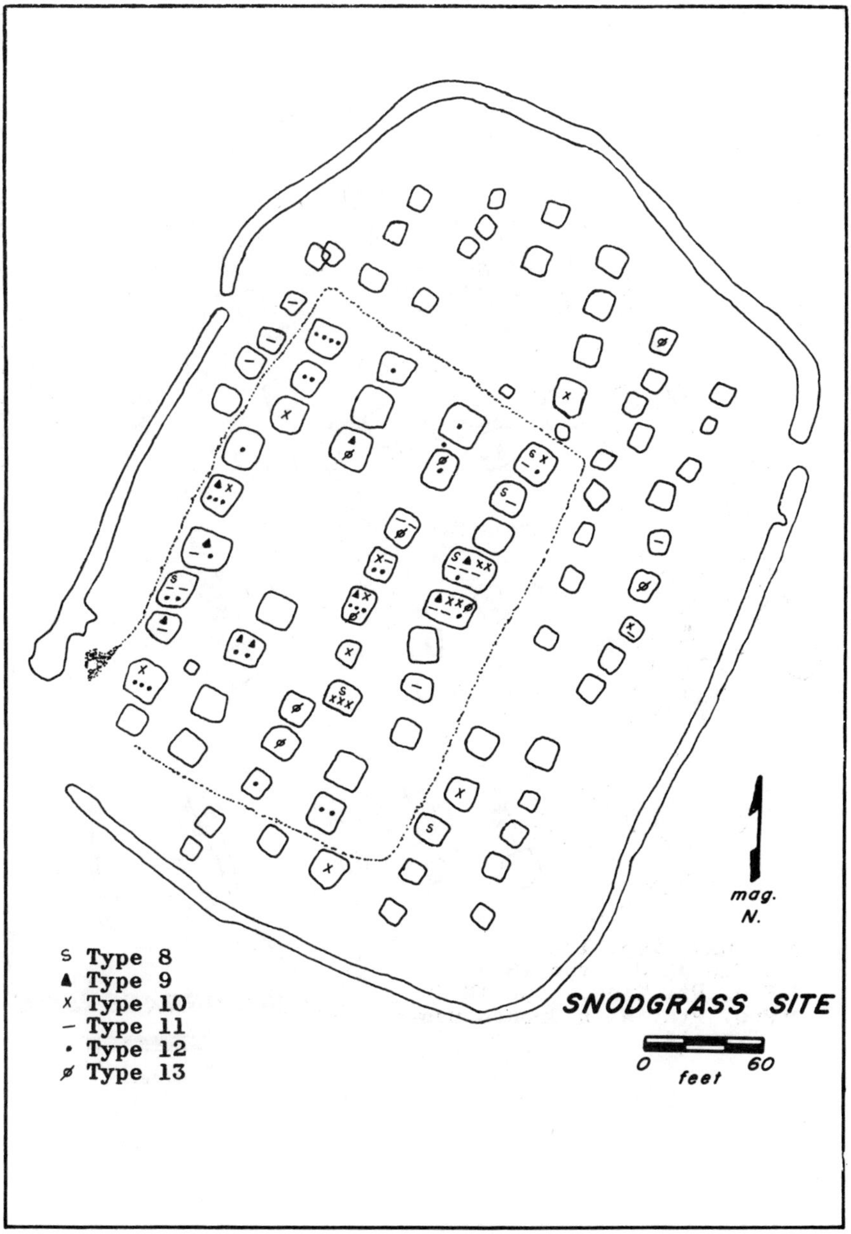

Figure 39. Distribution of projectile points: Types 8, 9, 10, 11, 12, and 13.

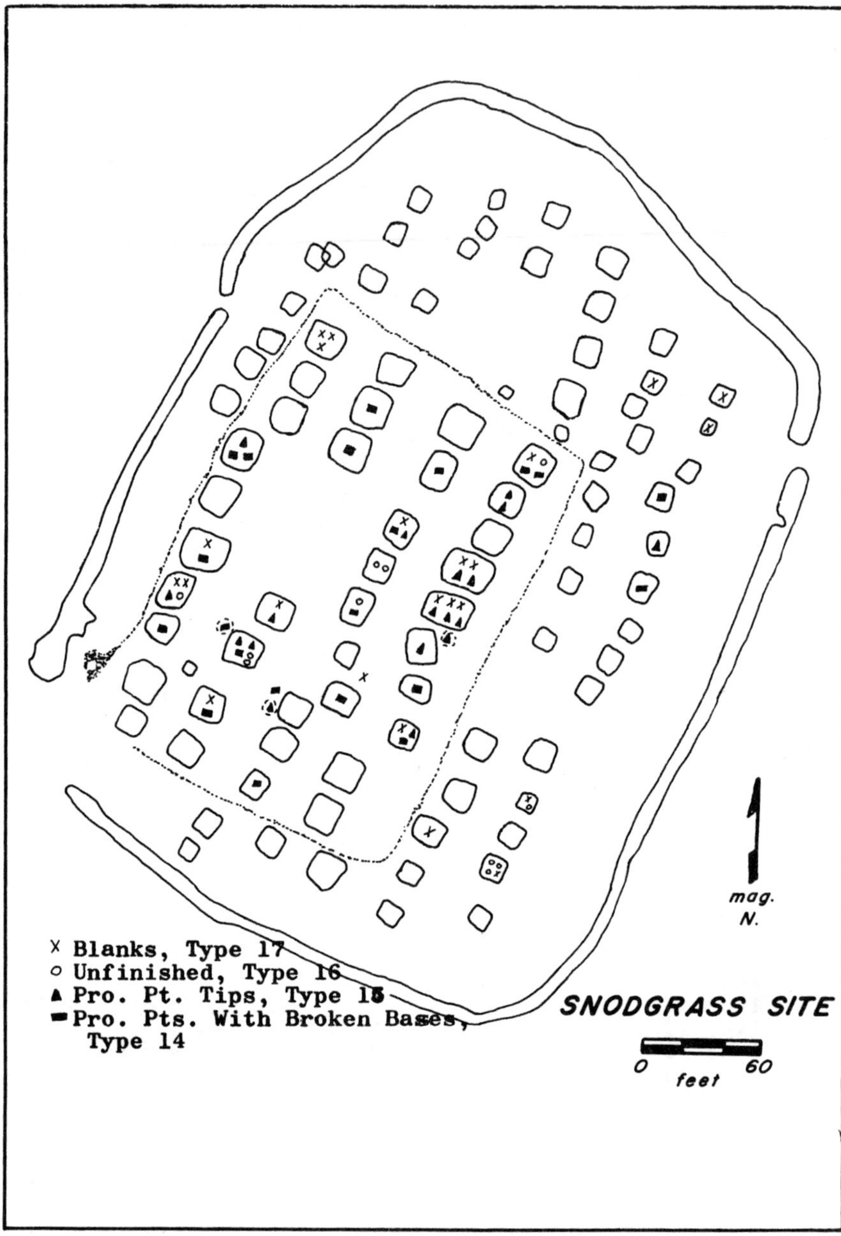

Figure 40. Distribution of projectile points: unfinished and broken specimens.

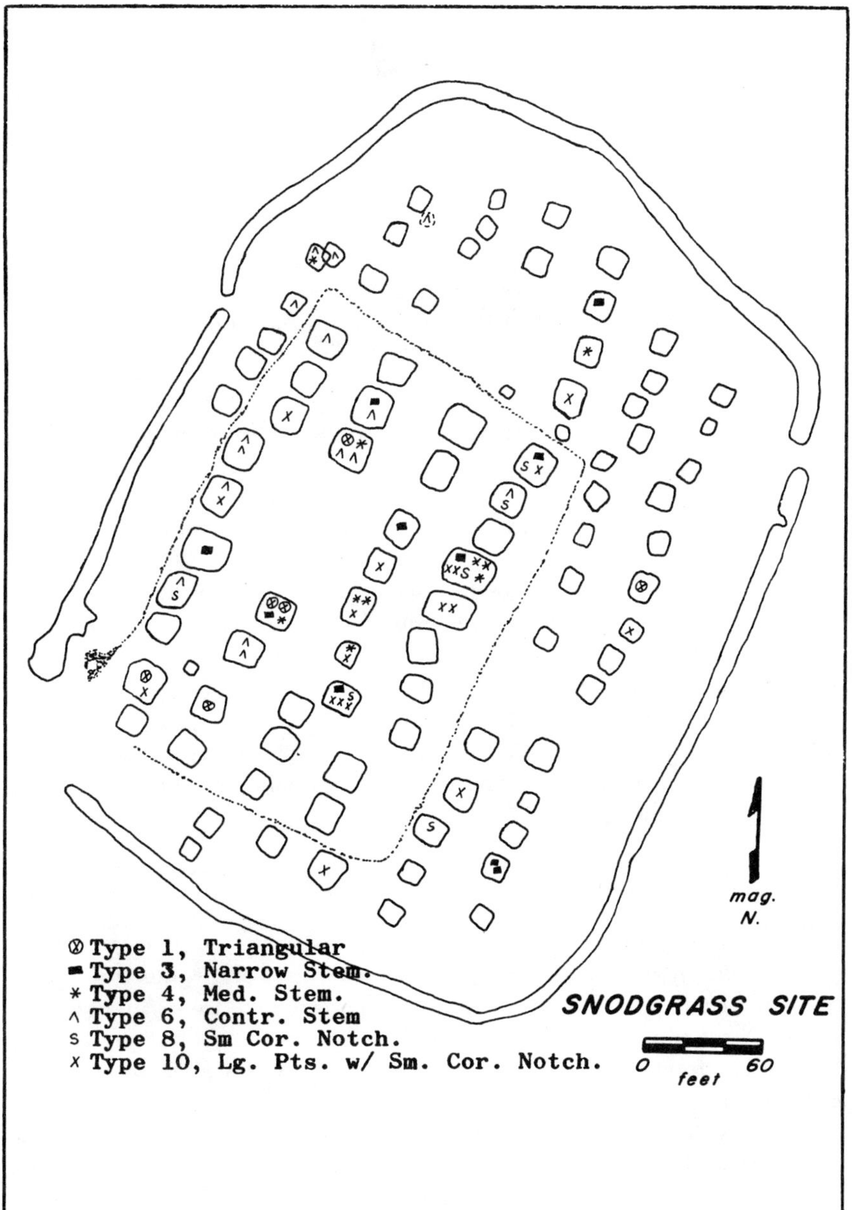

Figure 41. Distribution of projectile points: Types 1, 3, 4, 6, 8, and 10.

VI

DISTRIBUTION OF CERAMIC ARTIFACTS AND ATTRIBUTES

A number of ceramic artifacts and attributes have been selected from the total Snodgrass assemblage for distributional analysis. Artifacts chosen are sherd "arrowshaft abraders," Wickliffe "juice presses," pottery trowels, pottery discs, and ceramic ear ornaments. These were chosen for the following reasons:

1) Distribution of such goods might reflect functionally specific loci within the village. The first three types of artifacts are technological in nature in that they are presumed to have been used in manufacture of other artifacts or in the processing of foodstuffs.

2) Distributions of such items might reflect social organization of the village's inhabitants through restrictions placed on the use of some items by social classes or ranks of individuals in the population. Items of personal adornment might well have indicated social standing.

DISTRIBUTION OF WICKLIFFE "JUICE PRESSES"

Twenty-three sherds from "juice presses" were recovered from the site (Fig. 42; Pl. 5). Of these, 16 specimens came from a single structure, Structure 16. Two specimens came from Structure 17, 3 from Structure 55, 1 from Structure 51 and 1 from the surface just west of Structure 55. The distribution forms a tight cluster off the southwest corner of the courtyard of Segment 1.

Probably no more than 4 whole "presses" are represented by all these sherds. Many theories are extant as to the function of these artifacts, ranging from what the name implies, an implement to extract juice from fruits and berries, which is highly improbable, to a device for leaching hominy, perhaps slightly more plausible. It is best to state, however, that these are items of unknown function. Additional discussion is given in the section on Powers Phase ceramics.

Plate 5. Wickliffe "juice press" sherds.

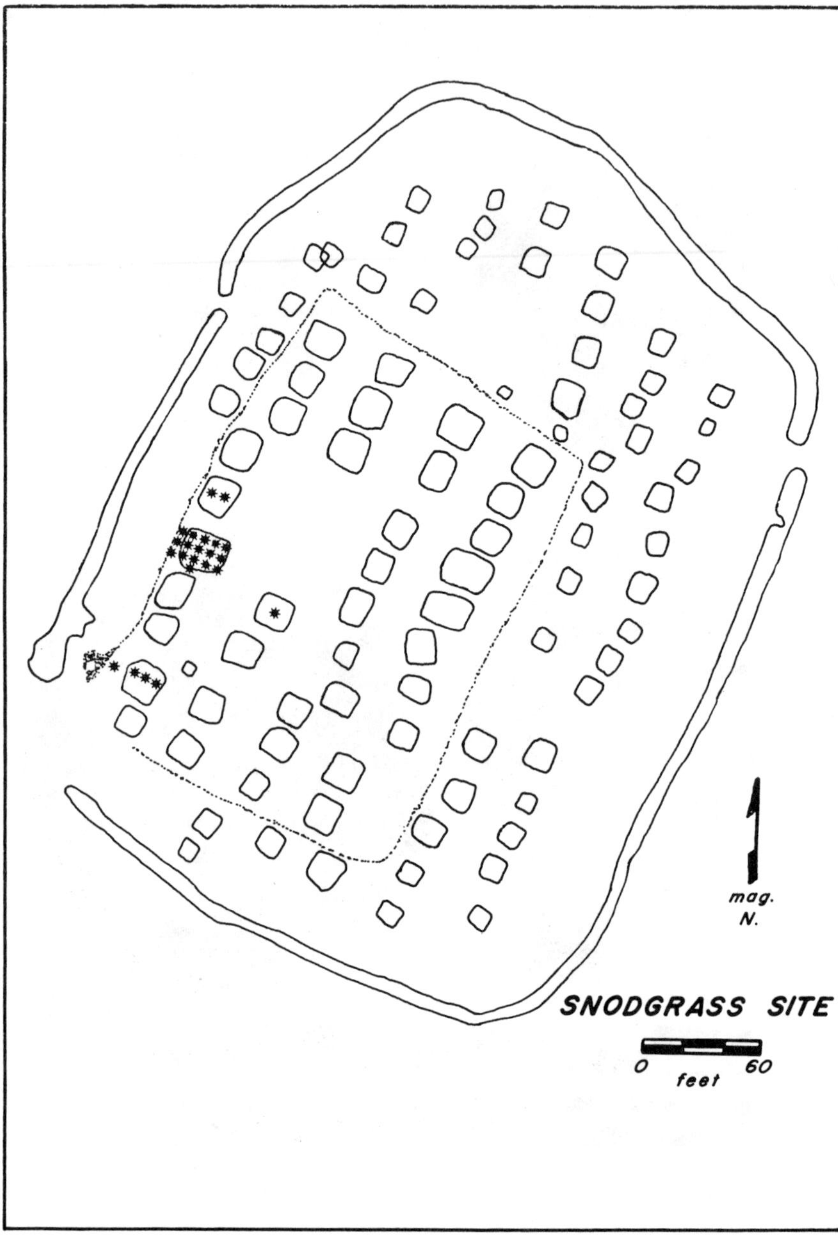

Figure 42. Distribution of Wickliffe "juice press" sherds.

Conclusions

The restricted distribution of this artifact on the Snodgrass site indicates it was used in a rather highly specialized task. This task was primarily performed in Structure 16 but also in structures in immediately adjacent areas. It is difficult to state whether or not the occupants of these structures were craft specialists, but it is safe to assert that very little use was made of the "juice press," a restricted number of people were involved in its use, and those persons lived only in a restricted area of Segment 1.

DISTRIBUTION OF SHERD "ARROWSHAFT ABRADERS"

These artifacts resulted from the secondary use of sherds from broken vessels. They were used as abraders for cylindrical objects, probably of wood, which left grooves across the interior surface of the sherds (Pl. 6). These grooves are about the diameter of arrow shafts, hence these artifacts have been called "arrowshaft abraders," which probably reflects their true function.

Two structures on the site contained larger quantities of these artifacts than did others (Fig. 43). These are Structure 18 on the west side of the courtyard in Segment 1 and Structure 26 at the south end of Segment 3. Structure 18 contained 7 specimens and 26, 5. This is not surprising for Structure 18, since its contents reveal that it was a craft-oriented structure, but Structure 26 had few remains other than the abraders. In Segment 1, single abraders were recovered from Structures 15, 16, 19, 21, 17, 20, 5, and 4 and from Pit 2. Two abraders each occurred in Structures 44 and 47 and in Pit 8. Single specimens were found at the surface near Structures 17 and 19.

In Segment 2 single abraders were found in Structures 1, 23, and 33 and two came from Structure 66. In Segment 3, 1 specimen each came from Structures 36 and 58, in addition to the 5 aforementioned specimens from Structure 26.

Conclusions

If these reflect the amount of arrow making activity, most arrow shafts were made inside Segment 1 mainly on the west and north sides of the courtyard. Most were made presumably in Structure 18. No evidence of arrow making activity came from the last two southern rows in Segment 1. Arrows were also made in Segments 2 and 3 but fewer man-hours appear to have been expended at these tasks. The occupant or occupants of Structure 26 in Segment 3 engaged heavily in arrow making.

Plate 6. Arrowshaft abraders.

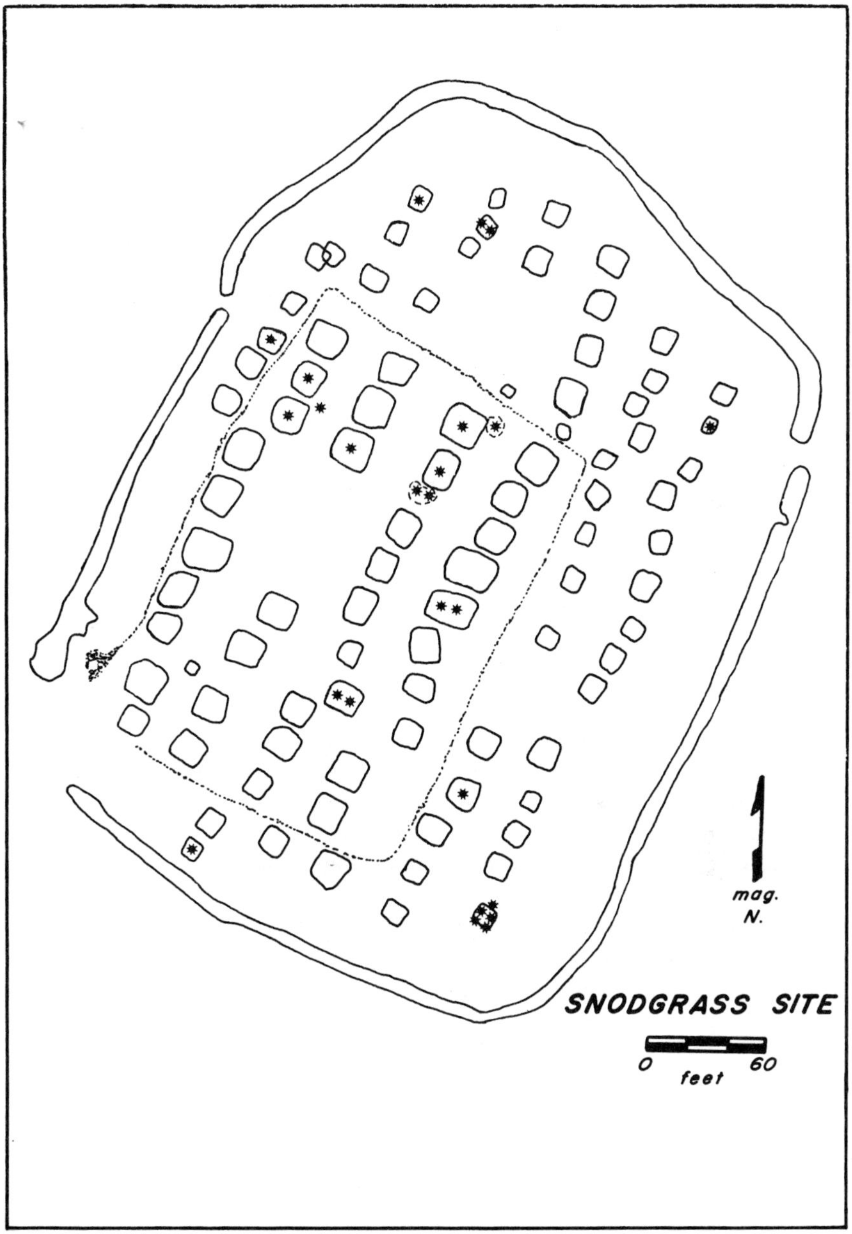

Figure 43. Distribution of arrowshaft abraders.

A contrast exists between the distribution of "arrowshaft abraders" and projectile points (Fig. 2). The heaviest concentration of projectile points is on the east side of the courtyard in Segment 1 where very few abraders occur. This would indicate that the distribution of projectile points was brought about by a phenomenon unrelated to arrow making, or that use of "arrowshaft" abraders is misunderstood.

DISTRIBUTION OF POTTERY TROWELS AND EVIDENCE OF POTTERY MAKING

Twelve pottery trowels were found on the Snodgrass site. They are mushroom-shaped solid ceramic objects composed of a disc with a handle extending from its center. Handles are either flat, oval, or bifurcated at the upper end of their stems (Pl. 7). They were used in conjunction with smooth stones to smooth vessel walls and to weld coils together. They would not have been used to work on wattle and daub walls on this site.

Single specimens came from Structures 8, 14, 16, 21, 82, 46, and 50 and from Pit 15 (Fig. 44). Two specimens each came from Structures 4 and 47. Although no trowels were found in Structure 25, the southernmost structure in the west row, it has more evidence of pottery making than any other structure on the site. It contained raw clay, tempered clay, ground shell, a mortar for grinding shell, and a huge stockpile of shell piled in the southwest corner. It appears as if a specialized pottery maker lived there. It is the only structure on the site that contained a ceramic elbow pipe and rattle. The occupant of this structure must have been involved in the making of rather specialized artifacts. What can be considered as pottery kits were found in Structures 47 and 14. In Structure 14 a trowel, 2 smoothing pebbles, tempered clay, and whole shells were found together in a pit. In Structure 47, two trowels were found in association with a smooth pebble and tempered clay. Piles of shell were also found in Structure 4 where 2 trowels were found. Shell was also found in Structure 65 in Segment 2, but there is no way of knowing whether it was destined for pottery temper.

Conclusions

Inhabitants of the Snodgrass site made their own pottery. Raw materials such as shell and clay were stockpiled in certain structures for use. More man-hours of pottery making took place inside Segment 1 since only two examples came from outside this area, Structure 25 in Segment 2 and Structure 14 in Segment 3. The making of specialized objects such as pipes and rattles appears to have been performed by a single individual or a limited

Plate 7. Pottery trowels.

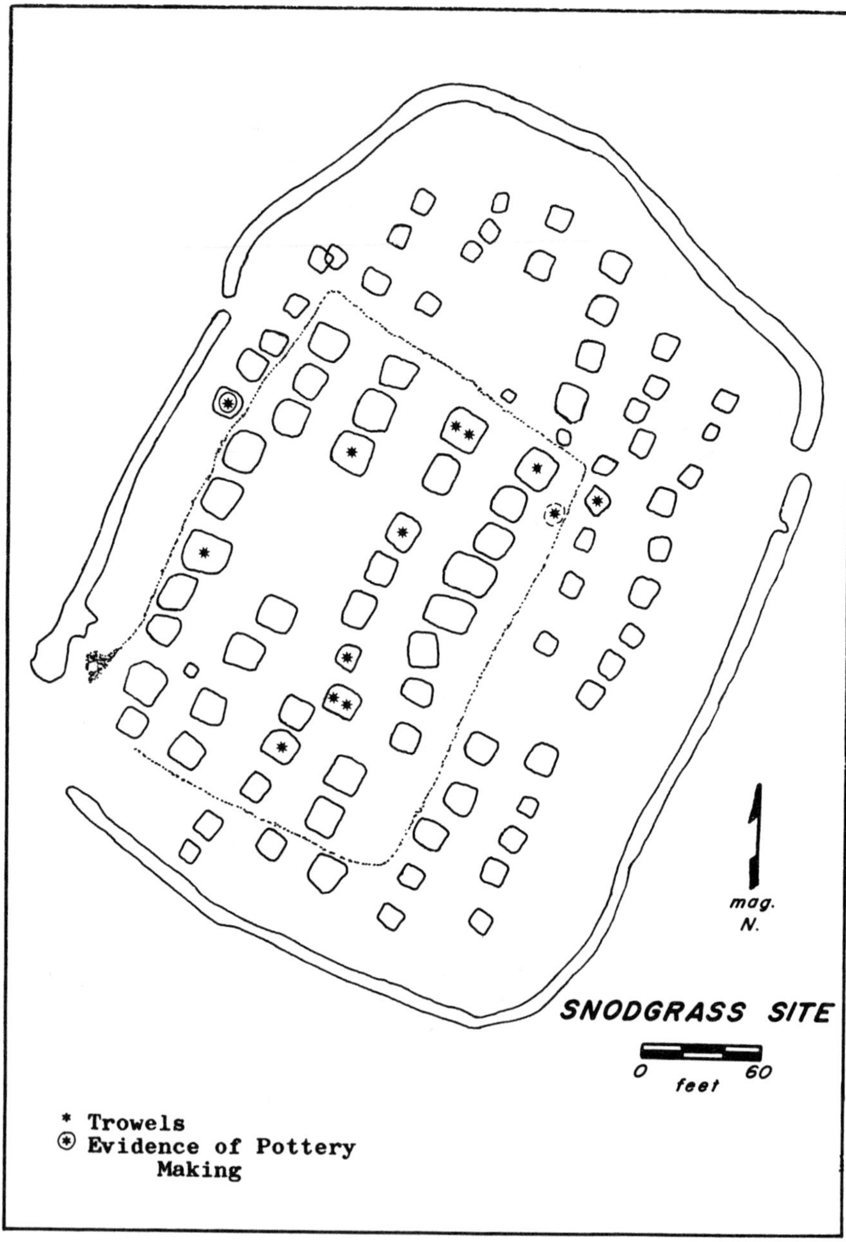

Figure 44. Distribution of pottery trowels and evidence of pottery making.

few. Most households show no evidence of ceramic manufacturing. It appears that only a few individuals made most of the pottery for the population. This suggests a slight degree of specialization or a situation under which members of several households went to another household to perform these tasks. It is also possible that not every household owned pottery trowels. They may have been shared by a number of households. Or, only a few individuals were making pottery when the site was destroyed. This same observation holds true for the other examples of limited distribution of various objects.

DISTRIBUTION OF POTTERY DISCS

Like sherd arrowshaft abraders, pottery discs indicate a secondary use of broken vessels. Pottery discs are of unknown function and were made from sherds from large vessels with little curvature. They are roughly circular in form but can be elongated and are never under 1 inch and seldom more than 3 inches in diameter (Pl. 8). One, three, or five holes were drilled through the sherds, each hole being drilled from both sides, hence they are biconical in form. If the disc has one hole it is drilled centrally. If it has three, which is very rare, they are drilled in a straight line. If the sherd possesses five holes they form a square surrounding a central perforation. Some are undrilled.

All categories of these artifacts cluster in the north half of Segment 1 (Fig. 45). There are too many to list individually in this text by provenience. The heaviest concentration occurs in Structures 16 and 17 on the west side of the Segment 1 courtyard. Structure 16 had 7 specimens and 17 had 11 specimens. Structures 7, 8, and 44 each contained 5 specimens, as did Pit 8. Structures 18 and 47 each contained 4 discs. Other structures contained less than four. No structures outside Segment 1 contained more than one. Five specimens came from Segment 2 and 5 from Segment 3. Twelve specimens, other than those mentioned in Pit 8, came from pits inside Segment 1.

Distribution of Discs by Categories

Unperforated

Twenty-six undrilled specimens were recovered. They form a rough circle around the courtyard of Segment 1, but not immediately adjacent to it (Fig. 46). Only 1 specimen came from the last two southern rows in Segment 1. Twenty of the 26 specimens occur within Segment 1. Four specimens came from Segment 2 and only 2 from Segment 3. In Segment 2,

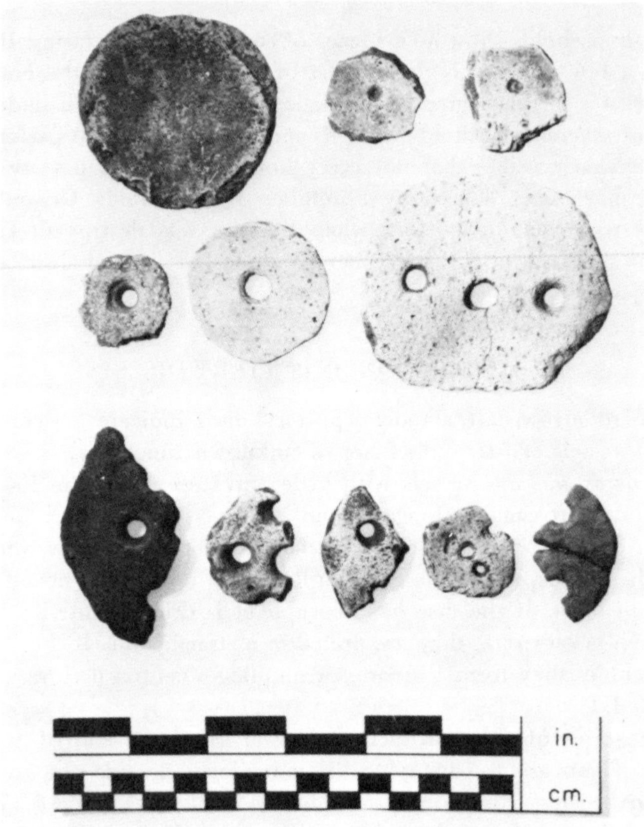

Plate 8. Pottery discs.

they cluster at the northwest and northeast corners of Segment 1. Only 1 specimen was found in a pit. Six specimens are quite large, over 4 inches in diameter (Fig. 46). These occur primarily on the west side of Segment 1.

Partially Perforated

These are discs in which the hole was started but never finished. Usually the hole is drilled from one side only. Fifteen specimens of this type were found (Fig. 47). Thirteen of these came from Segment 1 and 1 each came from Segments 2 and 3. Five of this type cluster on the west side of the courtyard in Segment 1. Two occur in Structure 16 and three in 17. Others are more or less randomly distributed throughout the segment.

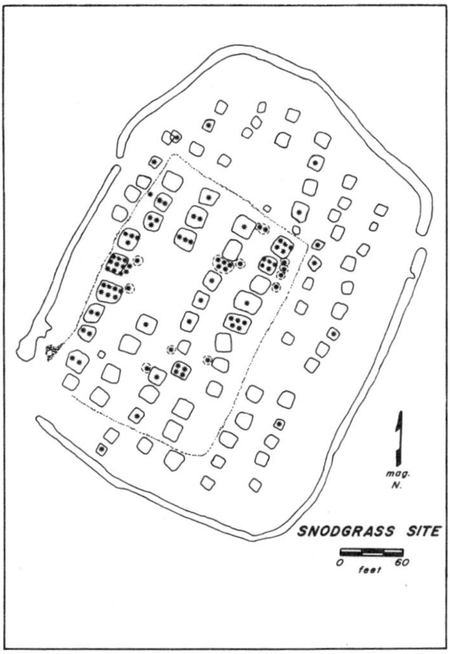

Figure 45. Distribution of pottery discs.

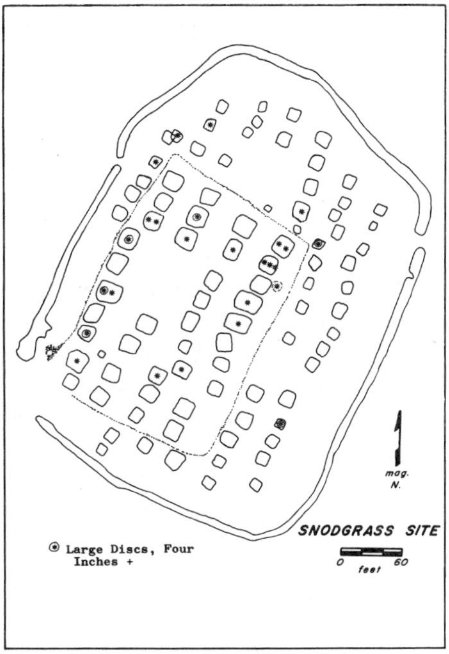

Figure 46. Distribution of unperforated pottery discs.

One Hole Completely Drilled

These are discs through which a hole is completely drilled. The largest concentration of these were found on the west side of the courtyard in Segment 1 in Structures 16, 17, 18, 19, and 20, as well as in pits adjacent to Structure 16 (Fig. 48). Others are scattered north and east of the courtyard but only 4 of the 27 specimens occur in Segment 1 south of the courtyard. Only 1 specimen occurs outside Segment 1. It is in Structure 58 in Segment 3.

Specimens with 3 Holes

Only 2 specimens of this type were found, both in Segment 1. One was located in Structure 5 and the other in Structure 51 (Fig. 49).

Specimens with 5 Holes

These specimens are for the most part broken, but enough remains to easily identify the 5 holes in the aforementioned pattern. These occur in the north half of Segment 1 (Fig. 49). Only 3 specimens (from Structures 51, 55, and 56) are south of the courtyard. A majority of the specimens cluster in the northeast corner of Segment 1. Six occur on the west side of the segment, whereas 15 occur on the east side, 4 of which came from Pit 8. It would appear that most five-holed discs were used in the northeast portion of Segment 1.

Differential Distribution of Pottery Disc Types

Figure 52 represents the distribution of discs with one partial or complete hole, and ones with 3 or 5 holes (multiple-drilled). It is quite apparent that the overwhelming majority of these types occur in the northern half of Segment 1. Most multiple-drilled discs cluster in the northeast quarter of Segment 1, whereas partially or completely drilled discs cluster west and southeast of the courtyard. Sixteen of the 26 multiple drilled discs occur in the northeast quarter. Only 9 specimens of the single-holed type occur on the north and west side of the courtyard and only 6 of the multiple-drilled discs occur in this area. A concentration of 11 single-holed types occurs east and southeast of the courtyard. Only 2 of the multiple-drilled discs occur here, and only 3 of the single-holed types occur outside Segment 1, 1 in Segment 2 and 2 in Segment 3.

When the distribution of all perforated discs (1, 3, or 5 holes) is considered (Fig. 50) it is quite apparent that they are confined to a rather

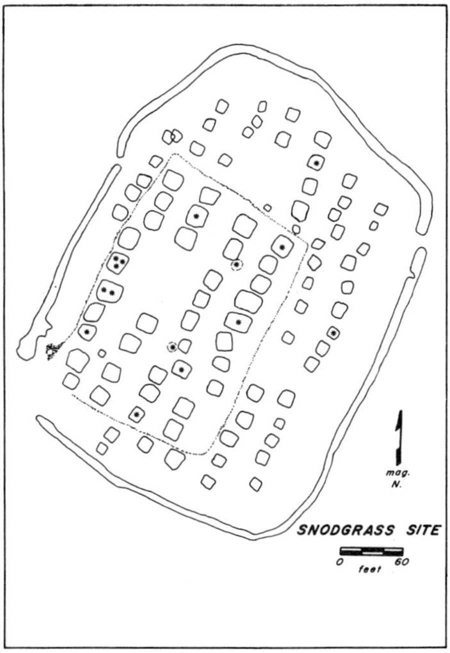

Figure 47. Distribution of partially perforated pottery discs (one hole).

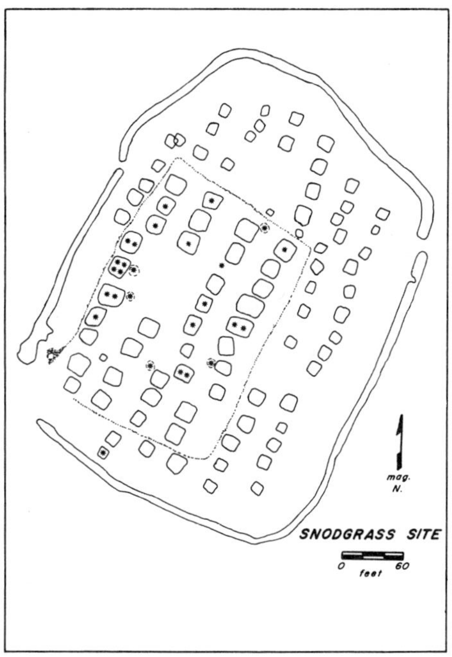

Figure 48. Distribution of pottery discs with one hole completely drilled.

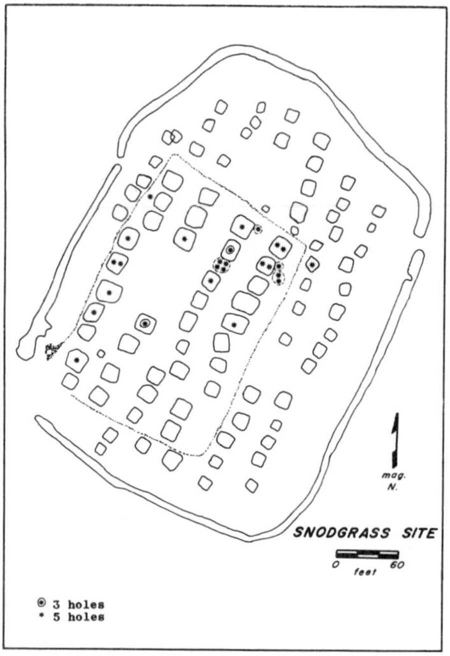

Figure 49. Distribution of pottery discs with three and five holes.

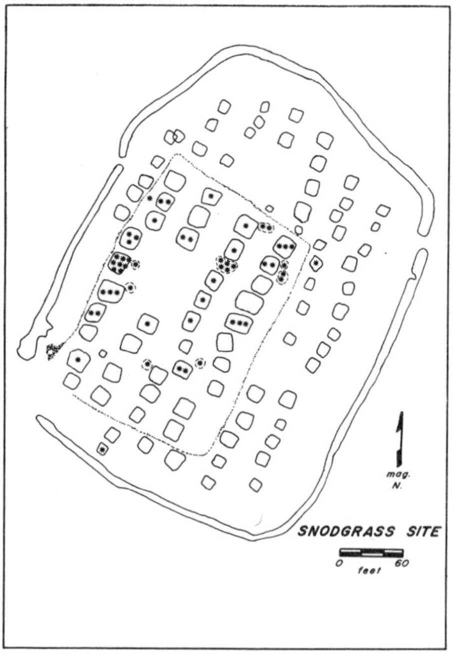

Figure 50. Distribution of completely perforated pottery discs—those with one, three, and five holes.

restricted area. In Segment 1, all but 6 specimens occur north of a northwest-southeast line just off the south side of the courtyard. Only 2 specimens occur outside Segment 1.

Conclusions Concerning the Distribution of Pottery Discs

1) Pottery discs are limited to roughly the northern half of Segment 1. This would indicate that households in this area contained essentially the only individuals in the village who made and used this type of artifact.

2) Within this area, households northeast of the courtyard used multiple-drilled discs whereas other households used discs with single perforations. If discs were used in some sort of task, the evidence indicates that this task was performed only in the north half of Segment 1 and that different types of discs were used by households in two different areas (Figs. 51, 52). Unperforated discs appear to be randomly distributed. This may be due to the fact that they represent a stage in making perforated ones or they may have had a separate function. Distribution of unperforated, partially perforated, and perforated discs is presented on a single map in Figure 53. If they are articles of personal adornment then only members in the northern half of Segment 1 would wear them. If only the function of such artifacts were known, a much clearer interpretation could be given.

DISTRIBUTION OF CERAMIC EAR ORNAMENTS

Two types of artifacts fall under this category. One is commonly known as an earplug and the other as an earspool (Pl. 9). Earplugs are small rivet-shaped ceramic objects usually fired quite black and often polished, which were worn through holes in the earlobe. Earspools are cylindrical ceramic objects with a groove around the middle and were worn in the same fashion as earplugs.

A total of 36 earplugs and 2 earspools were recovered from the site. Only 5 specimens were found outside Segment 1 (Fig. 54). The majority of them appear to be more or less randomly distributed within Segment 1. Structure 47 had 4 specimens, 39 had 3, and Structures 55, 8, and 44 had 2 each. Other structures had 1 or none. Several specimens were found in pits. Four earplugs were found in Segment 2. Three of these came from Structure 66 and the other from Structure 24. Structure 27 yielded the only specimen in Segment 3. A single red-painted earspool came from Structure 4 and an unpainted one came from Structure 56 in Segment 1.

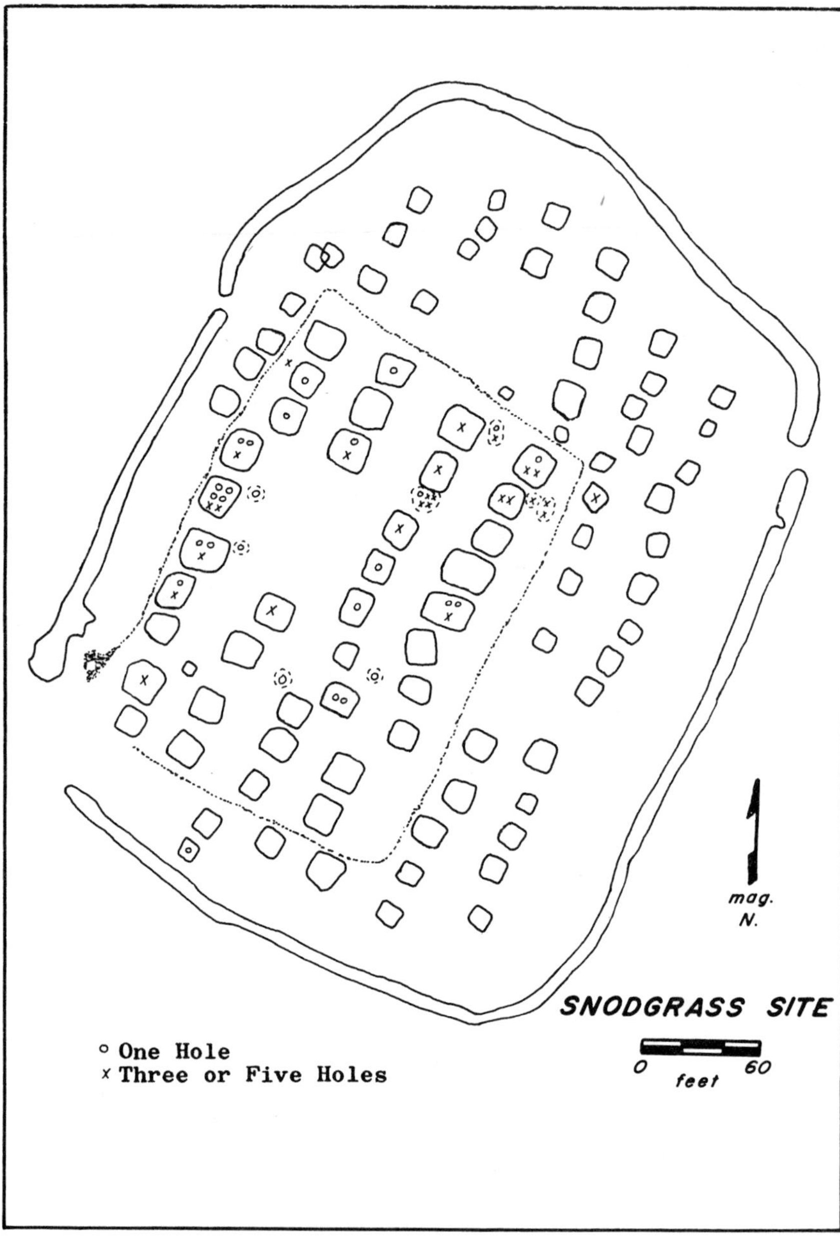

Figure 51. Distribution of perforated pottery discs with one hole and three or five holes.

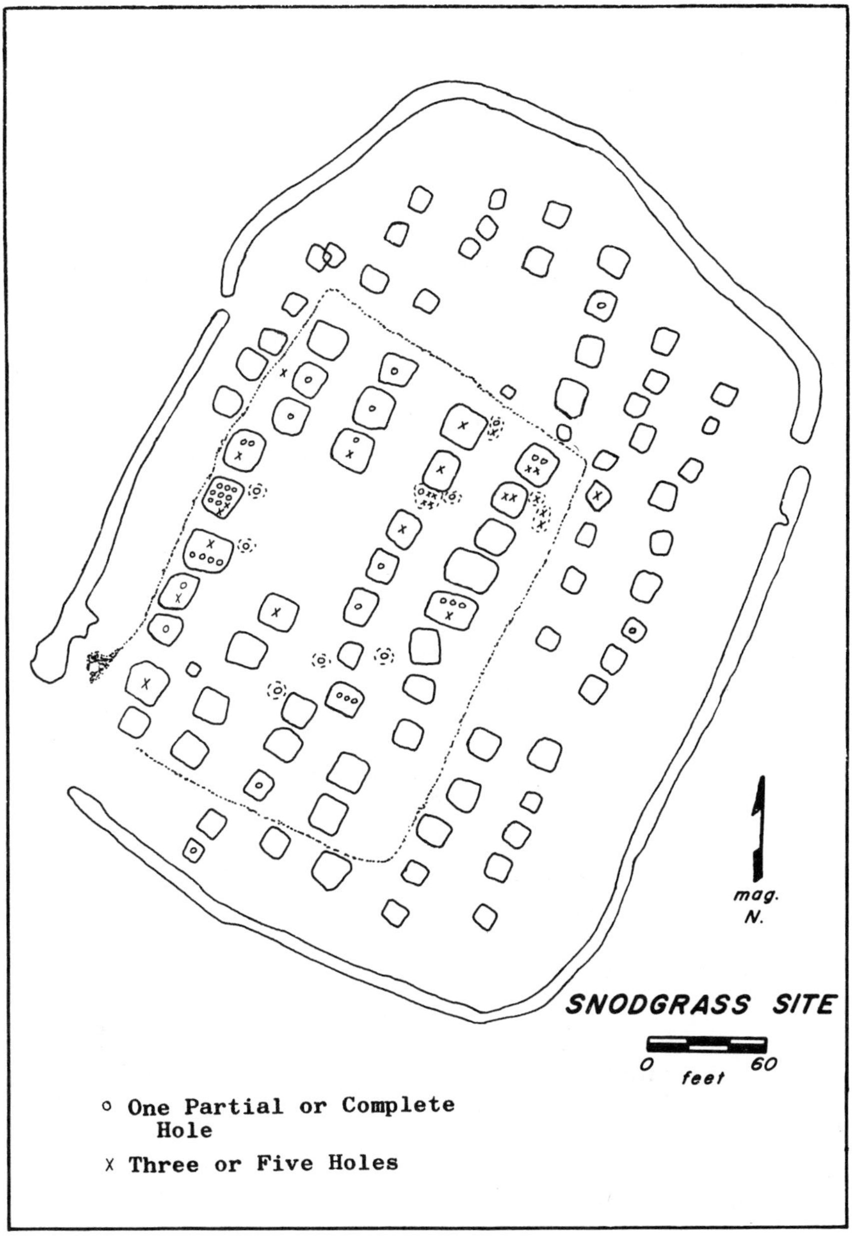

Figure 52. Distribution of pottery discs with one partial or complete hole and those with three or five holes.

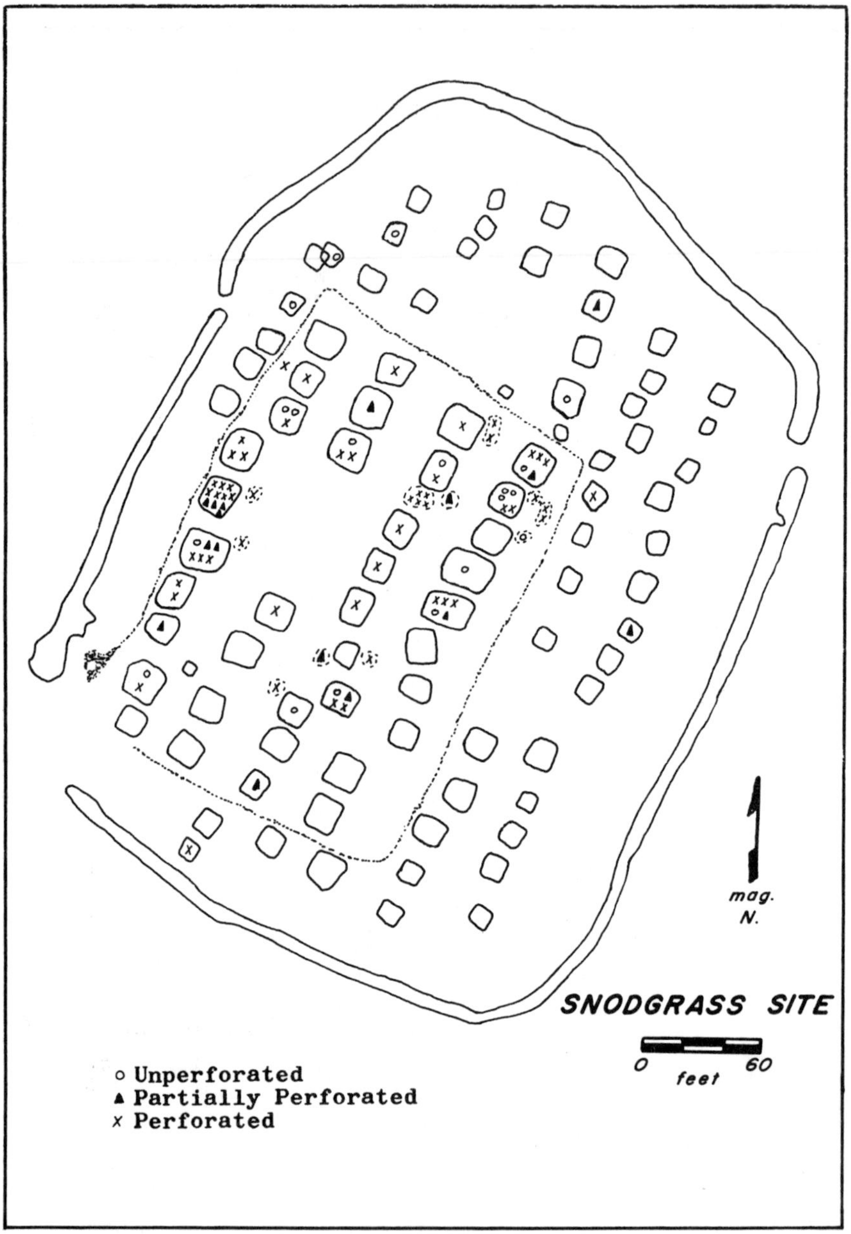

Figure 53. Distribution of unperforated, partially perforated, and completely perforated pottery discs.

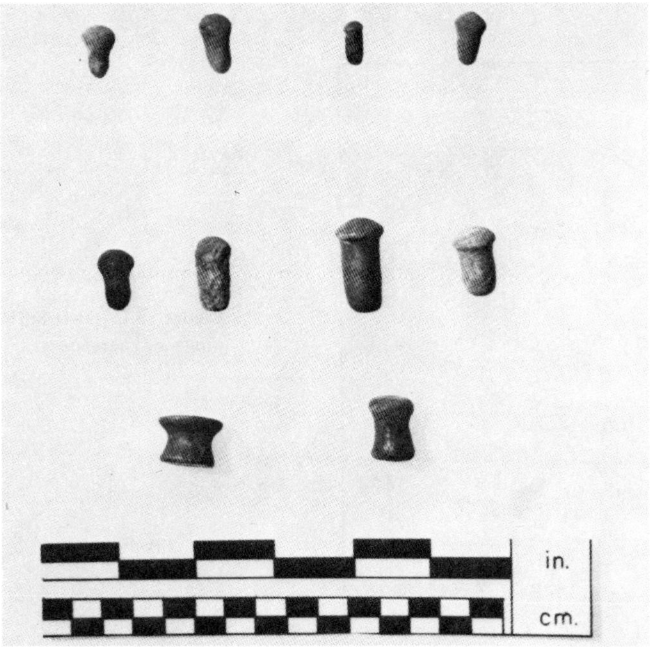

Plate 9. Earplugs and earspools.

Conclusions

Occupants of Segment 1 were essentially the only individuals in the village who made and used ceramic ear ornaments. There is no way to determine if these were worn by one or both sexes. These ornaments could very well have been used to identify social rank of individuals and only the higher ranking individuals were allowed to wear them. This would account for the presence of ear ornaments inside Segment 1 where the large houses, decorated pottery, and effigies occur. There is no absolute proof of this, however.

DISTRIBUTION OF EFFIGY APPENDAGES

Effigies are typically Mississippian in placement on vessels. They either occur as rimriders on small steep-sided bowls or as hoods on waterbottles (Pl. 10). Most can be identified as to the subject they were meant to depict. They occur in the form of humans, bears, birds, deer, frogs, conch shells, and unidentifiable zoomorphic forms. Collectively they cluster in the northern two-thirds of Segment 1, primarily to the north and east of the courtyard (Fig. 55). Only 5 of the 27 specimens fall outside Segment 1; 4 in Segment 2

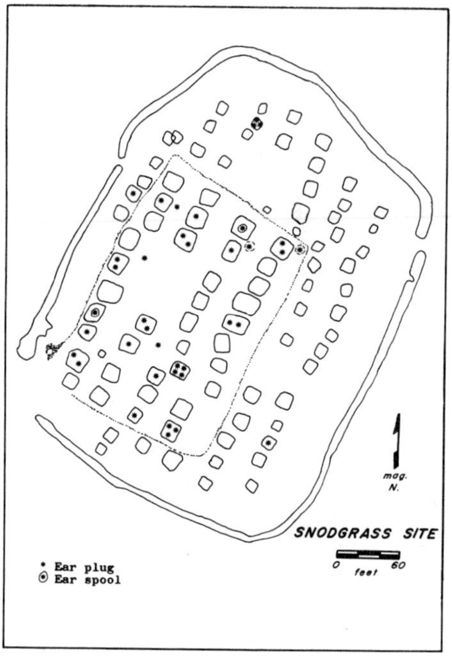

Figure 54. Distribution of earplugs and earspools.

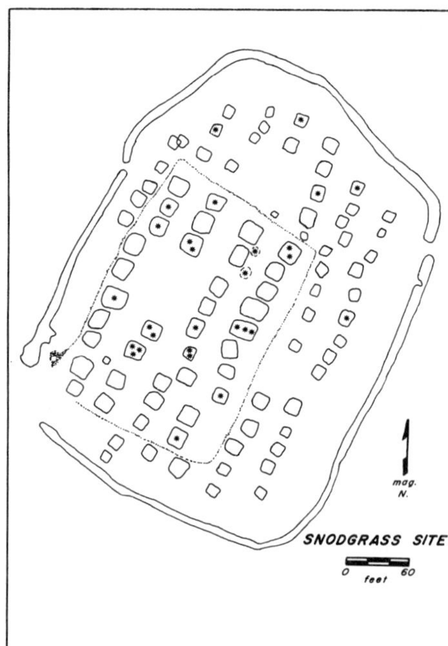

Figure 55. Distribution of effigies.

and 1 in Segment 3. Paste and workmanship would indicate they were made on the site and not procured by trade.

Human Effigies

Four human effigies came from the village (Fig. 56). Two are of the rimrider type and 2 are from hooded bottles. The 2 rimriders came from Structure 44 and the hooded specimens came from Structure 3 in Segment 1 and from Structure 10 in Segment 2. It appears that human effigies of the hooded type (Pl. 10:7) were broken at the northern end of Segment 1 and in adjacent areas of Segment 2 while rimrider specimens were broken east of the courtyard. Obviously the sample is too small to positively determine this.

Plate 10. Effigies.

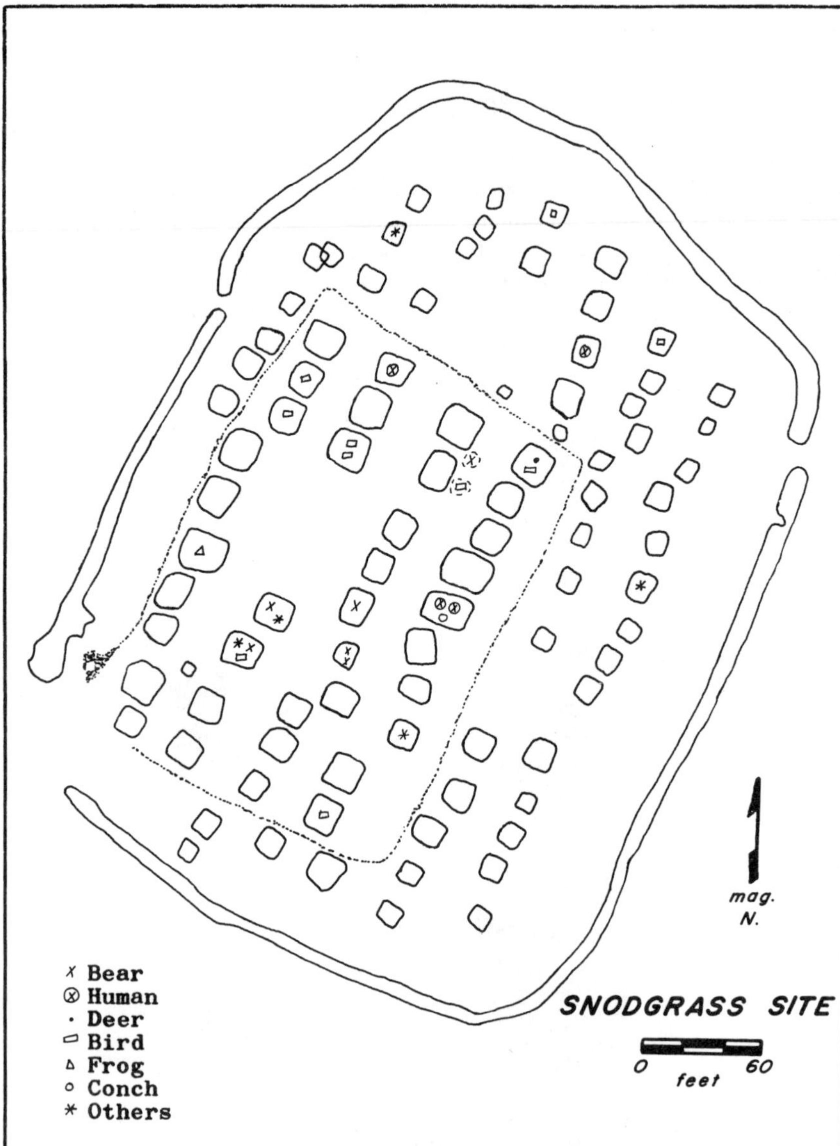

Figure 56. Distribution of effigies by type.

Bear Effigies

These cluster better than any other effigy form. Five of the 6 specimens were found in the same area. All occur within Segment 1. The 5 specimens were found 1 each in Structures 45, 51, and 52 and 2 in Structure 46 (Fig. 56). The other specimen was found in Pit 3. It would appear that a potter or potters living near the southeast corner of the courtyard made effigies of a single type. The nearest structure with pottery making equipment is Structure 47.

Bird Effigies

Eleven of these specimens were recovered, 8 from inside Segment 1, and 2 from outside in Segment 2 (Fig. 56). Another came from the surface. At least 2 depict ducks, but the others are rather nondescript bird forms. Six of the 8 specimens from Segment 1 cluster along a belt north of the courtyard in Structures 19, 20, 21, and 8 and in Pit 9. One specimen was found in Structure 39 in the southeast corner of the segment and another in Structure 52 south of the courtyard. Specimens from Segment 2 came from Structures 2 and 77. Distributional evidence indicates that the majority of bird effigies were made by households north of the courtyard in Segment 1.

Deer, Frog, and Conch Shell Effigies

Only 1 of each of these types was found (Fig. 56). The deer effigy came from Structure 8 and the frog from Structure 16. The conch effigy came from Structure 44.

Unidentifiable Effigies

These 3 specimens are so badly broken or so nondescript that they are unassignable to form. One of these came from Segment 1 and 1 each came from Segments 2 and 3.

Conclusions

1) Most effigies were made by households in the northern two-thirds of Segment 1. This might mean that effigies identified these households as a separate village social unit or that only these households had the right to make and use effigies. Or perhaps structures in the northern two-thirds of Segment 1 were occupied longer than other structures in the segment and village so there was more time for effigies to have been made, broken, and discarded.

2) Effigy types cluster within the village. In Segment 1, bear forms cluster in households southeast of the courtyard, birds cluster north of the courtyard, rimrider human effigies concentrate to the east, and hooded human effigies concentrate to the north. This must indicate that potters or users in these respective areas had their own effigy styles which were not shared with other households. It is not unreasonable to say that these may have been totemic in nature and identified different social units.

3) Most effigies occur inside Segment 1. Segment 2 had only 4 and Segment 3, 1. People who lived inside Segment 1 might have had the right to make effigies whereas people in other segments did not. If the presence of effigies is indicative of rank, the highest ranking individuals of the site lived in the northern two-thirds of Segment 1.

DISTRIBUTION OF LUGS AND TABTAILS

Lugs and tabtails are of similar form but the differentiating factor is the vessel form on which they occurred. Lugs occurred on jars and tabtails on effigy bowls (Pl. 11). Specimens used in this distributional analysis are only

Plate 11. Lugs and tabtails.

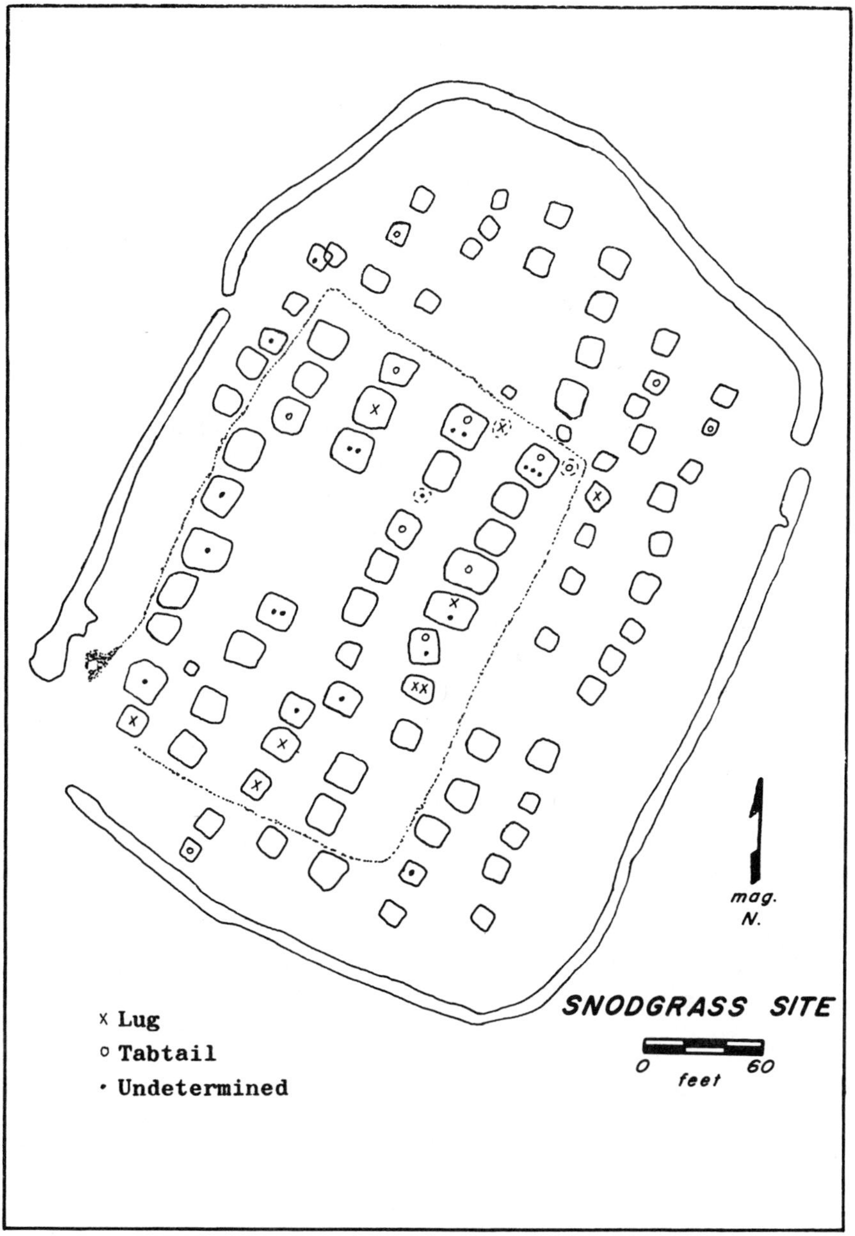

Figure 57. Distribution of lugs and tabtails.

those that are positively identifiable. Nine lugs were recovered from the site, all but 1 from within Segment 1. They occur in the northeast quarter and the last two southern rows of Segment 1 (Fig. 57). Two specimens came from Structure 42 and 1 each came from Structures 44, 22, 50, 48, and 54 and from Pit 2.

The distribution of tabtails is essentially limited to the northern half of Segment 1 (Fig. 57). Eight specimens came from this area. One each came from Structures 19, 3, 4, 8, 43, 84, 82, and Pit 11. Three specimens (1 from each) came from Structures 64, 76, and 33 in Segment 2 and 1 came from Structure 58 in Segment 3.

Conclusions

1) Lugs and tabtails cluster in the northern half of Segment 1 with the major clustering in the northeast quarter (Fig. 57). Tabtails are restricted to the north half. Potters either were more innovative in this area or they had social sanction for the making of these forms. Tabtails cluster essentially in the area where effigies clustered, as might be expected, and the same conclusion would apply.

2) Lugs are limited to the eastern portion of Segment 1. These may have been used as a socially identifying mark on pottery to separate it from pottery made by other social units on the site.

3) Tabtails were seldom made and used outside Segment 1. They have essentially the same distribution in Segments 2 and 3 as effigies and the same conclusions would apply.

DISTRIBUTION OF PERFORATED AND BIFURCATED JAR HANDLES

Perforated handles are strap handles from jars with a vertical hole through the strap near the rim (Pl. 12). Apparently this was for running a cord through for suspension. Bifurcated jar handles are strap handles on which the handle is bifurcated where it joins the shoulder of the vessel (Pl. 12). Ten perforated handle specimens were found on the site, of which 9 were inside Segment 1 (Fig. 58). A single specimen occurred in Segment 3 in Structure 14. The 9 specimens in Segment 1 occur essentially in the north half and are more or less randomly distributed. Structures 18 and 45 each had 2 specimens; other specimens occurred singly in structures.

Only 3 bifurcated specimens were found, all in the north half of Segment 1 (Fig. 58). The specimens were found in Structures 20 and 44 and Pit 16.

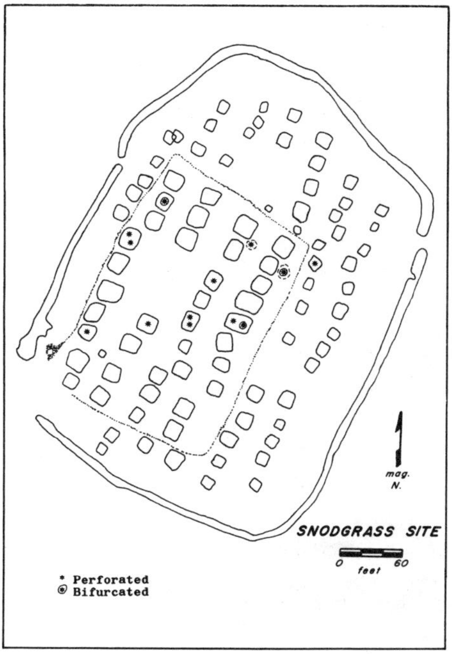

Figure 58. Distribution of perforated and bifurcated jar handles.

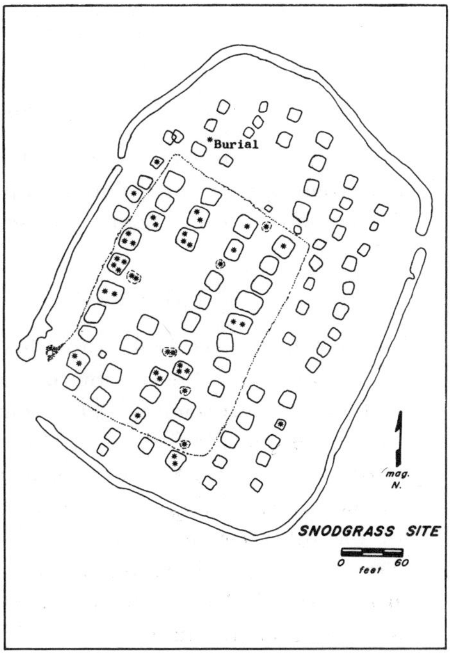

Figure 59. Distribution of scalloped-rim bowls.

Plate 12. Perforated and bifurcated jar handles.

Conclusions

Perforated and bifurcated jar handles were used by households in the north half of Segment 1. Potters in this area added these attributes to pottery for unknown reasons, perhaps because they were socially qualified to do so.

DISTRIBUTION OF SCALLOPED-RIM BOWLS

Small flaring rim bowls often have scallops on their rims. These occur in clusters of two or three on four opposing sides of the rim (Pl. 13).

Forty-three specimens came from the Snodgrass village. Only 6 of these came from outside Segment 1 (Fig. 59). This attribute clusters to the west, north, and southeast of the Segment 1 courtyard. Although more occur in the north half of Segment 1, there are many in the south half, unlike several of the other ceramic attributes. Three specimens came from Segment 2. Two came from Structures 24 and 61, and the only complete bowl came from Burial 7. Three specimens came from Segment 3, 2 from Structure 71 and one from Structure 28.

Conclusions

Potters throughout Segment 1 made scalloped-rim bowls, although most were made and used west and north of the courtyard. Extensive use of this attribute took place off the southeast corner of the courtyard. Essentially it was limited for use only by occupants of Segment 1. Its use might have been restricted to only one segment of the Snodgrass society.

DISTRIBUTION OF INCISED SHERDS

Incised decorations were used on jar shoulders by the Snodgrass potters. These are in every identifiable example and are composed of three parallel

Plate 13. Scalloped-rim bowls.

lines in a chevron design and occur on both large and small jars (Pl. 14). One example (Structure 21) is on a jar handle.

This motif is almost completely restricted to Segment 1. Only 5 of the 80 specimens occur outside Segment 1 (Fig. 60). In Segment 2, single specimens occur in Structures 24, 61, and 69 and in Segment 3 in Structure 14 and 58. The greatest concentration of specimens is in structures immediately adjacent to the courtyard in Segment 1. Most occur on the west and north sides of the courtyard. Structure 21 has by far the most specimens, totaling 14. Structures 17 and 18 each have 7 specimens. Elsewhere in the segment, Structure 55 has 4 specimens, and Structures 8, 44, and 82 and Pit 34 each

Plate 14. Incised sherds.

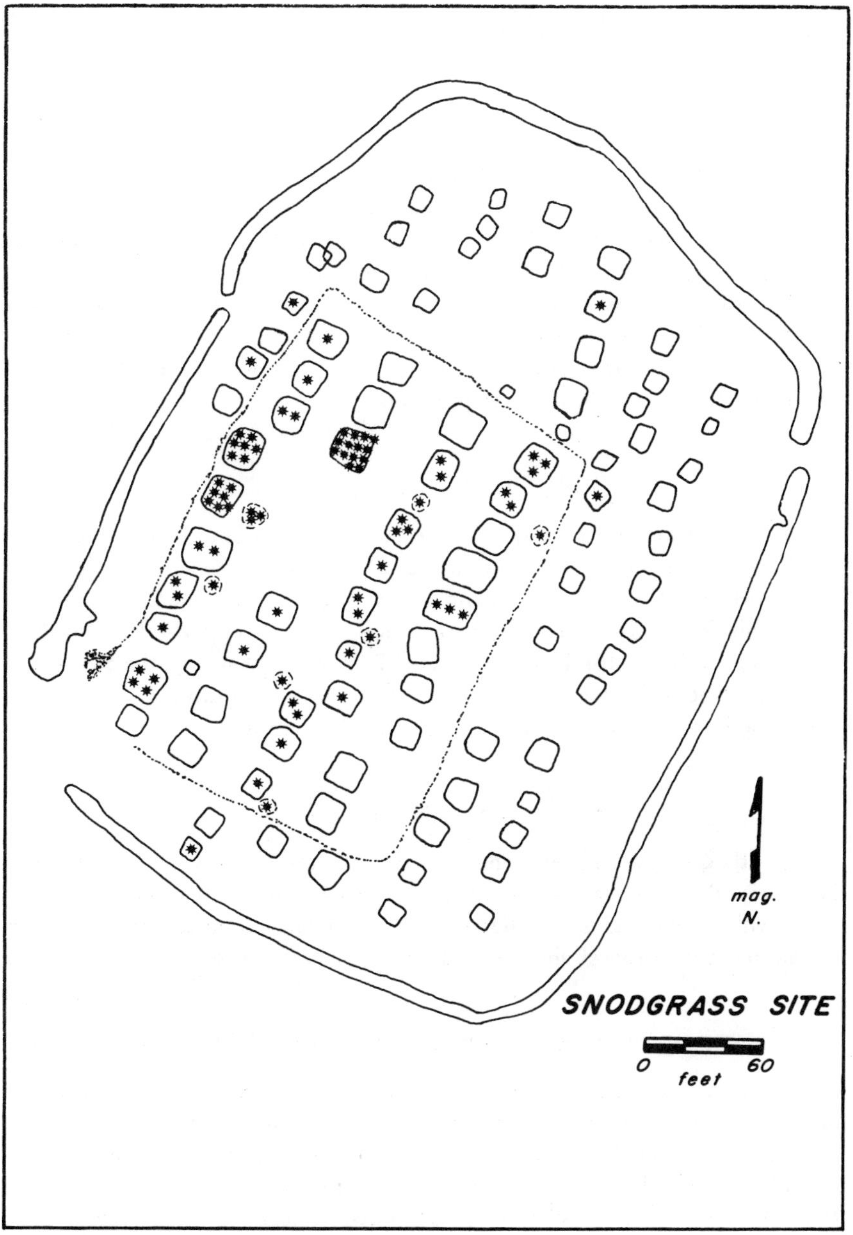

Figure 60. Distribution of incised sherds.

have 3. Two specimens occur in each of Structures 19, 16, 5, 45, 49, 56, and 7. Other structures or pits contain 1 or none.

Conclusions

The use of incised chevron designs was essentially limited to potters or households within Segment 1. It appears that they almost had exclusive right to the design. The greatest quantity of incised pottery was used in Structures 21, 18, and 17. It is possible that all incised pottery on the site was made by occupants of these households. This motif may have been used to identify the ceramics of a number of related households and could have been made by a mother and her daughters, or it could have identified some other social segment within the population.

DISTRIBUTION OF PUNCTATE SHERDS

Punctate motifs are very rare on the site. They appear as inverted triangles on the upper shoulder sherds from jars and in one instance, on the inside of a bowl (Pl. 15). On at least one jar they are bordered below by incised lines. Only 9 examples came from the Snodgrass site (Fig. 61). Four of these came from a single structure, Structure 17, at the west side of the Segment 1 courtyard. Other specimens came one each from Structures 7, 52, 56, and 50. A single specimen came from Structure 77 in Segment 2.

Conclusions

Essentially only one household used punctate pottery. It could easily have been that only one woman was responsible for all the punctate pottery in the village. Punctates may have been a distinguishing mark for the pottery of that particular household or just the potter's preference.

DISTRIBUTION OF NODED SHERDS

Noding occurs on small incurved-rim bowls and rarely on small handleless jars. Nodes are grouped in twos or threes on four opposing sides of the vessel, just below the rim (Pl. 16). Of the 24 specimens from the site, only 5 noded jars were found (1 in Structure 50, 1 in 84, 2 in 16, and 1 in 8). Only 2 of the 19 noded bowl specimens occurs outside Segment 1 (Fig. 62). They were in Structure 38 of Segment 3 and in Structure 23 of Segment 2. Most noded bowl specimens occur in the north half of Segment 1. In fact only 2 specimens occur in the southern half, 1 in Structure 39 and 1 in 50.

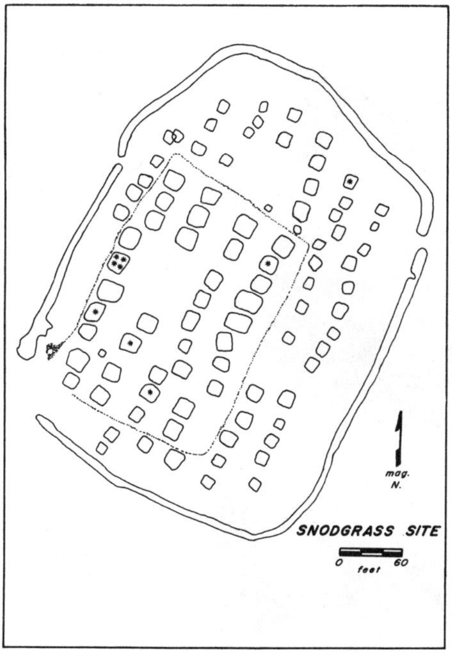

Figure 61. Distribution of punctate sherds.

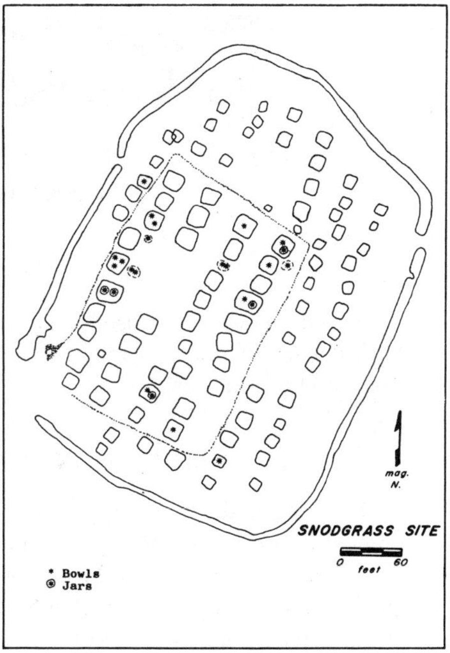

Figure 62. Distribution of noded sherds.

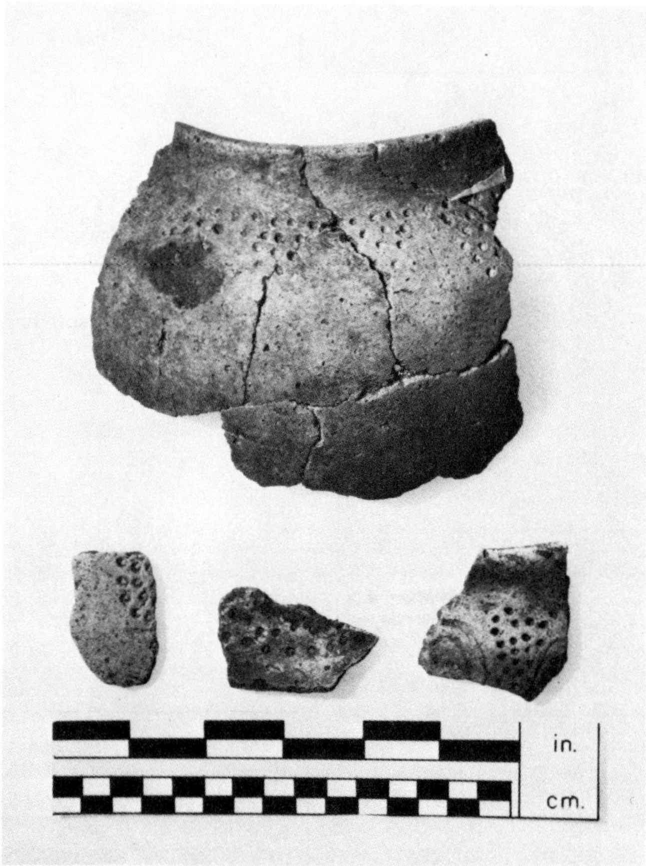

Plate 15. Punctate sherds.

Conclusions

Noded vessels were used only inside Segment 1 and only in its north half. Potters of this area may have had exclusive rights to the use of noding as a vessel decoration.

DISTRIBUTION OF NOTCHED RIMSHERDS

Notching is the most common rim motif used by the potters of the Snodgrass village (Pl. 17). It most frequently occurs on small flaring rim bowls but does occur on large flaring rim bowls and small and large jars. This rim treatment can be divided into 11 types based on angle of notching on top or side of rim, size of notches, shape of notches, and spacing of notches.

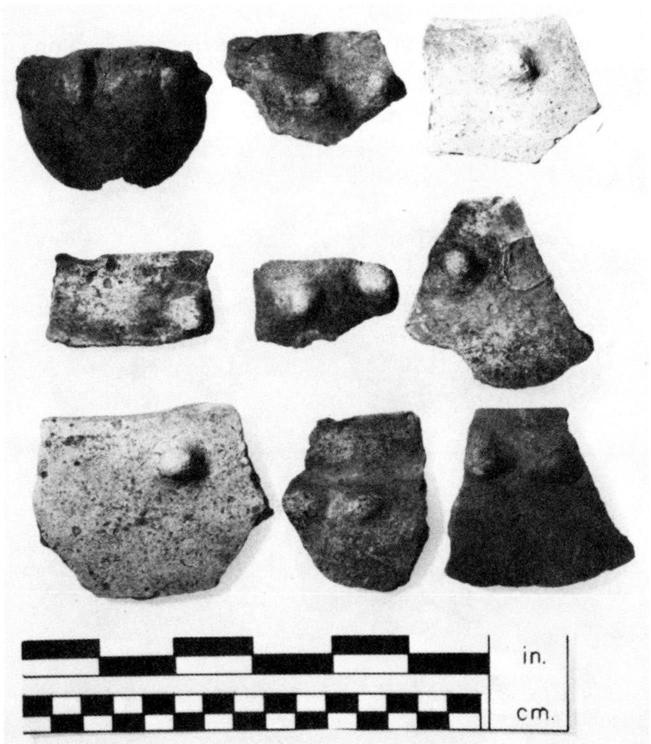

Plate 16. Noded sherds.

Notching Types

Type 1: Left Diagonal Topnotched (Fig. 63:A)

Position of Notch: Top of rim.
Angle: Diagonal slanting to the left.
Comments: These notches are as deep as they are wide and are uniformly spaced.
Number of Specimens:
Bowls: 5
Jars: 0

Type 2: Right Diagonal Topnotched (Fig. 63:B)

Position of Notch: Top of rim.
Angle: Diagonal slanting to the right.

Comments: Same as Type 1 except more closely spaced on jars.
Number of Specimens:
Bowls: 11
Jars: 4

Plate 17. Notched rims.

Type 3: Right Diagonal Sidenotched (Fig. 63:C)

Position of Notch: Side of rim.
Angle: Diagonally slanting to the right.
Comments: Same as for Type 1.
Number of Specimens:
Bowls: 2
Jars: 0

Type 4: Right Diagonal Side-Topnotched (Fig. 63:D)

Position of Notch: On both top and side of rim.
Angle: Diagonally to the right.
Comments: These notches are more widely spaced than on other types and cut through the vessel lip so that half is on top and half is on the side of the rim.
Number of Specimens:
Bowls: 5
Jars: 1

Type 5: Ninety-Degree Topnotched (Fig. 63:E)

Position of Notch: Top of rim.
Angle: Ninety degrees to main axis of rim.
Comments: These notches are very small and closely spaced.
Number of Specimens:
Bowls: 6
Jars: 5

Type 6: Rectangular Sidenotched (Fig. 63:F)

Position of Notch: Side of rim.
Angle: Vertical.
Comments: These notches are rather closely spaced and are small rectangular depressions made with a broad-edged tool.
Number of Specimens:
Bowls: 3
Jars: 0

Type 7: Left Diagonal Sidenotched Lip (Fig. 63:G)

Position of Notch: On side of rim in lip.
Angle: Diagonally to the left.
Comments: These are rather closely spaced notches that are as deep as they are wide.
Number of Specimens:
Bowls: 1
Jars: 0

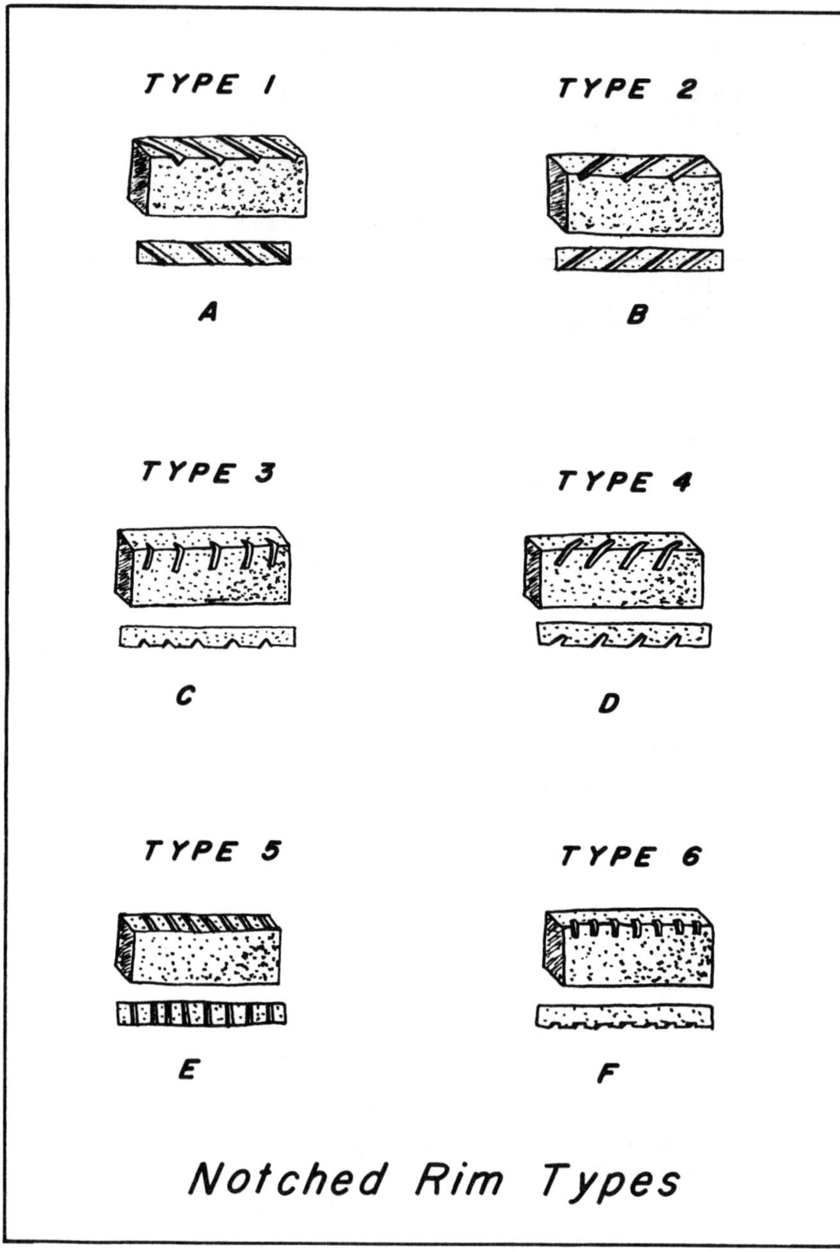

Figure 63. Notched rim types 1-6.

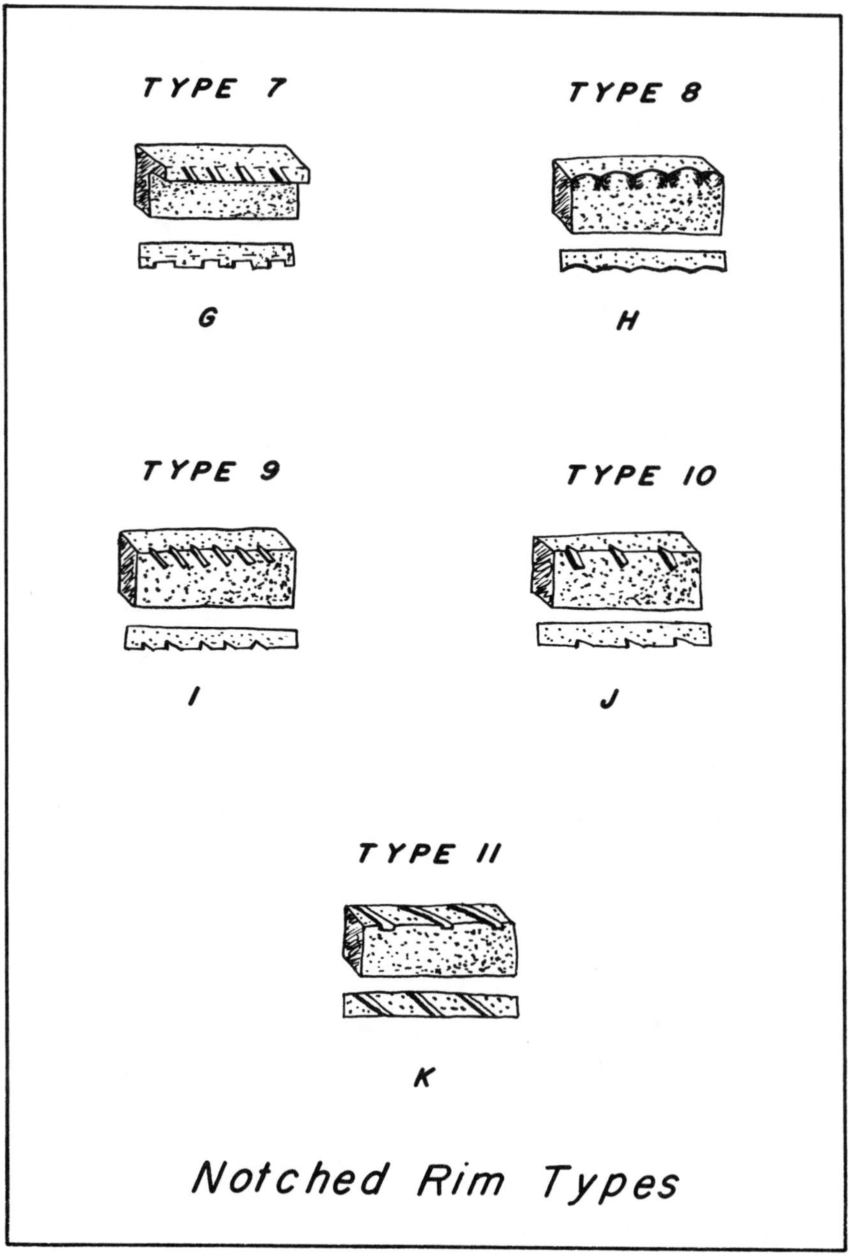

Figure 64. Notched rim types 7-11.

Type 8: Piecrust Sidenotched (Fig. 64:H)

Position of Notch: On side of rim.
Angle: Vertical.
Comments: These are broad depressions that were apparently formed with the potter's fingertips. The finished product has narrow vertical ridges between shallow depressions.
Number of specimens:
Bowls: 7
Jars: 0

Type 9: Closely-Spaced Left Diagonally Sidenotched (Fig. 64:I)

Position of Notch: On side of lip.
Angle: Diagonally to the left.
Comments: This is the same as Type 3 but angles in opposite direction.
Number of Specimens:
Bowls: 0
Jars: 2

Type 10: Broad Left Diagonally Sidenotched (Fig. 64:J)

Position of Notch: Side of rim.
Angle: Diagonally to the left.
Comments: These are much like Type 9 except the notches are much larger and a little more widely spaced.
Number of Specimens:
Bowls: 0
Jars: 1

Type 11: Left Diagonal Rectangular Topnotched (Fig. 64:K)

Position of Notch: Top of rim.
Angle: Diagonally to the left.
Comments: This is similar to Type 1 except the notches are more closely spaced and are as broad at the bottom as at the top indicating they were made with the edge of a rectilinear object.
Number of Specimens:
Bowls: 1
Jars: 0

Distribution of Notched Types (Fig. 65)

Distribution of Type 1

Five specimens of this type were found, but since 2 fit together they are counted as a single specimen. They were found in Structures 61 and 65 in Segment 2 some 140 feet apart (Fig. 66). Two other specimens occur in Structure 16 and 1 in Structure 84.

CONCLUSIONS. The sample is far too small to present a meaningful distribution.

Distribution of Type 2

Six of the 13 specimens of this type cluster in the vicinity of the northwest corner of the Segment 1 courtyard (Fig. 67). Two specimens were found in Structures 18 and 20, and 1 came from Structures 16 and 17. A single specimen came from just outside Segment 1 in Structure 24 in the same area. Three specimens came from Pit 34 in Segment 1. Single specimens occurred elsewhere in Segment 1 in Structures 43, 51, and 47. Structures 24 and 66 in Segment 2 and Structure 72 in Segment 3 yielded single specimens.

CONCLUSIONS. This motif is indigenous to structures on the west and northwest sides of the Segment 1 courtyard. This must have been a mode used by a single potter or a limited few living in adjacent households.

Distribution of Type 3

The 2 specimens of this type were found in Structures 21 and 84 (Fig. 68).

CONCLUSIONS. The 2 specimens are limited to Segment 1, but the sample is too small to be meaningful.

Distribution of Type 4

The 6 specimens of this type cluster more closely than any other type (Fig. 69). All specimens of this type came from within Segment 1. Three came from Structure 19 and 1 each came from Structure 18, Structure 84, and Pit 30, immediately adjacent to Structure 19. They probably represent only 2 complete specimens.

CONCLUSIONS. With one exception, this type is restricted to only a small area in Segment 1.

Distribution of Type 5

Seven of the 11 specimens of this type were found in the area near the north end of Segment 1 (Fig. 70). Single specimens came from Structures 17, 20, 5, 8, 45, 50, 55, and 62. A single specimen also came from Pit 34. In Segment 2, single specimens came from Structures 24 and 25.

CONCLUSIONS. This motif was used by households mostly in the northern end of Segment 1.

Distribution of Type 6

The 3 specimens of this type were found in the northeast quarter of Segment 1 (Fig. 71). One each came from Structures 8, 83, and 84.

CONCLUSIONS. This motif was used by a restricted number of households in the northeast quarter of Segment 1. It too must have been a localized style made by one person or a limited number of individuals.

Distribution of Type 7

Only 1 specimen of this type was found in Segment 1. It came from Structure 47.

CONCLUSIONS. The sample is far too small to be meaningful. This specimen is probably a variant of more common sidenotched types.

Distribution of Type 8

Five of the 7 specimens of this type were found on the east side of the Segment 1 courtyard, 3 in Structure 82 and 1 each in Structure 45 and Pit 19 (Fig. 72). Another specimen was found in the segment in Pit 34. A single specimen came from Structure 28 in Segment 3.

CONCLUSIONS. This type is almost completely limited to Segment 1. It must have been used by households on the east side of the courtyard.

Distribution of Type 9

One specimen of this type came from Structure 18 and 1 from Structure 8, both in Segment 1.

CONCLUSIONS. This is a very small sample, so there are insufficient data from which to draw any conclusions.

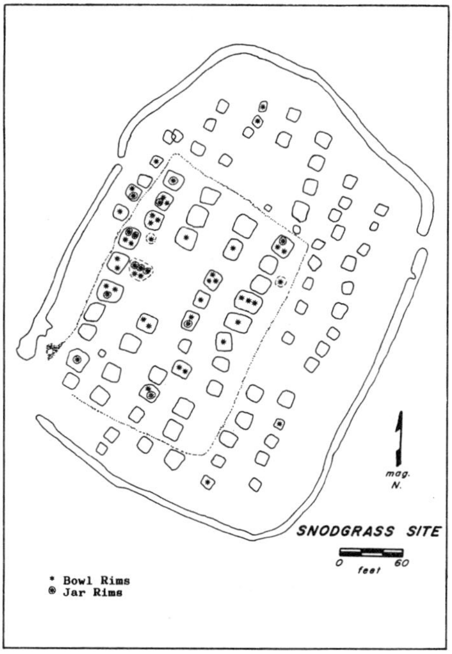

Figure 65. Distribution of notched bowl and jar rims.

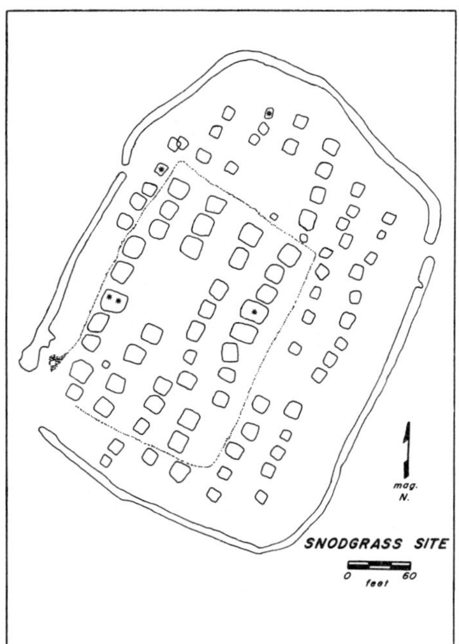

Figure 66. Distribution of notched bowl rims, Type 1.

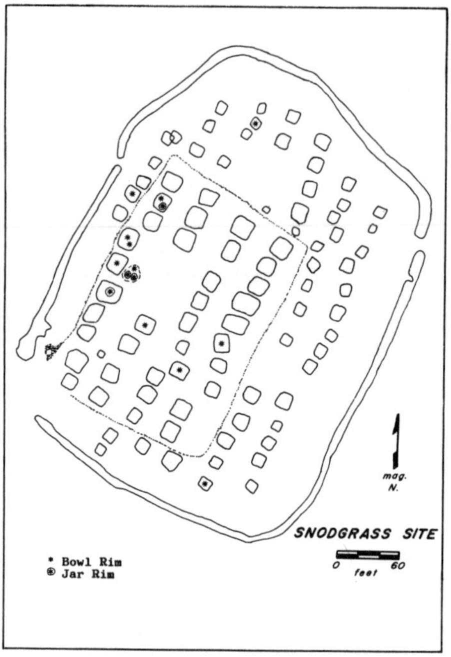

Figure 67. Distribution of notched bowl and jar rims, Type 2.

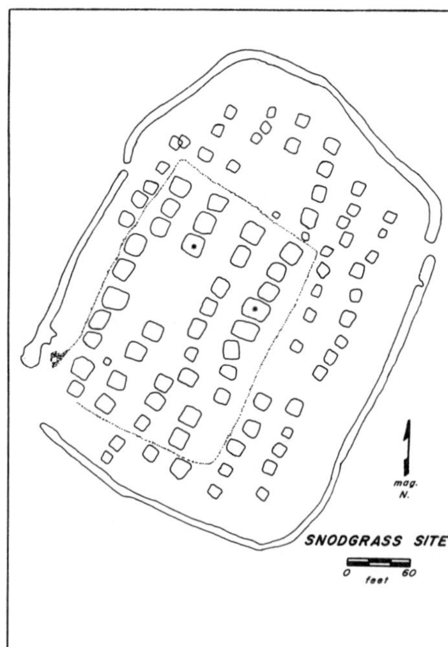

Figure 68. Distribution of notched bowl rims, Type 3.

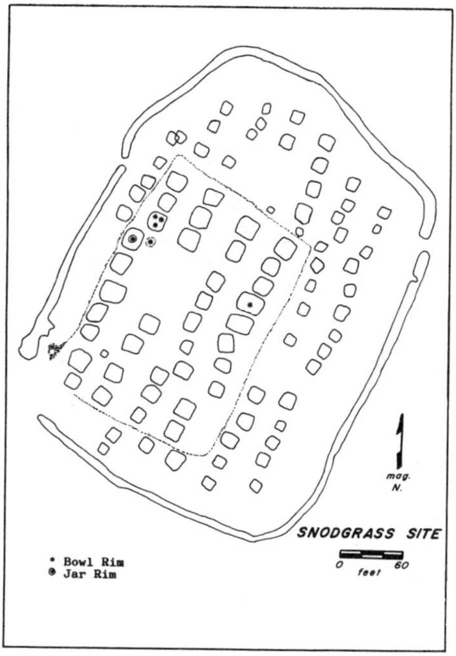

Figure 69. Distribution of notched bowl and jar rims, Type 4.

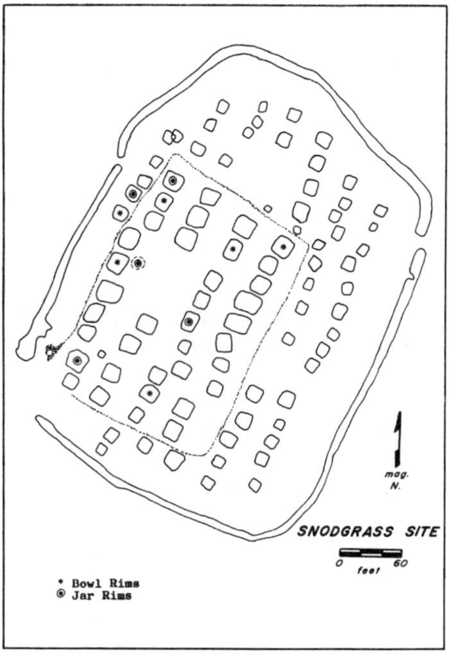

Figure 70. Distribution of notched bowl and jar rims, Type 5.

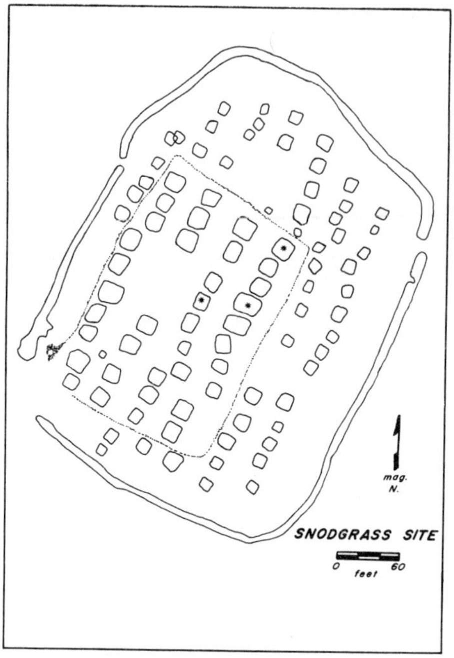

Figure 71. Distribution of notched bowl rims, Type 6.

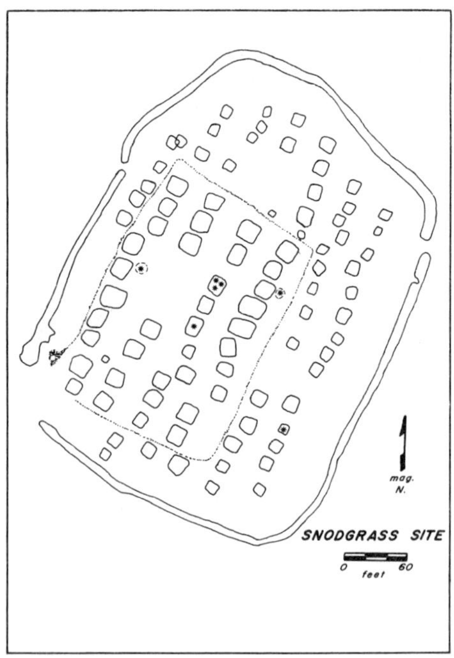

Figure 72. Distribution of notched bowl rims, Type 8.

Distribution of Type 10

A single specimen of this type was found in Structure 50. The sample is too small for any meaningful conclusions.

Distribution of Type 11

Only 1 specimen of this type came from the village. It was found in Structure 51. Conclusions are the same as for Type 10.

Distribution of Combination of Types

Notches oriented diagonally to the right on top or sides of rims, Types 2, 3, and 4

Bowls and jars decorated with these motifs cluster on the west side of the courtyard of Segment 1 (Fig. 73).

CONCLUSIONS. These types of motifs were almost exclusively used west of the Segment 1 courtyard.

Notches on top oriented to the right and notches on the top and side of rim, Types 2 and 4

Jars of Type 2 cluster in the vicinity of the southwest corner of the Segment 1 courtyard, while bowls of Types 2 and 4 cluster around the northwest corner of the courtyard (Fig. 74).

CONCLUSIONS. Households on the northwest corner of the courtyard made bowls of Types 2 and 4, while occupants at the southwest corner made mostly jars with Type 2 rim treatment.

Distribution of surface treatment on side of rim, Types 3, 6, and 8

Sidenotched or indented motifs occur on the east side of the Segment 1 courtyard (Fig. 75).

CONCLUSIONS. Occupants of households on the east side of the Segment 1 courtyard used side treatment motifs on rims while occupants on the west side used top-treated rims.

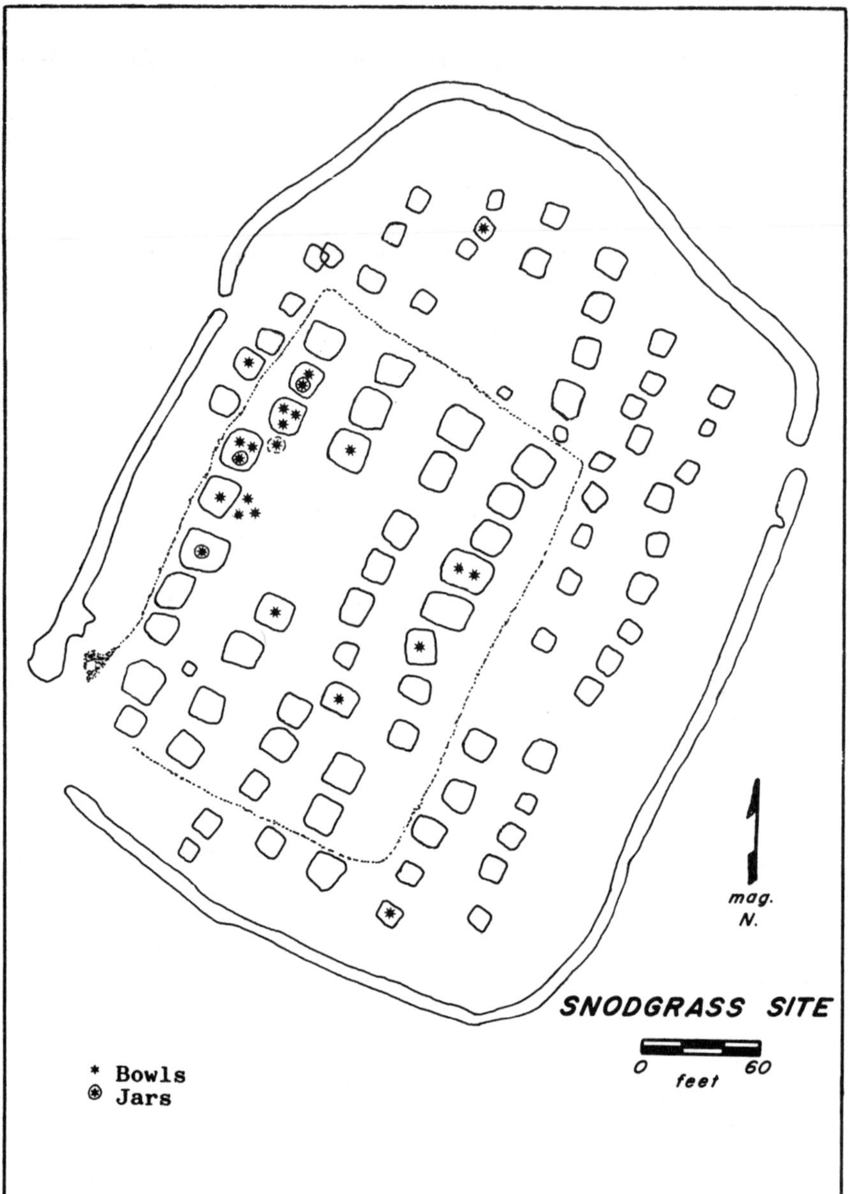

Figure 73. Distribution of notched bowl and jar rims, Types 2, 3, and 4.

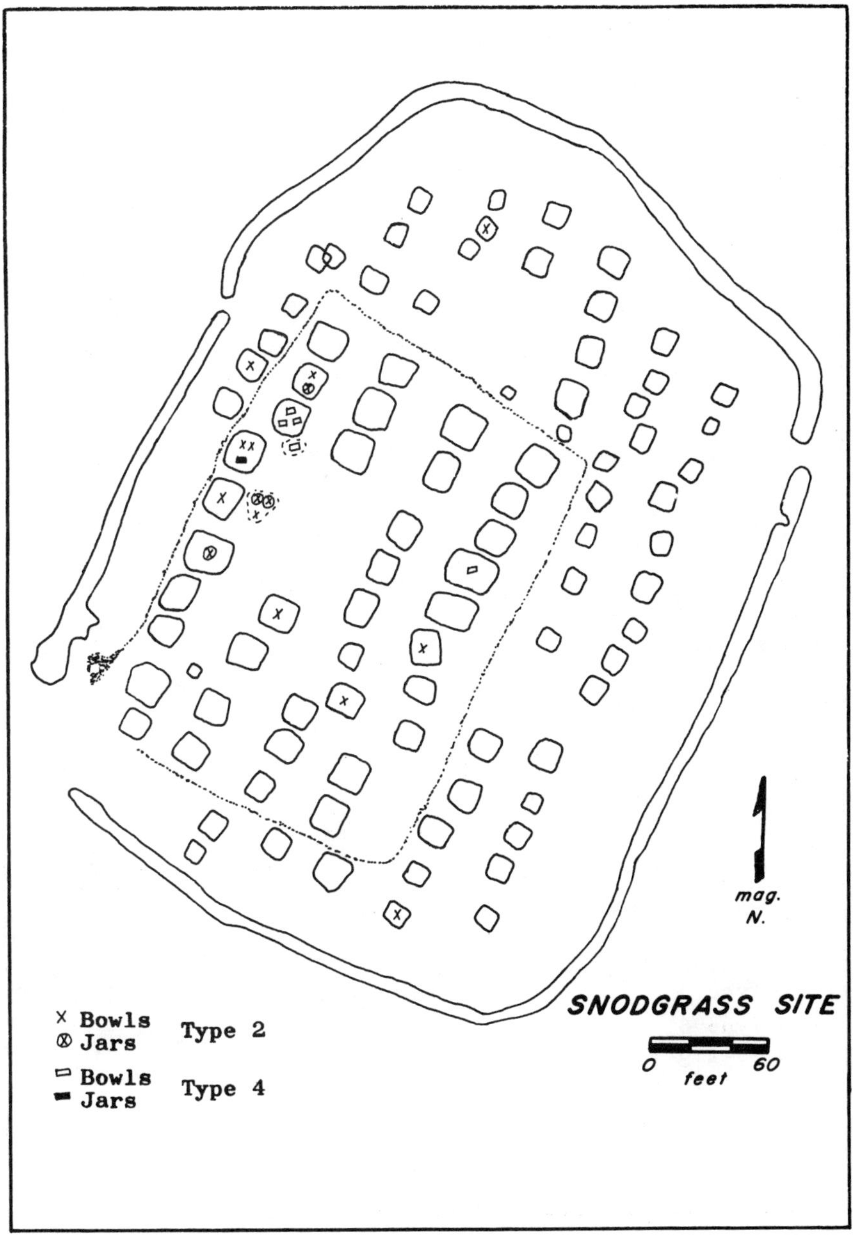

Figure 74. Distribution of notched bowl and jar rims, Types 2 and 4.

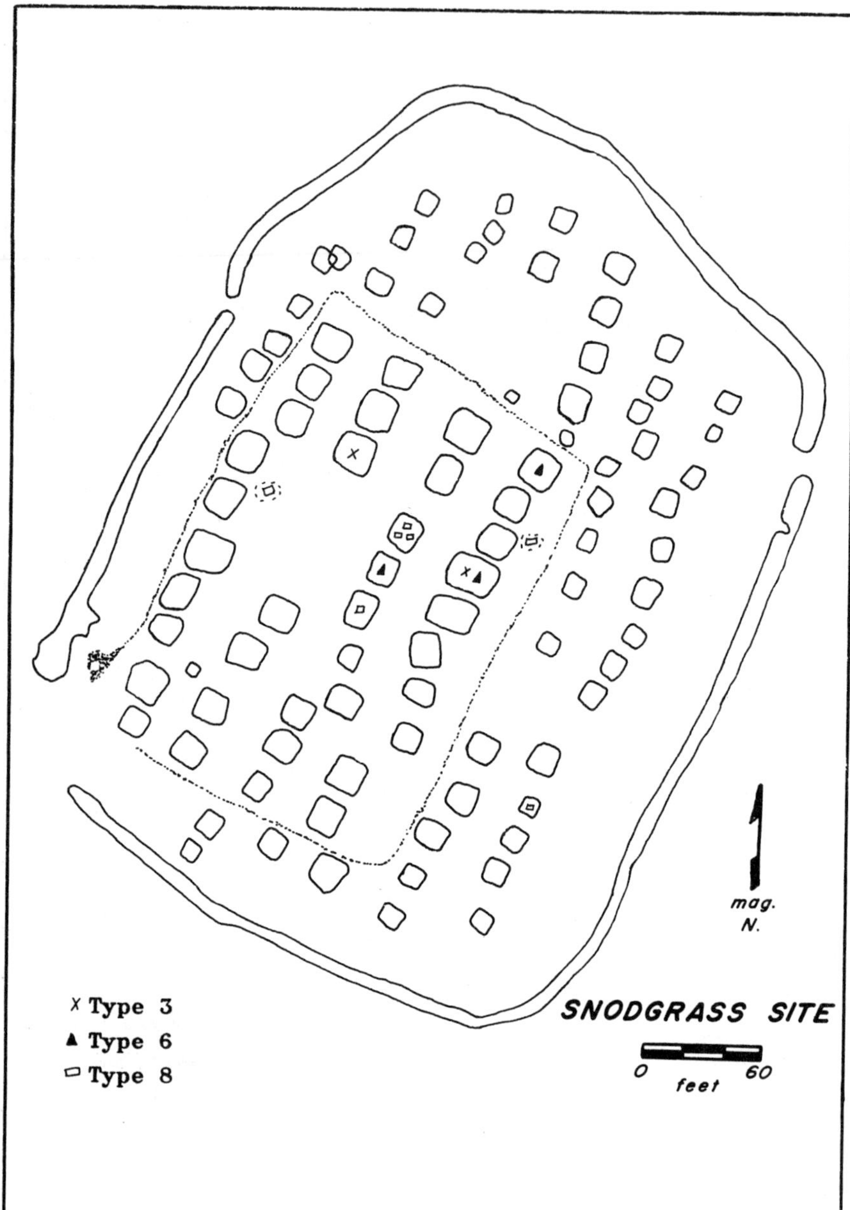

Figure 75. Distribution of notched bowl rims, Types 3, 6, and 8.

Distribution of all types of rim-top decorations on bowls compared and contrasted with all types of rim-side decorations on bowls

Bowls with decorations on the rim tops occur on the west side of Segment 1 courtyard and in adjacent structures in Segment 2, while bowls with side decorated rims occur on the east side of the courtyard (Fig. 76).

CONCLUSIONS. Individuals of either side of the courtyard used placement of notching on bowl rims to differentiate their ceramics.

Distribution of all rim-top decorations on bowls and jars compared and contrasted with all rim-side decorations on bowls and jars

Bowls and jars with rim-top decoration occur on the west side of Segment 1 courtyard, while bowls and jars with rim-side decorations occur on the east side (Fig. 77).

CONCLUSIONS. Potters on the west side of Segment 1 used rim-top decorations on both bowls and jars, while potters on the east side used side decorations primarily on bowls.

Distribution of top and sidenotched jars compared and contrasted

With only one exception, jars with notches on top of the rim occur on the west side of Segment 1. Only 3 specimens of sidenotched types were found; 2 were on the east side of the Segment (Fig. 78).

CONCLUSIONS. Individuals on the west side of Segment 1 used jars decorated with top notches; while those on the east side seldom used notched jar rims, and if they did they were placed on the side of the rim.

Distribution of right-oriented notching of any type compared and contrasted to left-oriented notching of any type

Right-oriented specimens cluster on the west side of the northern half of Segment 1. Left-oriented specimens occur randomly (Fig. 79).

CONCLUSIONS. Left-oriented specimens may have resulted from left-handed potters. Lefthanded people would probably have been rather randomly distributed among the potters.

Distribution of left-oriented types (Types 1, 7, 9, 10, and 11) compared and contrasted to right-oriented types (Types 2, 3, and 4) and straight notching (Types 5, 6, and 8)

Left-oriented types (1, 7, 9, 10, and 11) occur randomly but they are found

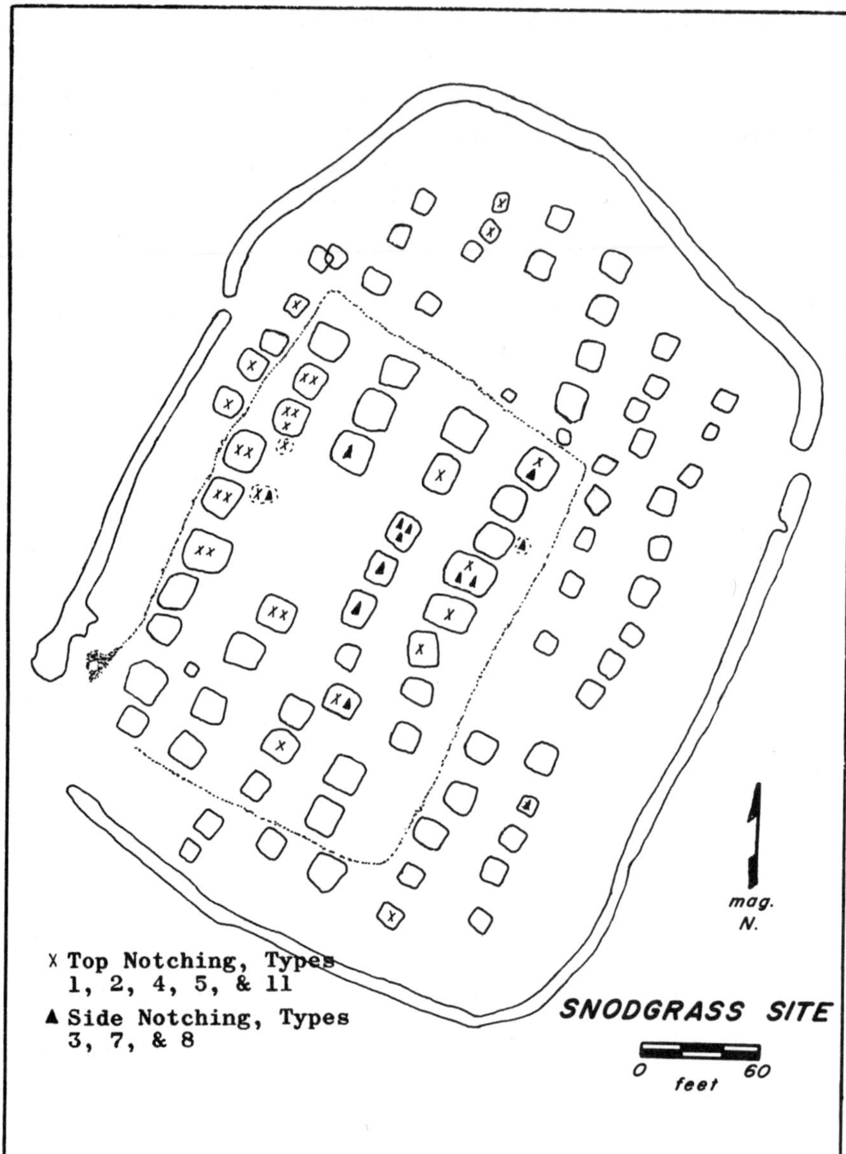

Figure 76. Distribution of notched bowl rims—top notching and side notching.

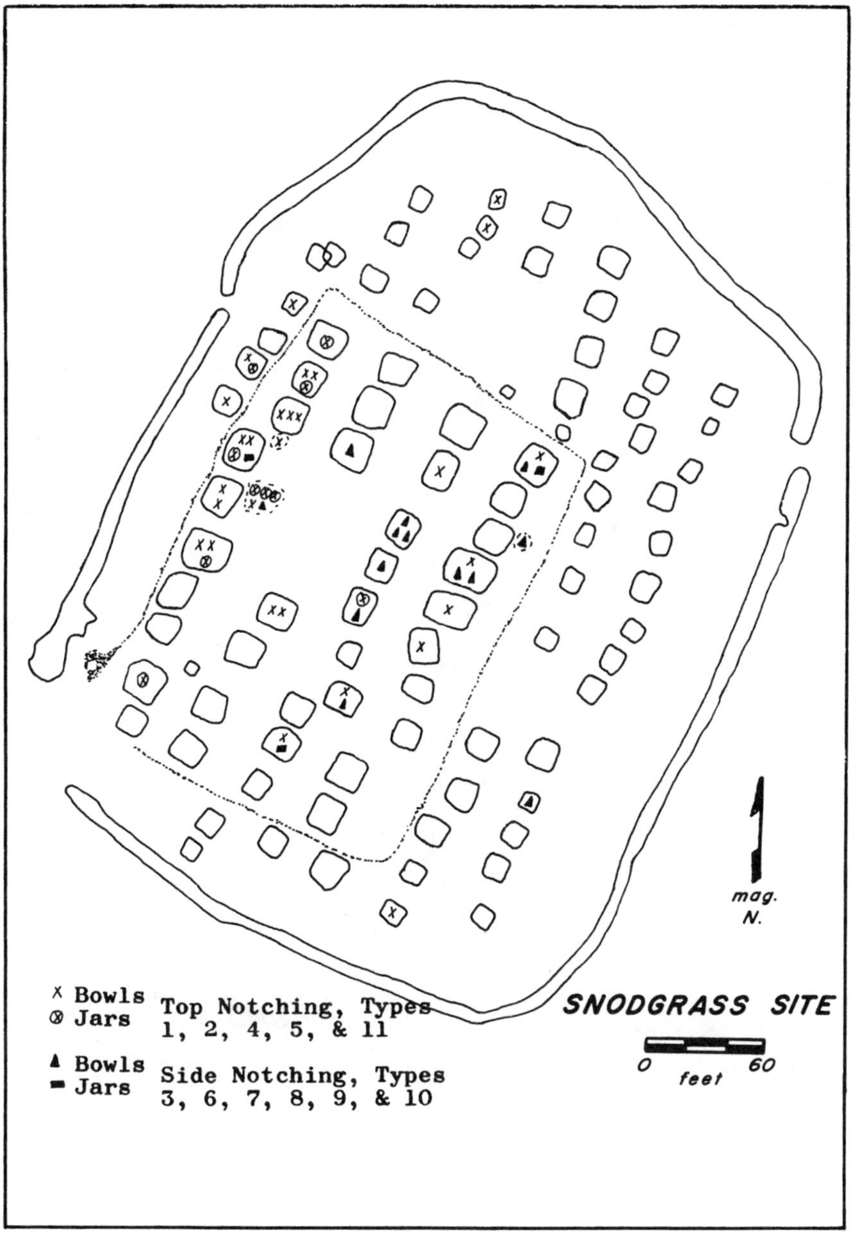

Figure 77. Distribution of notched bowl and jar rims—side notching and top notching.

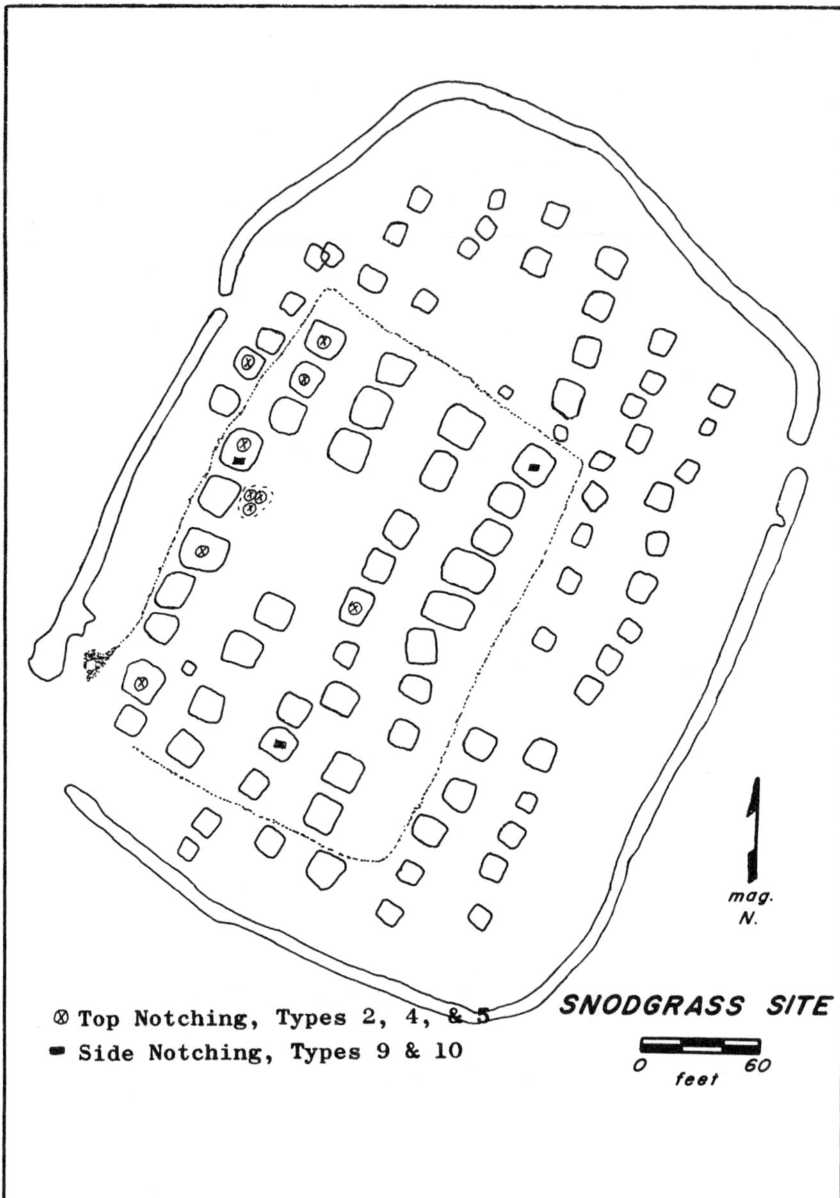

Figure 78. Distribution of notched jar rims—top notching and side notching.

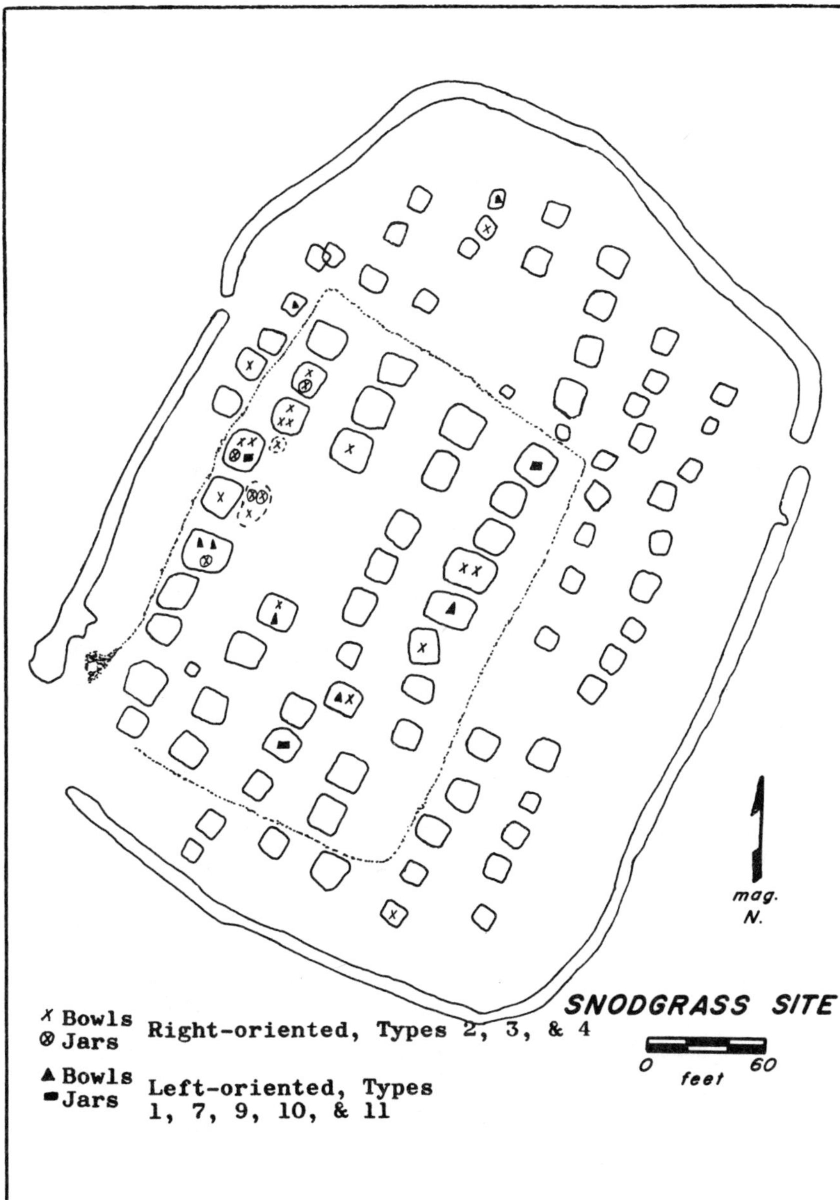

Figure 79. Distribution of notched bowl and jar rims—right-oriented and left-oriented notching.

more frequently off the southeast corner of the Segment 1 courtyard (Fig. 80). Right-oriented types (2, 3, and 4) cluster west of the Segment 1 courtyard, while straight-notched types (5, 6, and 8) cluster more consistently in isolation in the northeast quarter of Segment 1 but also occur west of the courtyard.

CONCLUSIONS. Potters in various areas around the Segment 1 courtyard produced different rim treatment forms. These may have been employed by members of different social units to differentiate their pottery.

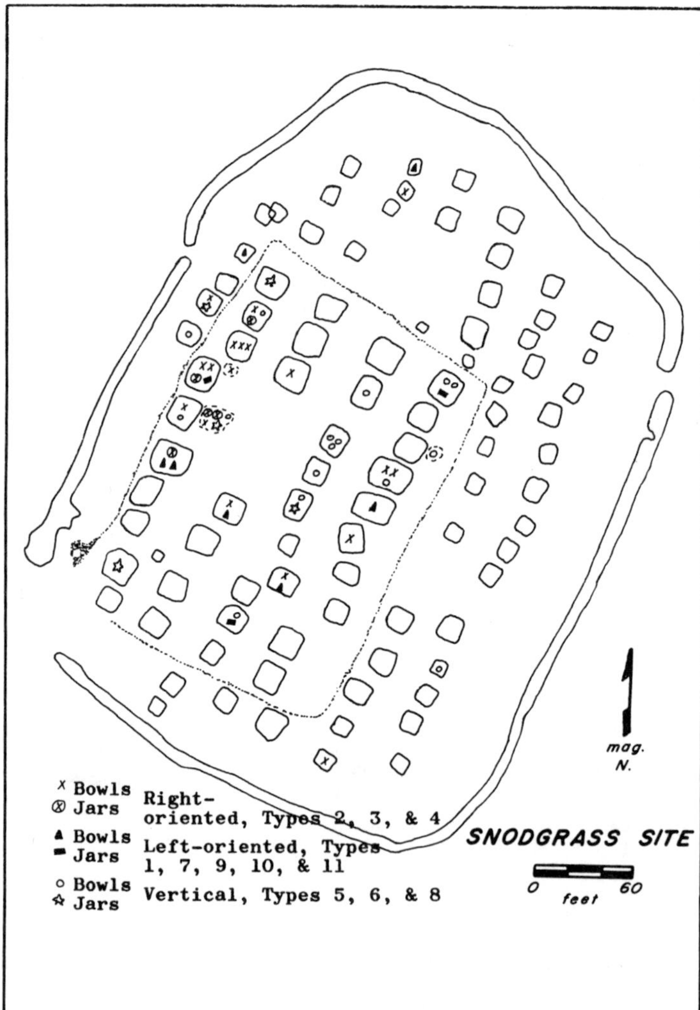

Figure 80. Distribution of notched bowl and jar rims—right-oriented, left-oriented, and vertical notching.

VII

SUMMARY

It is well known that Mississippian societal units were divided into segments or divisions of greater and lesser political force, as is witnessed by the early historical accounts and analyses of Mississippian societies. One way that this is reflected in the archaeological data is in the clear distinction in site size among the several living and working locations of this distinctive complex in Southeast Missouri.

The Powers phase settlement pattern certainly demonstrates differential site size. The major site of the Powers phase, Powers Fort, has platform mounds and extensive fortification ditches and embankments and is four times larger than any subsidiary Powers phase village. There are more exotic goods at Powers Fort in the form of painted, polished, and engraved pottery (Surface collections conducted from 1964 to 1972). Motifs on vessels reflect involvement in the Southeastern Ceremonial Complex. Very few burials have been excavated at Powers Fort, so as yet it is undetermined whether there is differential distribution of status goods with burials.

There was also too little data on burials at Snodgrass to make a judgment. At the Turner site, however, as will be described in Thomas Black's monograph, the burial patterns for this "sister" site of Snodgrass did not suggest much status differentiation. Such indications of a higher level of ascribed status are likely to be found in the major town of a Mississippian community.

At the Snodgrass site, however, there are the indications of some sort of social or living segmentation and of behavioral practices associated with them. An internal compound surrounds the largest structures on the site. Structures outside this area are smaller and are built on less favorable locations. Each of the three segments of house groupings surrounds a courtyard.

The structures in the internal compound or Segment 1, are much larger than the other two and required much more building material. They are located on the flattest and highest ground and have the largest courtyard. From the standpoint of desirable living quarters, this was surely the favored area of the site. If there are significant social divisions within the site, they should be also reflected in the various types of items found.

Segment 1 at the Snodgrass site contains an overwhelming majority of items of adornment and decorated items. All the earplugs except 5 specimens, occur within the segment (see Fig. 54). Almost all effigies (Fig. 55), tabtails (Fig. 57), perforated and bifurcated jar handles (Fig. 58), punctate sherds (Fig. 61), noded sherds (Fig. 62), and notched bowl and jar rims (Fig. 65) occur within Segment 1. These items are almost totally absent outside the segment. There is likewise differential distribution of designs within Segment 1, which may reflect further social subdivisions or merely family preference. Projectile points concentrate around the courtyard, with a majority in large structures on the east side. Bear effigies concentrate in structures adjacent to the southeast corner of the courtyard while bird effigies concentrate in structures adjacent to the northwest corner. Lugs and tabtails concentrate east of the courtyard in the segment as do perforated and bifurcated jar handles, whereas scalloped-rim bowls occur rather randomly throughout the segment. Incised sherds concentrate around the courtyard with a greater density around the northwest corner. Punctate sherds occur around the southwest corner of the courtyard. Noded sherds concentrate off the west side and northeast corner of the courtyard. Notches on top of bowl and jar rims concentrate on the west side of the courtyard, while notches occur on the side of rims on the east side. Obviously these distributions have social connotations but whether they reflect family styles or some form of dual division is open to question.

Since all these attributes and items occur predominantly within Segment 1, it may be inferred that they demonstrate that the people who occupied the most favorable location on the site and lived in the largest structures made and used decorated items. This seems to indicate differential social status stemming from political power, but it would seem a bit premature to reach such a conclusion on the basis of the Snodgrass data alone.

It is possible that the people who occupied Segment 1 controlled and farmed the arable land around the site, and occupants of Segments 2 and 3 seasonally occupied farmsteads away from the village. This would help explain the low frequency of items outside Segment 1. However, there is no direct evidence for seasonality as differential use of land. The only evidence for control of resources in the Powers phase comes from a corn storage structure on the Turner site. Central storage facilities may indicate a surplus and perhaps some kind of redistribution practices, but the excavated evidence for this is slim indeed.

The validity of the conclusions resulting from this study depends on a demonstration of contemporaneity of all structures within the village and throughout all segments. Due to the destruction of the village by fire, we know that all structures were contemporaneous for at least one day, the day the village burned. From the occurrence of refuse pits adjacent to structures both inside and outside the internal compound, we know that these village segments existed side by side for a period of time prior to the fire. There are more refuse pits inside the internal compound (Segment 1) than outside, which indicates that either more people lived in Segment 1, or it was occupied longer than Segments 2 and 3, or that occupants of Segment 1 had more refuse for disposal. Fewer refuse pits outside the internal compound could indicate that fewer people lived in these segments, that Segments 2 and 3 were occupied a shorter period of time than Segment 1, or that they had less refuse for disposal. Another obvious explanation of fewer refuse pits in Segments 2 and 3 is that the occupants may have thrown their refuse into the fortification ditch. Tests in the ditch in 1968, 1969, and 1970 demonstrated that the bottom of the ditch is littered with refuse. It is quite possible that people living adjacent to the fortifications threw their refuse in the ditch. Occupants in the internal compound could not have easily done this, since they were in the center of the site and surrounded by a wall.

It cannot be proved that all structures in the village were built at the same time, but it can be safely stated that they existed side by side for at least a period of time before they were destroyed. During this time, cultural activities were carried out in structures both inside and outside the internal compound, Segment 1. It is assumed that the contents of structures and adjacent pits reflect at least a portion of the material goods used by the inhabitants and that these goods reflect the style of vessels and tools used. Material found associated with structures outside the compound must represent the kinds of goods used there. If they had made and used decorated pottery we would have found remains of it in the structures and refuse pits.

Almost all structures in the village apparently were dwellings of small social units, probably in the form of nuclear families, if small houses are an indication of this. Hearths in these domestic dwellings are surrounded by ceramic cones and utilitarian cooking vessels. Structures both inside and outside the internal compound contain remains of large jars, bowls, bottles, and other utilitarian items. Differences between the segments lie in elaboration of articles in Segment 1—by decoration in the form of incising, punctating, and noding and by the presence of effigies and earplugs. The segments existed side by side, and people inside Segment 1 decorated pottery and wore earplugs, while inhabitants outside did not. If people outside the wall used these articles, they hid them so well that either we did not find them, or they threw them far into the swamp when they broke, or they threw them over the wall into the internal compound, or they ground them up to temper pottery. These ideas are, of course, highly unlikely. These objects occur in such small frequency outside the internal compound that their occurrence is insignificant. For example, 33 earplugs and earspools were found inside Segment 1, while only five specimens came from Segments 2 and 3. These specimens could have been lost by members of Segment 1, or moved by rodents or natural forces, or actually used by members of Segments 2 and 3 even though there was social sanction against it.

Since there is a dichotomous distribution of these selected items between Segments 1 and Segments 2 and 3, there has to be an explanation. Such a phenomenon could not happen by chance. The reason these items (decorated pottery, earplugs, effigies, etc.) were selected for distributional plots in this presentation is that they demonstrate the most differentiation between the segments. If plain utilitarian wares had been selected for a distributional plot, they would have occurred both inside and outside the internal compound, with slightly more inside. This distribution was not used because it was desired to emphasize differential distributions, not similarities.

When the distributions of all the above goods are considered, it is obvious that more items of each category are found in Segment 1. The people who lived inside Segment 1 used more and a greater variety of each category of items. Why the people inside used items such as perforated pottery discs and Wickliffe "juice presses" while those outside did not is open to question. None of the items found at the Snodgrass site can be called true status items in the sense that they are made of exotic materials or demonstrate a high degree of artistic skill. The distributional analysis demonstrates one fact: inhabitants of Segment 1 had decorated utilitarian items and possessed more material goods than those in Segments 2 and 3. Occupants of Segments 2 and 3 owned only the basic domestic necessities and nothing more. It is suggested that this is good evidence of social differentiation between two groups living side by side in a single village.

This report on the Snodgrass site and the one on the Gypsy Joint site prepared by Bruce Smith are the first of a series resulting from the Powers Phase Project. As the initial investigations were made known to anthropological and archaeological conferences during the late 1960s and early 1970s, the complex nature of the Mississippian settlement pattern came as a distinct surprise. Quite a few projects have since been modeled to investigate the same patterns that were first recovered in some depth by the Powers Phase Project crews. We have also found a certain disbelief among our colleagues about the short lifespan of these sites and this society in this area—until they visit and see for themselves.

In the late 1960s, we were quite sure that the Powers phase people had moved into the area from the St. Francis area, or at least Griffin felt fairly sure of this. Perhaps now we are somewhat less certain of their precise background and immediate derivation. There are some jar design similarities to vessels in the Cairo Lowlands rather than the St. Francis area. Publication of the data on the Turner site by Cynthia and James Price and eventual future works at Powers Fort should contribute to this question and also to the equally puzzling question as to the problem of what happened to the Powers phase population when they abandoned the area in the fourteenth century.

BIBLIOGRAPHY

Adams, Robert McC.
1968 Archaeological Research Strategies: Past and Present. Science 160:1187-92.

Ballinger, Homer J. and Paul Pesones
1948 Investigations of Southeast Missouri Secondary Limonite Deposits, Wayne, Butler, and Ripley Counties, Missouri. U.S. Bureau of Mines Report of Investigations, No. 4314.

Beardsley, Richard K. et al.
1956 Functional and Evolutionary Implications of Community Patterning. Society for American Archaeology Memoirs, No. 11.

Binford, Lewis R. and Sally R. Binford
1966 A Preliminary Analysis of Functional Variability in the Mousterian of Levallois Facies. Recent Studies in Paleoanthropology, American Anthropologist 68(2, pt. 2):238-95.

Binford, Lewis R. and Sally R. Binford (eds.)
1968 New Perspectives in Archaeology. Chicago: Aldine Publishing Company.

Brown, James A.
1971 The Dimensions of Status in the Burials at Spiro. In: Approaches to the Social Dimensions of Mortuary Practices, Society for American Archaeology Memoirs, No. 25.

Chapman, Carl H. and Leo O. Anderson
1955 The Campbell Site: A Late Mississippi Town and Cemetery in Southeast Missouri. The Missouri Archaeologist 17(2-3):1-140.

Cole, Fay-Cooper, et al.
1951 Kincaid, A Prehistoric Illinois Metropolis. Chicago: University of Chicago Press.

Decennial Census of U.S. Climate Monthly
1963 Averages for State Climatic Divisions 1931-1960. Missouri Climatography of the U.S., No. 85.

Deetz, James
1960 An Archaeological Approach to Kinship Change in Eighteenth Century Arikara Culture. Unpublished Ph.D. Dissertation. Harvard University.
1965 The Dynamics of Stylistic Change in Arikara Ceramics. Urbana: University of Illinois Press.

Fisk, Harold N.
1944 Geological Investigations of the Alluvial Valley of the Lower Mississippi. Vicksburg: Mississippi River Commission.

Freeman, Leslie and James A. Brown
1964 Statistical Analysis of Carter Ranch Pottery. In: Chapters in the Prehistory of Eastern Arizona II, by Paul S. Martin, et al. Fieldiana: Anthropology 55.

Fried, Morton H.
1960 On the Evolution of Social Stratification and the State. In: Culture in History: Essays in Honor of Paul Radin, edited by Stanley Diamond. New York: Columbia University Press.

Fritz, John and Fred T. Plog
1970 The Nature of Archaeological Explanation, American Antiquity 35:405-12.
Fundaburk, Emma Lila
1958 Southeastern Indians, Life Portraits, A Catalogue of Pictures, 1564-1860. Luverne, Alabama: Emma Lila Fundaburk, Publisher.
Griffin, James B.
1967 Eastern North American Archaeology: A Summary. Science 156:175-91.
Hill, James N.
1966 A Prehistoric Community in Eastern Arizona. Southwestern Journal of Anthropology 22:9-30.
1967 Structure, Function, and Change at Broken K Pueblo. In: Chapters in the Prehistory of Eastern Arizona, III, by Paul S. Martin, William A. Longacre, and James N. Hill. Fieldiana: Anthropology 57.
1968 Broken K Pueblo: Patterns of Form and Function. In: New Perspectives in Archaeology, edited by L. R. Binford and S. R. Binford. Chicago: Aldine Publishing Company.
1970 Broken K Pueblo: Prehistoric Social Organization in the American Southwest. University of Arizona Papers in Anthropology, No. 18.
Hole, Frank and Robert F. Heizer
1965 An Introduction to Prehistoric Archaeology. New York: Holt, Rinehart and Winston.
Hutton, J. H. and Henry Herman Krusekopf
1916 The Soils of Missouri. M.A. Thesis. University of Missouri.
Krusekopf, H. H.
1962 Major Soil Areas of Missouri. University of Missouri Agricultural Experiment Station Bulletin B785.
Larson, Lewis H.
1971 Archaeological Implications of Social Stratification at the Etowah Site, Georgia. In: Approaches to the Social Dimensions of Mortuary Practices, edited by James A. Brown. Society for American Archaeology Memoirs, No. 25.
Leach, Edmund
1954 Political Systems of Highland Burma. Boston: Beacon Press.
Longacre, William A.
1963 Archaeology as Anthropology: A Case Study. Unpublished Ph.D. dissertation. Department of Anthropology, University of Chicago.
1964a Archaeology as Anthropology: A Case Study. Science 144:1454-55.
1964b Sociological Implications of the Ceramic Analysis. In: Chapters in the Prehistory of Eastern Arizona, II, by Paul S. Martin, et al. Fieldiana: Anthropology 55.
1966 Changing Patterns of Social Integration: A Prehistoric Example from the American Southwest. American Anthropologist 68:94-102.
Magill, Arthur Clay
1958 Geography and Geology of Southeast Missouri Lowlands. Cape Girardeau, Missouri.
Marshall, Richard A.
1965 An Archaeological Investigation of Interstate Route 55 Through New Madrid and Pemiscot Counties, Missouri, 1964. Highway Archaeology Report No. 1, in Cooperation with the Missouri State Highway Department and the U.S. Department of Commerce, Bureau of Public Roads.
McCracken, Mary H. (comp.)
1961 Geological Map of Missouri.
McQuigg, James D. and Wayne L. Decker
1963 Climate of the Southeast Lowlands of Missouri. University of Missouri Agricultural Experiment Station Bulletin B794.

Mochon, Marion J.
1972 Language, History, and Prehistory: Mississippian Lexico Reconstruction. American Antiquity 37:478-503.

Morse, Dan F.
1973 Nodena: An Account of 75 Years of Archaeological Investigations in Southeast Mississippi County, Arkansas. Arkansas Archaeological Survey, Research Series 4.

Moselage, John H.
1962 The Lawhorn Site. The Missouri Archaeologist 24:1-110.

Peebles, Christopher S.
1971 Moundville and Surrounding Sites: Some Structural Considerations of Mortuary Practices II. In: Approaches to the Social Dimensions of Mortuary Practices, edited by James A. Brown. Society for American Archaeology Memoirs, No. 25.

Phillips, Philip, James A. Ford and James B. Griffin
1951 Archaeological Survey in the Lower Mississippi Alluvial Valley, 1940-1947. Papers of the Peabody Museum of American Archaeology and Ethnology XXV.

Rohn, Arthur H.
1965 Postulation of Socio-Economic Groups from Archaeological Evidence. In: Contributions of the Wetherill Mesa Archaeological Project, assembled by Douglas Osborne. Society for American Archaeology Memoirs No. 19.

Rouse, Irving
1953 The Strategy of Archaeology. In: Anthropology Today, edited by A. L. Kroeber. Chicago: University of Chicago Press.

Sahlins, Marshall D.
1958 Social Stratification in Polynesia. The American Ethnological Society, Monograph 29.
1968 Tribesmen. Englewood Cliffs, New Jersey: Prentice-Hall.

Saucier, Roger T.
1974 Quaternary Geology of the Lower Mississippi Valley. Arkansas Archaeological Survey Research Series 6.

Sauer, Carl Ortwin
1920 The Geography of the Ozark Highland of Missouri. The Geographic Society of Chicago, Bulletin No. 7.

Sears, William H.
1956 Settlement Patterns in the Eastern United States. In: Prehistoric Settlement Patterns in the New World, edited by Gordon Willey. Viking Fund Publications in Anthropology No. 23.

Service, Elman R.
1962 Primitive Social Organization, An Evolutionary Perspective. New York: Random House.

Settergreen, Carl and R. E. McDermott
1962 Trees of Missouri. University of Missouri Agricultural Experiment Station Bulletin B767.

Smith, Bruce
1972 Comparisons of Fort Ancient-Mississippian Faunal Utilization. Paper read at the Southeastern Archaeological Conference, Morgantown, West Virginia, October 1972.
1978 Prehistoric Patterns of Human Behavior, A Case Study in the Mississippi Valley. New York: Academic Press.

Smith, M. A.
1955 The Limitations of Inference in Archaeology. The Archaeological Newsletter 6(1):3-7.

Steward, Julian H.
1955 Theory of Culture Change. Urbana: University of Illinois Press.

Thomas, Cyrus
1894 Report on the Mound Explorations of the Bureau of American Ethnology. Bureau of American Ethnology 12th Annual Report.

Thompson, Raymond H.
1956 The Subjective Element in Archaeological Inference. Southwestern Journal of Anthropology 12:327-32.

Thruston, Gates P.
1890 The Antiquities of Tennessee. Cincinnati.

Tuggle, H. David, Alex Townsend, and Thomas J. Riley
1972 Laws, Systems, and Research Designs: A Discussion of Explanation in Archaeology. American Antiquity 37:3-12.

Webb, William S.
1952 The Jonathan Creek Village, Site 4, Marshall County, Kentucky. University of Kentucky Reports of Anthropology VIII(1):1-141.

White, Leslie A.
1949 The Science of Culture: A Study of Man and Civilization. New York: Grove Press.

Willey, Gordon R.
1966 An Introduction to American Archaeology Vol. 1. Englewood Cliffs, N.J.: Prentice-Hall, Inc.

Williams, James Raymond
1966 Fortified Towns of Southeast Missouri. M.A. Thesis, Department of Anthropology, University of Missouri.

Williams, Stephen
1954 An Archaeological Study of the Mississippian Culture in Southeast Missouri. Ph.D. Dissertation on microfilm, Yale University.

APPENDIX A

METRIC DATA AND LOCATION OF STRUCTURES ON THE SNODGRASS SITE

SNODGRASS SITE
STRUCTURE DIMENSIONS, AREA, AND LOCATION

Structure	Length NE-SW	Width NW-SE	Number of Square Feet	Location in Relation to White Wall
1	12.0	12.0	144.00	outside
2	16.0	16.0	256.00	outside
3	17.0	18.0	306.00	inside
4	21.0	21.5	451.50	inside
5	20.5	20.0	410.00	inside
6	16.5	16.0	264.00	inside
7	18.0	19.0	342.00	inside
8	21.0	19.0	399.00	inside
9	7.5	8.0	60.00	outside
10	19.0	15.5	217.00	outside
11	17.5	17.0	297.50	outside
12	13.0	10.5	136.50	outside
13	13.5	12.0	162.00	outside
14	13.0	13.0	169.00	outside
15	16.5	17.0	280.50	inside
16	21.0	20.5	430.50	inside
17	19.0	19.0	361.00	inside
18	20.0	19.0	380.00	inside
19	19.0	18.0	342.00	inside
20	15.0	16.0	240.00	inside
21	21.0	20.0	420.00	inside
22	18.0	20.5	369.00	inside
23	12.0	12.0	144.00	outside
24	14.0	14.5	203.00	outside
25	14.5	15.0	217.50	outside
26	10.0	12.0	120.00	outside
27	11.5	12.5	143.75	outside
28	14.0	14.0	196.00	outside
29	16.5	15.0	247.50	outside
30	16.5	14.5	239.25	outside
31	12.0	11.5	138.00	outside
32	10.0	11.0	110.00	outside
33	9.0	10.0	90.00	outside
34	16.0	16.0	256.00	outside
35	14.0	14.0	196.00	outside

SNODGRASS SITE
STRUCTURE DIMENSIONS, AREA, AND LOCATION (Continued)

Structure	Length NE-SW	Width NW-SE	Number of Square Feet	Location in Relation to White Wall
36	15.0	15.0	225.00	outside
37	14.0	15.0	210.00	outside
38	16.0	16.0	256.00	outside
39	18.5	19.5	360.75	inside
40	18.0	18.0	324.00	inside
41	14.5	14.5	210.25	inside
42	14.0	16.0	224.00	inside
43	18.5	18.0	333.00	inside
44	18.0	24.0	432.00	inside
45	20.5	16.5	338.25	inside
46	16.0	16.0	256.00	inside
47	18.0	17.5	315.00	inside
48	14.5	16.0	232.00	inside
49	15.0	15.5	232.50	inside
50	16.5	15.0	247.50	inside
51	18.0	17.5	315.00	inside
52	18.0	18.0	324.00	inside
53	15.5	16.5	255.75	inside
54	14.5	15.0	217.50	inside
55	19.5	19.0	370.50	inside
56	20.0	18.0	360.00	inside
57	16.0	15.0	240.00	inside
58	15.0	14.5	217.50	outside
59	14.5	14.5	210.25	outside
60	14.5	16.5	239.25	outside
61	12.5	11.0	137.50	outside
62	16.0	18.0	288.00	inside
63	13.0	15.0	195.00	outside
64	12.0	13.0	156.00	outside
65	12.0	12.5	150.00	outside
66	11.0	12.0	132.00	outside
67	12.0	12.0	144.00	outside
68	15.5	15.5	240.25	outside
69	13.5	13.0	175.50	outside
70	13.0	13.0	169.00	outside

SNODGRASS SITE
STRUCTURE DIMENSIONS, AREA, AND LOCATION (Continued)

Structure	Length NE-SW	Width NW-SE	Number of Square Feet	Location in Relation to White Wall
71	20.0	15.5	310.00	outside
72	14.5	12.5	181.25	outside
73	10.0	11.0	110.00	outside
74	12.0	13.0	156.00	outside
75	13.0	11.0	143.00	outside
76	11.5	12.5	143.75	outside
77	13.5	13.5	182.25	outside
78	14.5	14.5	210.25	outside
79	12.5	13.0	162.50	outside
80	12.5	14.5	181.25	outside
81	11.0	12.0	132.00	outside
82	16.0	17.0	272.00	inside
83	17.5	16.5	288.85	inside
84	21.0	22.5	472.50	inside
85	13.5	14.5	195.75	outside
86	15.5	16.0	248.00	outside
87a	12.0	13.5	162.00	outside
87b	13.5	14.5	195.75	outside
88	4.0	5.0	20.00	outside
89	12.0	13.0	156.00	outside
90	13.5	11.5	155.25	inside

Total sq. ft.: 21,550.10

SNODGRASS SITE
VILLAGE SEGMENTS AND STRUCTURE SIZE

Segment #1: Inside White Wall	
Structure	Square Feet
3	306.00
4	451.50
5	410.00
6	264.00
7	342.00
8	399.00
15	280.50
16	430.50
17	361.00
18	380.00
19	342.00
20	240.00
21	420.00
22	369.00
39	360.75
40	324.00
41	210.25
42	224.00
43	333.00
44	432.00
45	338.25
46	256.00
47	315.00
48	232.00
49	232.50
50	247.50
51	315.00
52	324.00
53	255.75
54	217.50
55	370.50
56	360.00
57	240.00
62	288.00
82	272.00
83	288.85
84	472.50
90	155.25
Total 38	12,060.10 29.5% of total area inside white wall

SNODGRASS SITE
VILLAGE SEGMENTS AND STRUCTURE SIZE (Continued)

Segment #2: North End of Site	
Structure	Square Feet
1	144.00
2	256.00
9	60.00
10	217.00
11	297.50
23	144.00
24	203.00
25	217.50
32	110.00
33	90.00
34	256.00
61	137.50
63	195.00
64	156.00
65	150.00
66	132.00
67	144.00
68	240.25
69	175.50
75	143.00
76	143.75
77	182.25
78	210.25
81	132.00
87a	162.00
87b	195.75
88	20.00
89	156.00
Total 28	4,670.25

$\bar{x}$ structure size: 166.79 square feet

SNODGRASS SITE
VILLAGE SEGMENTS AND STRUCTURE SIZE (Continued)

Segment #3: East Side of Site

Structure	Square Feet
12	136.50
13	162.00
14	169.00
26	120.00
27	143.75
28	196.00
29	247.50
30	239.25
31	138.00
35	196.00
36	225.00
37	210.00
38	256.00
58	217.50
59	210.25
60	239.25
70	169.00
71	310.00
72	181.25
73	110.00
74	156.00
79	162.50
80	181.25
85	195.75
86	248.00
Total 25	4,819.75

$\overline{x}$ structure size: 192.79 square feet

SUMMARY OF STRUCTURE DIMENSIONS, AREA, SIZE

Segment Number	Location	Number of Structures	Total Area of Structure Basins	Number of Structures Over 240 Sq. Ft.	$\overline{x}$ Structure Size
1	inside white wall	38	12,060.10 sq. ft.	32	322.63 sq. ft.
2	north end of site	28	4,670.25 sq. ft.	4	166.79 sq. ft.
3	east side of site	25	4,819.75 sq. ft.	4	192.79 sq. ft.

APPENDIX B

PROVENIENCE OF MATERIAL USED IN THE DISTRIBUTIONAL ANALYSIS

WICKLIFFE JUICE PRESS SHERDS

Structure No.	Field Specimen No. or Location
Structure 16	FS 59 rim
	FS 300 rim
	FS 36 lip
	FS 36 body
	FS 39 bottom rim
	FS 596 body
	16-6*body
	16-7 body
	16-7 body
	16-12 body
	16-12 body
	16-13 body
	16-13 body
	16-13 body
	16-20 body
	16-20 body
Structure 17	FS 68 body
	FS 355 body
Structure 51	FS 106 rim
Structure 55	FS 371 body
	FS 582 body
	FS 878 body
Skimmed Surface	735.2 east/316.2 south upper rim

*16.-6. 16 = Structure number. 6 = Square number. This numbering style is used to show provenience for specimens not assigned Field Specimen numbers. These generally are items that were not piece-plotted, whereas field specimens were.

ARROWSHAFT ABRADERS

Structure No.	Field Specimen No. or Location	No. of Grooves
Structure 1	FS 39	1
Structure 4	FS 553	2
Structure 5	FS 289	2
	FS 483	2
Structure 15	FS 31	1
Structure 16	FS 258	2
Structure 17	SS 235s/795e	4
Structure 18	FS 429	2
	FS 436 jar rim	2
	FS 536 jar rim	3
	FS 924	4
	FS 1128 awl abrader	8
	18-6	1
	18-10	1
Structure 19	19-4	1
Structure 20	FS 186	2
Structure 21	FS 631	3
Structure 23	FS 31	4
Structure 26	FS 10	2
	FS 23	2
	26-5	4
	26-5	2
	26-9	2
Structure 33	33-8	2
Structure 36	FS 553	2
Structure 44	285s/900e	1
	280s/900e	2
Structure 47	FS 607	2
	330s/865e	2
Structure 58	415s/770e	2 two pieces fit together
Structure 66	66-4	2
	66-7	1
Skimmed Surface	170s/840e	3
Skimmed Surface	230s/795e	1
EEP* #2		1
EEP #8		1
EEP #8		4

*Extra-edificial pit

POTTERY TROWELS

Structure No.	Description or Location
Structure 4	Pottery trowel fragments in pot hole in SE corner and whole trowel exposed after weathering all winter
Structure 8	FS 708
Structure 14	FS 7 intraedificial pit #1
Structure 16	FS 61
Structure 21	FS 36, FS 281, 21-11 three pieces of trowel
Structure 46	305s/865e
Structure 47	FS 130
	FS 131
Structure 50	360s/820e
Structure 82	FS 83
EEP #14	SE quarter

LARGE POTTERY DISCS

Structure No.	Field Specimen No. or Location
Structure 13	FS 20
Structure 15	FS 332
Structure 16	FS 22
Structure 18	FS 866
Structure 22	FS 49
Structure 28	FS 80

SMALL POTTERY DISCS

Structure No.	Field Specimen No. or Location	Without Perforations	Number of Partial Perforations	Number of Complete Perforations
Structure 3	FS 22			1
Structure 4	4-18			2
Structure 5	FS 21			3
	FS 460	x		
Structure 7	7-7	x		
	7-12	x		
	230x/940e SS			2
	220x/950e SS			3
	Skimmed Surface	x		
Structure 8	FS 155		1	
	FS 736	x		
	8-2			1
	8-10			1
	8-12			3
Structure 11	FS 165	x		
Structure 14	14-6			2
Structure 15	FS 51		1	
Structure 16	FS 131		1	
	FS 595			1
	16-8	x incised		
	16-14		1	
	16-20			1
	260s/790e SS			2
Structure 17	FS 72			1
	FS 110			2 bowl rim

SMALL POTTERY DISCS (Continued)

Structure No.	Field Specimen No. or Location	Without Perforations	Number of Partial Perforations	Number of Complete Perforations
Structure 17 (cont'd.)	FS 283	(plus 1 either partial or complete)		3
	FS 307		1	
	FS 310*		1 from both sides	
	FS 441			1 large
	17-7		1	
	17-14		1	1
	235s/795e SS			1
	Skimmed Surface			1
	Skimmed Surface			3
Structure 18	FS 1084			1
	18-5			2
	18-20 SS			1
Structure 19	FS 40			1
	FS 583	x		
	19-13	x		
Structure 20	FS 275*		1	1
	20-8			1
Structure 21	FS 270	x		
	FS 476			3
	21-8 SS			1
Structure 22	22-5		1	
Structure 44	FS 217	x		
	44-16			5
	280s/900e		1 from both sides	
	280s/905e			1

	280s/920e			1
Structure 45	FS 28			1
Structure 47	FS 633		1	
	FS 736			1
	47-6	x		
	47-20			1
Structure 48	FS 29		1 from both sides	
Structure 49	Pit #1	x		
Structure 51	290s/820e			3
Structure 55	FS 239			2
	55-10	x		
Structure 56	56-4			2, probably 5
	56-4			1
Structure 58	420s/780e			1 bowl rim
Structure 61	125s/835e	x		
Structure 64	FS 37	x		
Structure 69	125s/985e		1	
Structure 82	245s/895e			2
Structure 83	260s/875e			1
Structure 84	FS 29	x		
Structure 85	290s/1000e		1	
Structure 87	100s/840e	x		

SMALL POTTERY DISCS (Continued)

Structure No.	Field Specimen No. of Location	Without Perforations	Number of Partial Perforations	Number of Complete Perforations
EEP #2	Surface to pit floor			2
EEP #2				1
EEP #8				2
EEP #8				3
EEP #8				3
EEP #8			2	
EEP #8				1
EEP #9			1 from both sides	
EEP #12				1
EEP #14				2
EEP #14				4
EEP #19		x		
EEP #33	West half			1
EEP #34				1
EEP #37				1
EEP #43			1	
EEP #46				1
Skimmed Surface	150s/830e			3

*red stain–iron from water

TYPES OF POTTERY DISCS IN SPECIFIC STRUCTURES

Type	Structure No.	Field Specimen No. or Location
Unperforated	Structure 5	FS 460
	Structure 7	7-7
		7-12
		Skimmed Surface
	Structure 8	FS 736
	Structure 11	FS 165
	Structure 16	16-8
	Structure 19	FS 583
		19-13
	Structure 21	FS 270
	Structure 44	FS 217
	Structure 47	47-6
	Structure 49	Pit #1
	Structure 55	55-10
	Structure 61	125s/835e
	Structure 64	FS 37
	Structure 84	FS 29
	Structure 87	100s/840e
	EEP #19	
One partial perforation	Structure 8	FS 155
	Structure 15	FS 51
	Structure 16	FS 131
		16-14
	Structure 17	FS 307
		17-7
		17-14
		FS 310
	Structure 22	22-5
	Structure 44	280s/900e
	Structure 47	FS 633
	Structure 48	FS 29
	Structure 69	125s/985e
	Structure 85	390s/1000e
	EEP #9	
	EEP #43	
One complete perforation	Structure 3	FS 22
	Structure 8	8-2
	Structure 16	FS 595
		16-20
	Structure 17	FS 72
		FS 441
		235s/795e SS
		Skimmed Surface

TYPES OF POTTERY DISCS (Continued)

Type	Structure No.	Field Specimen No. or Location
One complete perforation (cont'd.)	Structure 18	FS 1084
		18-20 SS
	Structure 19	FS 40
	Structure 20	20-8
	Structure 21	21-8 SS
	Structure 44	280s/905e
		280s/920e
	Structure 45	FS 28
	Structure 47	FS 736
		47-20
	Structure 56	56-4
	Structure 58	420s/780e
	Structure 83	260s/875e
	EEP #2	
	EEP #8	
	EEP #33	
	EEP #34	
	EEP #37	
	EEP #46	
Three-hole type	Structure 51	290s/820e
	Structure 5	FS 21
Five-hole type	Structure 4	4-18
	Structure 7	220s/950e
		230s/940e
	Structure 8	8-12
		8-10
	Structure 14	14-6
	Structure 16	260s/790e SS
	Structure 17	FS 283
		Skimmed Surface
	Structure 18	18-5
	Structure 21	FS 476
	Structure 44	44-16
	Structure 55	FS 239
	Structure 56	56-4
	Structure 82	245s/895e
	EEP #2	
	EEP #8	
	EEP #8	
	EEP #8	
	EEP #8	
	EEP #12	
	EEP #14	

TYPES OF POTTERY DISCS (Continued)

Type	Structure No.	Field Specimen No. or Location
Five-hole type (cont'd.)	EEP #14 Skimmed Surface	 150s/830e
Undetermined	Structure 17	FS 110 (2 complete perforations)
One complete and one partial perforation	Structure 17 Structure 20	17-4 FS 275

DISTRIBUTION OF EAR PLUGS

Structure No.	Field Specimen No. or Location
Structure 5	215s/910e
Structure 8	FS 476
	8-10
Structure 15	FS 336
Structure 17	FS 170
Structure 20	160s/845e SS
Structure 21	FS 597
	Skimmed Surface
Structure 22	FS 199
Structure 24	160s/800e SS
Structure 27	Surface
Structure 39	400s/850e
	400s/845e
	405s/850e
Structure 44	FS 66
	44-13
Structure 47	FS 74
	FS 693
	FS 609
	325s/855e
Structure 48	FS 44
Structure 49	49-1
Structure 51	FS 87
	285s/820e
Structure 52	315s/805e
Structure 55	320s/745e
	325s/745e

DISTRIBUTION OF EAR PLUGS (Continued)

Structure No.	Field Specimen No. or Location
Structure 66	FS 10
	FS 73
	FS 89
EEP #3	
EEP #11	
Skimmed Surface	230s/790e
Skimmed Surface	160s/850e
Skimmed Surface 1969 Collection	310s/840e
Skimmed Surface 1969 Collection	210s/820e

DISTRIBUTION OF EAR SPOOLS

Structure Number	Field Specimen Number
Structure 4	FS 617 red painted
Structure 56	FS 129

DISTRIBUTION OF EFFIGIES

Structure No.	Field Specimen No. or Location	Description
Structure 2	backfill	bird?
Structure 3	FS 236	human face
Structure 8	FS 499	duck head
	FS 1105	deer or antelope head
Structure 10	FS 74	human head
Structure 16	FS 261	frog head
Structure 19	19-1	bird head
Structure 20	FS 98	bird? head
Structure 21	FS 329 & 825	bird head (effigy bowl)
	FS 790	bird
Structure 30	below house floor	part of bowl rim
Structure 39	FS 8	bird with comb
Structure 41	FS 31	miniature bowl, head-tail missing
Structure 44	FS 202	human head
	FS 487	conch shell
	FS 507	human head
Structure 45	FS 15	bear head
Structure 46	FS 212	bear
	305s/870e	bear
Structure 51	FS 70	bear head
	FS 35	squash effigy—hooded water bottle
Structure 52	NE	bat
	FS 270	bear
	FS 272	bird
Structure 64	FS 1	most of bowl rim—effigy gone
Structure 77	FS 71	bird
EEP #3		bear
EEP #9a		bird (turkey)
Skimmed Surface		bird? incised

DISTRIBUTION OF TABTAILS AND LUGS

Structure No.	Field Specimen No. or Location	Description
Structure 3	FS 194	tabtail
Structure 4	FS 55	undetermined
	4-17	tabtail
	4-2	undetermined
Structure 8	FS 1032	undetermined
	FS 829	undetermined
	FS 206	tabtail
	8-13	undetermined
Structure 14		lug
Structure 16	16-368	undetermined
Structure 17	17-12	undetermined
Structure 19	FS 380	tabtail
Structure 21	21-12	undetermined
	145s/865e	undetermined
Structure 22	FS 279	lug
Structure 23	FS 62	undetermined
Structure 33	FS 47	tabtail
Structure 38	430s/900e	undetermined
Structure 42	FS 186	lug
	325s/885e	lug
Structure 43	FS 129	tabtail
	43-10	undetermined
Structure 44	285s/900e	lug
	285s/910e	undetermined
Structure 47	47-5	undetermined
Structure 48		lug
Structure 49	49-4	undetermined
Structure 50	355s/830e	lug
Structure 51	290s/820e	undetermined
	290s/820e	undetermined
Structure 54	54-82	lug
Structure 55	320s/750e	undetermined
Structure 58	FS 20	tabtail
Structure 64	FS 1	tabtail
Structure 76	FS 19	tabtail
Structure 82	FS 64	tabtail
Structure 84	FS 20	tabtail
Structure 87B	105s/840e	undetermined
EEP #2		lug
EEP #8		undetermined
EEP #11	SW quarter	tabtail

PERFORATED JAR HANDLES

Structure No.	Field Specimen No. or Location
Structure 14	FS 55
Structure 15	15-5
Structure 18	18-18
	half jar in IE pit
Structure 44	285s/910e lug
Structure 45	275s/865e notched
	280s/865e
Structure 51	290s/820e
Structure 82	FS 126
EEP #3	

BIFURCATED JAR HANDLES

Structure No.	Field Specimen No. or Location
Structure 20	FS 207
Structure 44	FS 435
EEP #16	NW quarter

SCALLOPED RIM BOWLS

Structure No.	Field Specimen No. or Location
Structure 4	FS 337
Structure 5	FS 145
Structure 8	FS 164
Structure 16	FS 555
	16-543
Structure 17	FS 26
	FS 260
	FS 394 punctate and perforated
	FS 423
Structure 18	FS 456
	FS 473
	18-18

SCALLOPED RIM BOWLS (Continued)

Structure No.	Field Specimen No. or Location
Structure 19	FS 90
	FS 169
Structure 21	FS 448
	FS 607
	21-18
Structure 22	FS 189
	FS 492
Structure 24	FS 835
Structure 28	380s/950e
Structure 44	285s/910e
	final skim
Structure 47	FS 278
	47-16
	47-9
Structure 48	FS 22 ½ bowl, 7 scallops not grouped
Structure 49	49-9
	340s/825e
Structure 55	55-13
	FS 272
Structure 61	FS 50
Structure 71	FS 201
	71-3
EEP #2	E half
EEP #8	NW Quad
EEP #34	
EEP #34	
EEP #43	
EEP #43	
EEP #48	W half
EEP #81	bowl rim
Burial 7	FS 1, 8 scallops grouped in twos, whole bowl

INCISED SHERDS

Structure No.	Field Specimen No. or Location
Structure 5	FS 629
	5-14
Structure 7	7-13
	7-15
Structure 8	FS 39
	FS 524 jar rim
	FS 806
Structure 14	14-12
Structure 15	initial skim
Structure 16	FS 500 incised jar rim, also notched rim
	16-15
Structure 17	FS 398
	17-2
	17-6
	17-6
	17-13
	17-13
	17-17
Structure 18	FS 171
	FS 1198
	18-6
	18-15
	18-17
	18-17
	18-18
Structure 19	19-5
	19-22
Structure 20	20-8
Structure 21	FS 455
	FS 712
	FS 892
	21-6 rim sherd
	21-6
	21-10
	21-11
	21-12
	21-12 notched rim
	21-14
	21-15
	21-16
	21-18
	FS 676B jar handle with nodes

INCISED SHERDS (Continued)

Structure No.	Field Specimen No. or Location
Structure 24	FS 383
Structure 44	44-6
	285s/900e pit #1
	285s/905e
Structure 45	final skim
	275s/865e
Structure 46	46-5 jar shoulder
Structure 47	FS 600
Structure 48	375s/820e jar
Structure 49	49-2
	49-9
Structure 50	360s/820e also punctated and notched rim
Structure 51	290s/815e handle
Structure 52	52-10 also punctate
Structure 55	55-13
	55-13
	FS 593 handle, also notched
	general
Structure 56	FS 154 also punctate
	56-8
Structure 58	FS 36
Structure 61	125s/835e
Structure 62	62-18 handle with incising on shoulder, also notched
Structure 69	final skim jar shoulder
Structure 82	FS 76 jar rim
	final skim
	final skim
Structure 83	265s/885e
EEP #8	NW Quad
EEP #17	curvilinear
EEP #33	E half
EEP #34	4 lines
EEP #34	
EEP #34	
EEP #52	W half
EEP #68	S half
EEP #88	276.5s/784.7e large section of large jar with handle, fits with 56-8
Skimmed Surface	bird head bowl rim

PUNCTATE SHERDS

Structure No.	Field Specimen No. or Location
Structure 7	FS 55, 75, 169, 178, and 235s/945e two-thirds of a jar
Structure 17	FS 176 bowl rim
	FS 394 also perforated with scalloped rim
	17-12
	17-17
Structure 50	360s/820e jar with incising and notched rim
	17-12
	17-17
Structure 50	360s/820e jar with incising and notched rim
Structure 52	52-10 jar shoulder, also incised
Structure 56	FS 154 jar shoulder, incised
Structure 77	150s/102e jar shoulder

NODED BOWLS AND JARS

Structure No.	Field Specimen No. or Location	Description
Structure 4	FS 413	rim
Structure 7	7-6	rim
Structure 8	FS 277	rim
	8-6	shoulder sherd
Structure 16	16-15	shoulder sherd
	16-20	shoulder sherd
Structure 17	FS 459	rim
	FS 468	rim
	FS 508	rim
Structure 19	FS 542	notched rim (may be same vessel as EEP 30)
	FS 96	
Structure 23	FS 23	rim
Structure 38	425s/885e	node only
Structure 39	390s/855e	
Structure 50		miniature jar
	820e/350s	notched rim
Structure 84	FS 53, 18	almost complete bowl
	FS 104	jar
EEP #8		rim
EEP #8		rim
EEP #12	SW quarter	rim
EEP #30		notched rim (may be same vessel as Structure 19 FS 542)
EEP #34	quad BC	
EEP #34		rim

NOTCHED BOWL RIMS AND JAR RIMS

Structure No.	Field Specimen No. or Location	Description
Structure 5	FS 172	bowl
Structure 8	FS 776	jar
	8-7	bowl
	8-10	bowl
Structure 16	16-7	bowl
	16-417	bowl
	FS 500	jar, also incised
Structure 17	17-6	bowl
	17-17	bowl
Structure 18	FS 31	jar
	18-17	bowl
	18-20	bowl
	FS 1024	whole jar, small, notched rim
Structure 19	FS 409	bowl
	FS 542	bowl, noded
	FS 609	bowl
Structure 20	FS 207	jar
	20-3	bowl
	20-8	bowl
Structure 21	21-12	bowl
Structure 24	FS 837	bowl
	FS 160, 731, 161, 739	whole jar, notched rim
Structure 25	FS 140	bowl
Structure 28	380s/950e	pie crust bowl
Structure 43	43-10	bowl (fits with Structure 47, FS 374)
Structure 44	44-5	bowl
Structure 45	275s/865e	jar, perforated handle
	FS 7A, 7B	pie crust bowl
Structure 47	47-6	bowl
	FS 374	bowl (fits with Structure 43, 43-10)
Structure 50	360s/820e	jar, incised and punctate
	350s/820e	bowl, noded
Structure 51	290s/820e	bowl
	285s/830e	incurving bowl
Structure 55	FS 593	jar (handle), also incised
Structure 61	FS 25, 27, 31, 33, 51, 52, 53, 54, 56	large bowl (Structure 65, FS 25 fits also)
Structure 62	62-18	on jar handle sherd
Structure 65	FS 25	bowl (fits onto Structure 61 bowl)
Structure 66	FS 77	bowl
Structure 72	72-6	bowl
Structure 82	FS 11	pie crust bowl
	245s/885e	two sherds bowl
Structure 83	270s/875e	bowl

NOTCHED BOWL RIMS AND JAR RIMS (Continued)

Structure No.	Field Specimen No. or Location	Description
Structure 84	FS 46	bowl
	255s/920e	bowl
	FS 137	almost whole bowl
EEP #19	SE quarter	bowl
EEP #30		bowl, also noded
EEP #34	quad AD	bowl
EEP #34		jar
EEP #34		pie crust bowl
EEP #34	quad BC	large jar
EEP #34	quad BC	medium jar

NOTCHED BOWL AND JAR RIM TYPES

Type	Structure No.	Field Specimen No. or Location	Description
Type 1	Structure 16	16-7	bowl
		16-417	bowl
	Structure 44	44-5	bowl
	Structure 61	FS 25, 27, 31, 35, 51, 52, 53, 54, 56	bowl
	Structure 65	FS 25	bowl (fits with Structure 61 bowl)
Type 2	Structure 16	FS 500	jar, also incised
	Structure 17	17-6	bowl
	Structure 18	18-17	bowl
		18-20	bowl
	Structure 20	20-3	bowl
		FS 207	jar
	Structure 24	FS 837	bowl
	Structure 43	43-10	bowl (fits with Structure 47, FS 374)
	Structure 47	FS 374	bowl (fits with Structure 43, 43-10)
	Structure 51	290s/820e	bowl
	Structure 66	FS 77	bowl
	Structure 72	72-6	bowl
	EEP #34	quad BC	jar, medium
	EEP #34		jar
	EEP #34	quad AD	bowl
Type 3	Structure 21	21-12	bowl
	Structure 84	255s/920e	bowl

NOTCHED BOWL AND JAR RIM TYPES (Continued)

Type	Structure No.	Field Specimen No. or Location	Description
Type 4	Structure 18	FS 31	jar
	Structure 19	FS 409	bowl
		FS 542	bowl, noded
		FS 609	bowl
	Structure 84	FS 137	bowl, almost whole
	EEP #30		bowl, also noded
Type 5	Structure 5	FS 172	bowl
	Structure 8	8-7	bowl
	Structure 17	17-17	bowl
	Structure 20	20-8	bowl
	Structure 24	FA 160, 161, 731, 739	whole jar, notched rim
	Structure 25	FS 140	bowl
	Structure 45	275s/865e	jar, perforated handle
	Structure 50	350s/820e	bowl, noded
	Structure 55	FS 593	jar (handle) also incised
	Structure 62	62-18	jar (handle sherd)
	EEP #34	quad BC	jar, large
Type 6	Structure 8	8-10	bowl
	Structure 83	270s/875e	bowl
	Structure 84	FS 46	bowl
Type 7	Structure 47	47-6	bowl
Type 8	Structure 28	380s/950e	pie crust bowl
	Structure 45	FS 7A, 7B	pie crust bowl
	Structure 82	FS 11	pie crust bowl
		245s/885e	bowls, 2 sherds
	EEP #19	SE quarter	bowl
	EEP #34		pie crust bowl
Type 9	Structure 8	FS 776	jar
	Structure 18	FS 1024	whole jar, small, notched rim
Type 10	Structure 50	360s/820e	jar, incised and punctated
Type 11	Structure 51	285s/830e	incurving bowl

APPENDIX C

PROJECTILE POINT FREQUENCY AND DISTRIBUTION BY TYPES

PROJECTILE POINT FREQUENCY AND DISTRIBUTION BY TYPES

Structure Number	Projectile Point Types 1	2	3	4	5	6	7	8	9	10	11	12	13	14	15	16	17	Unclassified	Total
1																			0
2																			0
3												1							1
4					1							1							2
5												1	1	1					3
6																			0
7						1		1			1				2				5
8			1		3			1		1	1	1		2		1	1	1	13
9																			0
10				1															1
11										1								1	2
12																			0
13																			0
14																			0
15									1		1			1					3
16			1				1		1		1	1		1			1	1	8
17					1	1			1	1		3							7
18						2						1		2	1				6
19					1					1									2
20												2							2
21	1			1		2			1				1	1					7
22			1			1								1					3
23											1								1
24											1								1
25					2														2
26																			0

27					1															1
28																1	1			2
29																				0
30	1				1								1	1						4
31											1				1					2
32																				0
33																	1			1
34																				0
35																				0
36										1										1
37								1									1		1	3
38		1																		1
39												2								2
40																				0
41														1	1		1			3
42											1			1						2
43															1					1
44		1							1	2	2	1	1		3		3			14
45				2	1		1		1	1		3	1	1		1				12
46				1						1										2
47			1					1		3				1						6
48												1		1						2
49													1							1
50													1							1
51	2		1	1											1		1			6
52						2			2			2		1	2	2				11
53	1													1			1			3
54																				0
55	1									1		3								5
56						1		1			2	2			1	1	2		2	12
57																				0

PROJECTILE POINT FREQUENCY (Continued)

Structure	Projectile Point Types																		
Number	1	2	3	4	5	6	7	8	9	10	11	12	13	14	15	16	17	Unclassified	Total
58																			0
59																			0
60																			0
61						1					1								2
62						1						4					3		8
63																			0
64																			0
65																		1	1
66																			0
67																			0
68																			0
69			1																1
70			2		1											3	1	1	8
71										1									1
72																			0
73																			0
74																			0
75																			0
76																			0
77													1		1				2
78																			0
79																			0
80																			0
81																	1		1
82			1				1				2		1	1	1		1		8
83										1	1	2				2		2	8

84			1	3	1			1	1	2	3	1			2		2		17
85										1	1								2
86														1					1
87a						1										1			2
87b				1		1													2
88																			0
89																			0
90					1														1
EEP 33															1				1
EEP 77						1													1
EEP 78					1														1
EEP 86														1					1
Surface W of 49														1					1
298.8s-912.7e															1				1
190.0s-920.0e												1							1
316.3s-873.2e																	1		1
Total	6	2	10	10	15	15	3	6	9	18	20	32	9	21	19	12	23	10	241

APPENDIX D

RADIOCARBON DATES OF THE POWERS PHASE

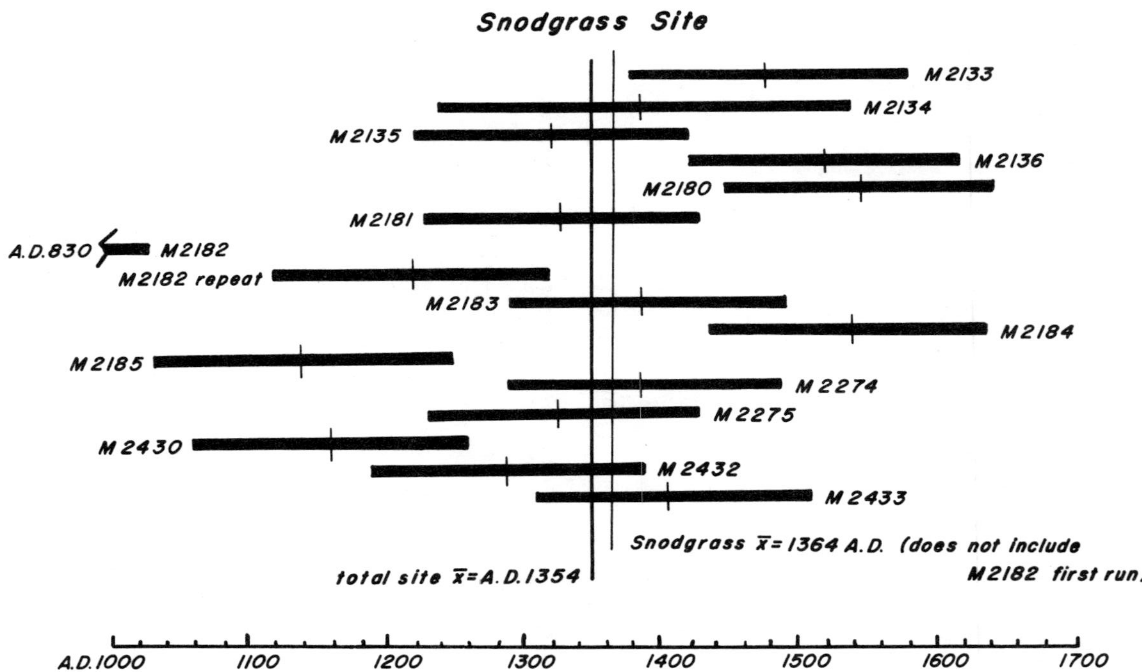

Radiocarbon Dates for the Powers Phase

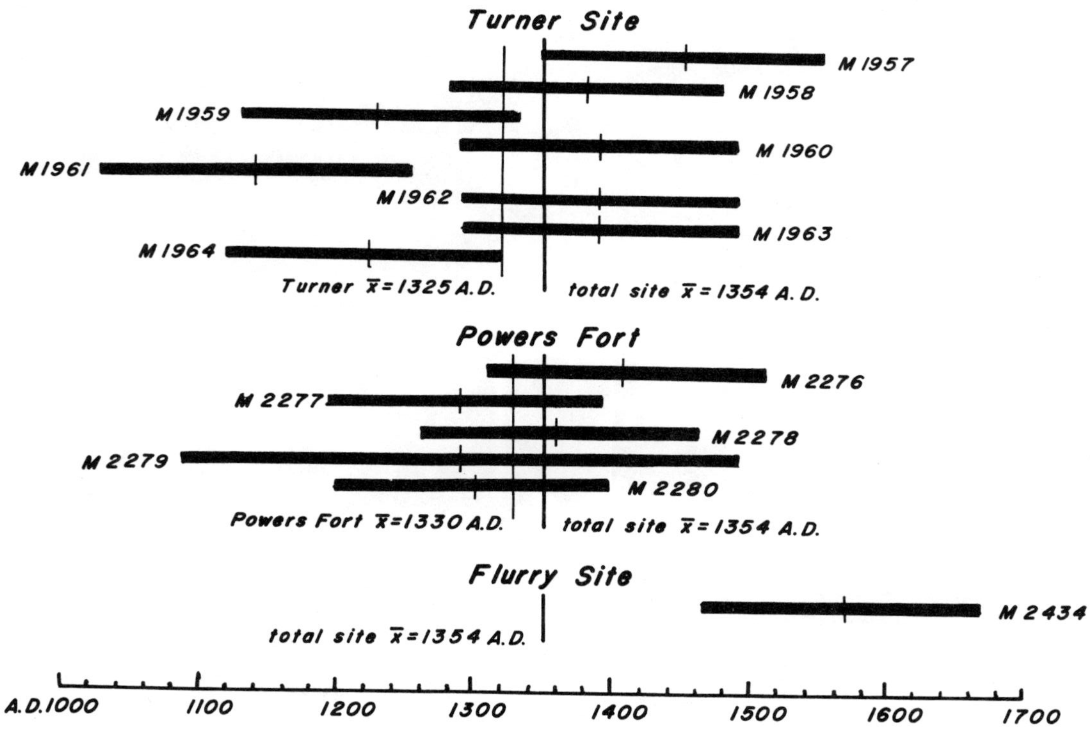

Radiocarbon Dates for the Powers Phase

APPENDIX E

DIFFERENTIAL JAR SIZE IN THE POWERS PHASE

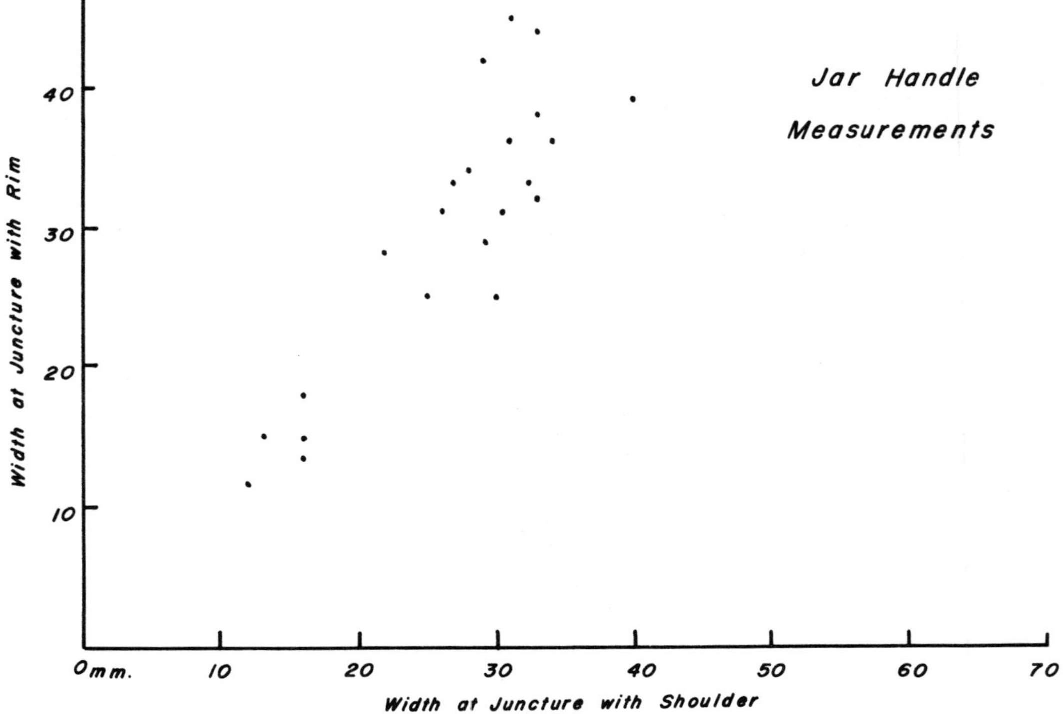

Differential Jar Size in the Powers Phase

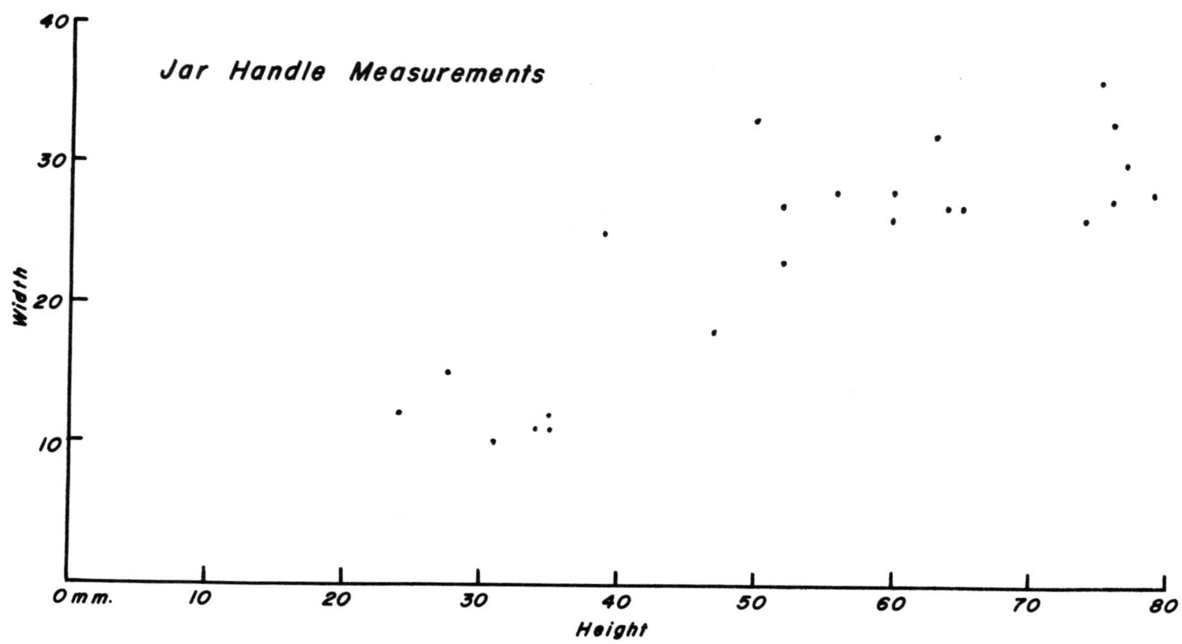

Differential Jar Size in the Powers Phase